Philip Henry Smith

Legends of the Shawangunk (Shon-Gum) and Its Environs

Including Historical Sketches, Biographical Notices, and Thrilling Border....

Philip Henry Smith

Legends of the Shawangunk (Shon-Gum) and Its Environs
Including Historical Sketches, Biographical Notices, and Thrilling Border....

ISBN/EAN: 9783337019204

Printed in Europe, USA, Canada, Australia, Japan

Cover: Foto ©ninafisch / pixelio.de

More available books at **www.hansebooks.com**

Legends

OF THE

SHAWANGUNK

(SHON-GUM)

AND ITS ENVIRONS,

INCLUDING

HISTORICAL SKETCHES, BIOGRAPHICAL NOTICES,
AND THRILLING BORDER INCIDENTS AND ADVENTURES

RELATING TO THOSE PORTIONS OF

THE COUNTIES OF ORANGE, ULSTER AND SULLIVAN

LYING IN THE SHAWANGUNK REGION.

ILLUSTRATED BY

NUMEROUS ENGRAVINGS AND PEN SKETCHES BY THE AUTHOR.

By PHILIP H. SMITH.

AUTHOR OF

"ACADIA: A LOST CHAPTER IN AMERICAN HISTORY", "THE GREEN MOUNTAIN BOYS, OR VERMONT
AND THE NEW YORK LAND JOBBERS", "HISTORY OF DUTCHESS COUNTY",
"THE STATESMEN OF POUGHKEEPSIE", ETC., ETC.

PREFACE.

WHEN for the first time an Old World trave'er is permitted to behold an American landscape in Autumn, he is transported at the array of gorgeous hues of which he had formed no conception. Nowhere does Nature take on a brighter livery than in the vicinity of the Shawangunk; and there needs but the rendering of its history into story by a Scott or a Cooper to immortalize the locality. Here, beneath the effulgent rays of the October sun, there burns, not one bush, but thousands, as with fire, yet are not consumed; and here the maple, the sumac, the Virginia creeper, and the expanses of golden-rod and purple asters flood the forests and fields with their matchless coloring.

It requires no great effort of the fancy to picture the bark canoes of the aboriginals still plying upon the bosoms of the many romantic lakes, or swiftly coursing along the beautiful streams that, like sinuous bands of silver, wind among the verdant meadows. One would be pardoned for being deceived into the belief that the smoke from an embowered cottage arose from the embers of an Indian wigwam; and the traveler half expects to meet troops of goblin warriors, as in the Moorish legend, painted and equipped for battle, silently threading the forest over the Indian trails yet clearly traceable through the mountain fastnesses

Does the reader desire details of the more tragic sort ? Then lend your attention while are told tales of midnight marauders, both white and red, who fell upon unsuspecting and unprotected families along the frontier; listen while scenes are depicted of by-gone times, when the silence of night was wont to be broken by the screams of affrighted women and children, as the murderous tomahawk was brandished over its victims, and when scalps reeking with gore were borne away in triumph. Every locality in the Shawangunk region has its legend of Indian atrocity, or its story of Revolutionary barbarity; the chain of stone forts yet standing along the river valleys bear testimony to the general insecurity of life in those troublous times.

Or if the reader delights in tales of adventures with the wild animals of the forest, of encounters with the nomadic bear, the ferocious panther, or the prowling wolf, and all the exciting experiences of a woodland life, it is hoped the hunting stories of the Shawangunk will constitute a source of thrilling interest.

It may be that he who has leisure and inclination to scan this volume is of a philosophic turn of mind, and would prefer to trace a reflex of the religious sectarianisms and feudal customs of the Old World in the unsettled society of the New. For such a one the history of Robert Chambers and the Baronetcy of Fox Hall, the story of Lewis Du Bois the Walloon, and the narrative of the Hardenburgh war, all of which are considered at length in these pages, will afford abundant material for reflection.

Then, too, the more humble but no less heroic virtues of the pioneer settler, enduring the hardships and privations of a frontier life to the end that he might carve for himself a home in the wilderness—such will form a theme no less fruitful and interesting.

It is the usual thing for history to deal exclusively with great events. The conduct of armies, the description of battles, and a record of matters involving the interest of the many, are the topics which absorb the attention of the historian, while the individual experiences in the every-day life of the common people are lost sight of altogether. The knowledge that a battle was fought is of less value than a knowledge of the causes that led to it and the issues resulting from it; and how can one understand the causes except he enter into sympathy with the masses involved; or how can he sympathize unless he is familiar with their individual sufferings, and with their manner of life and mode of thinking? We know that the battle of Monmouth was fought; the number and disposition of the contending forces, at what time and by whom the charges were made; the repulses and all the details of the action are matters of record; but the individual experiences and home life of the sterling patriots in the lower ranks that participated in the fight are topics yet undeveloped. In the preparation of this volume the end is kept in view of supplying this deficiency, and thus, in a measure, supplementing the more pretentious histories.

The most fascinating chapters of the past are those so remote that well-established fact and dim tradition become so blended that one can hardly be distinguished from the other. It may be asserted that history then loses its value as an educator, as it no longer stands a truthful transcript of the human character. But we should not forget that there can be no more interesting and valuable study of the general character and standing of a community than a research into its current beliefs and traditions, even though the subjects should partake of the nature of myths and fables. The poems of Ossian possess a rare value in that they delineate the habits and experiences of the people of ancient Ireland and Scotland centuries beyond the limit of so-called authentic history; the same may be said of the works of Homer, however wild and chimerical the stories may appear. It has been said that the most conscientious history is but the development or maintenance of a theory. No man ever witnessed a battle unbiased; it is to this biased source that the historian turns for his facts; these facts are liable to undergo a still further change in the crucible of his pet theory, and the public must accept the result. Compare the works of English writers on the causes and conduct of the war of 1812 with the versions of the same war by American authors, and, but for the names and dates, one would hardly recognize the same event.

But let not the matter-of-fact reader be dismayed. Though the term "legend" has been made use of in the present volume, no narrative has been inserted without the authority of contemporaneous history, or well-authenticated tradition.

"Legend" has a less repulsive sound to the superficial reader than "history;" while the genuine student will readily discern and accept a means of instruction under whatever guise it is found. For a like reason each topic is complete in itself, thus doing away with the necessity of a consecutive reading of the book. Inasmuch as the vicinity of the Shawangunk is attracting the attention of the public as a desirable place in which to spend the summer, it has been thought a work of this kind, possessing the value of history and the charm of romance, would be acceptable.

While there is much that is here found in print for the first time, all available published sources have been laid under contribution in its compilation. Ancient records have been rigidly searched with a view of obtaining such facts not only as were new to the public, but such as would be of general interest. The aim has been to make a book as attractive to a citizen of a distant locality as to a resident of the Shawangunk region, and by a judicious selection of topics and a careful revision of the text, to expunge whatever may have been of a local and common-place nature.

Several standard local works have been freely quoted, and many of their interesting features embodied in this volume. Of this class we make mention of Stickney's History of Minisink; the Bevier pamphlet, from which is obtained much that is valuable of the Revolutionary history of Ulster; Eager's History of Orange County; Quinlan's Life of Tom Quick, etc. These books are now out of print, and some of them command fabulous prices, such is the demand for them. The matter contained in these favorite works may possess a value in the present dress above that of new facts. We make an especial acknowledgment of the courtesy of E. F. Quinlan, M. D., and also of Hon. George M. Beebe, both of Monticello, N. Y., who kindly consented to our use of the writings of James Eldridge Quinlan, the author of Tom Quick and of the History of Sullivan county. Mr. Quinlan possessed within himself the rare combination of indefatigable research and a pure and forcible diction that claimed the attention of the reader; and his efforts are justly regarded as a standard authority on the subjects of which he has treated. Space would fail were we to mention all the favors and facilities afforded us in the works of research. Not the least of the results hoped for in the production of this volume is that this romantic and interesting region may, though its instrumentality, come to be better known to the outside world. We shall always treasure the reminiscences of a summer spent in climbing the mountains, sailing over the lakes, and tracing out the Indian trails in the forests, in our search for the rare and quaint in the annals of the Shawangunk.

CONTENTS.

The Shawangunk and its Environs,
The Delawares,
The First Esopus War,
The Second Esopus War,
The Esopus Mutiny,
The War with the Jerseymen,
The Mastodon,
Catherine DuBois,
Greycourt Inn,
Minisink Battle,
Brant and the School-girls,
Claudius Smith,
Edward Roblin,
Lieutenant Burt,
The DuBois Homestead,
Massacre at Fantinekill,
Burning of Warwarsing,
Kortright's Expedition,
Anderson and Osterhout,
Polly Tidd,
Captivity of Mrs. Coleman,
Phebe Reynolds and the Tories,
Miss Land's Midnight Journey,
The Tories after the Revolution,
Tom Quick, the Indian Slayer,

Tom Quick and the Indian Muskwink,
Tom Quick and the Buck with Seven Skins,
Tom Quick's Indian Exploits,
Indian Stratagem to Slay Tom Quick,
The Savages plan Tom Quick's Capture,
Early Settlers of the Shawangunk Region,
A Border Alarm,
Sam's Point, or the Big Nose of Aioskawasting,
"Gross" Hardenburgh,
Little Jessie Mitteer and the Bear-trap,
A Rival of Israel Putnam,
Panther Hunting at Long Pond,
Bear Hunt on the Mongaup River,
Casualty on Blue Mountain,
Nelson Crocker and the Panthers,
The Disappointed Groom,
New Paltz,
Needderduytse Taal te Schawankonk,
The Traps,
Shanks Ben,
Facts and Fancies,

LEGENDS OF THE SHAWANGUNK.

THE SHAWANGUNK AND ITS ENVIRONS.

THE Shawangunk is a vast amphitheatre of rocks piled into the most fantastic shapes, with forests covering its crests and slopes, and sporting the exuberance of Nature's own flower-garden. Here the arbutus, the azalea, and the laurel, successively clothe the sides with vernal beauty.

The summits overlook the valleys of the Rondout and Walkill, beautiful as Paradise, where lie the great grazing and dairy farms of world-wide celebrity; while eastward can be traced the valley of the Hudson, from Cornwall to the mountains about Lake George.

From these airy heights mountain views may be seen such as will strike the beholder with astonishment. On the south the view is bounded by the mountains of New Jersey; the highlands of the Hudson lie to the southeast, with the white sails of sloops and smoke of steamers in Newburgh bay, plainly visible to the naked eye; the Housatonic mountains of Connecticut bound the horizon on the east; the whole line of the Berkshire mountains of Massachusetts, and portions of the Green mountains of Vermont, may be seen to the northeast; while the Helderbergh mountains on the north, the Catskill and Shandaken mountains on the northwest, and the Neversink mountains on the west, complete a panorama in some respects unrivalled in America.

If we are moved with emotions of grandeur at the sublime power of the Creator as manifested in this great panorama of mountains, what must be our feelings, when, under the light of geology, we have presented for our contemplation the convulsions that have brought these mountains into being, and the mutations that have marked their history for unnumbered ages?

The Shawangunk was old before God had formed Adam out of the dust of the ground, and had breathed into him the breath of life; it has witnessed changes in the earth's condition of which the mind can form no adequate conception.

This globe, geologists say, was once in a fluid state; that in cooling, the unequal contraction of the earth's crust caused some parts to rise above surrounding portions, producing mountain ranges. The whole Appalachian system, of which the Shawangunk forms a part, owes its existence to this agency.

They tell us, also, that this continent, mountains and all, was once submerged beneath the ocean. Marine shells are to this day found imbedded in the rocky crests of Shawangunk; no theory other than that the waves of old Ocean once beat above it can account for their presence there.

This submerging process antedates the period of the deluge of Noah's time, as is indicated by the organic remains, which are those of extinct animals. Palæontologists estimate the number of species of fossil remains to be more than 12,000, yet scarcely one of this number has been identified with any creature now living.

Gradually the land was elevated to its present level, the ocean receded, and drainage took place from the surface of the earth. Lay bare to-day the rock on which the soil of Sullivan county rests, and it will be found to be furrowed and grooved as the agency of flowing water carried on for successive ages is now known to effect. The general direction of these grooves, together with other evidences, show these vast currents to have come from the north and northwest. Some of the natural depressions, as, for instance, the Mamakating valley, are filled to a great depth by masses of sediment deposited by the water before it receded.

There are examples of denudation in this vicinity; that is to say, the hills have been worn away and lowered, and the deep valleys made still deeper, by tremendous cataracts and surges, as the water rushed violently over high ledges, and fell hundreds of feet into the valley below. While contemplating such a scene, the imagination must fall far short of the reality. The tidal wave that destroyed the port town of Lima, or the surge that overwhelmed the Turkish fleet in Candia, destructive as they were, but faintly shadow the terrific scene.

It requires considerable stretch of the fancy to imagine immense icebergs floating over these mountain peaks, as, swayed by the combined action of wind and current and tide, they impinged against the sides and tops of the elevations, causing those huge rents and fissures that constitute a distinguishing feature of the mountain scenery of this locality.

When the water partially subsided, the ice-floes may have rested on the surface, and were congealed to whatever they came in contact with; and, as they were subsequently borne up on the flow of the tide, they detached tons of rock from its parent bed; then, floating over mountain and valley, the *débris* was deposited when the wasting away of the ice loosened its hold. This seems to be the most plausible theory in accounting for the fact that masses of Shawangunk grit, weighing many tons each, were carried up the western slope and over the tops of the Shawangunk mountain, and deposited near Newburgh, where we now find them.

The series of elevations composing the Shawangunk have a decided Alpine character; that is to say, there are numerous peaks elevated above general summits, while the summits themselves are broad, wild and rocky. In many places the declivities are precipitous and rugged in the extreme. There are occasional depressions, or passes, which are locally known as "cloves." The "Pass of the Mountains," at Otisville, on the line of the Erie railroad, is well worthy of study.

Near the point where the Millbrook stream flows down into the Walkill valley, is a series of remarkable mural precipices, from 300 to 600 feet in perpendicular height. This adamantine wall of parti-colored rock, constitutes one of the distinguishing features of the mountain; and a ramble upon its dizzy heights, where a walk has been laid out along the very brink, provided one's nerve is strong enough, is an achievement long to be remembered. On the top of this ledge are found the finest specimens of the far-famed Shawangunk huckleberries.

This mountain range, so near to the crowded thoroughfare, yet characterized by such wild and picturesque scenery, with deep intervening valleys, and abounding in natural lakes, has much to interest the artist and the seeker after rest and health. The shades of tint and color, varying with the course of the seasons and the daily changes of the weather, are not to be surpassed in any quarter of the world.

Lying at intervals on the very summit of this mountain, are several considerable lakes of remarkable depth and clearness. Lake Mohonk is especially a romantic body of water, surrounded by masses of huge rocks piled in heaps a hundred and fifty feet high. When twilight descends upon the bosom of the lake, and the great rocks that bend over it send out their shadows athwart its dark expanse, it blends the gloomy, the grand, and the picturesque in a scene that is full of sublimity.

Washington Irving, who once journeyed over this mountain in company with Martin Van Buren, thus describes his impressions:

"The traveler who sets out in the morning from the beautiful village of Bloomingburgh, to pursue his journey westward, soon finds himself, by an easy ascent, on the summit of the Shawangunk. Before him will generally be spread an ocean of mist, enveloping and concealing from his view the deep valley and lovely village which lie almost beneath his feet. If he reposes here for a short time, until the vapors are attenuated and broken by the rays of the morning sun, he is astonished to see the abyss before him deepening and opening on his vision. At length, far down in the newly revealed region, the sharp, white spire of the village church is seen, piercing the incumbent cloud; and as the day advances, a village, with its ranges of bright-colored houses and animated streets, is revealed to the admiring eye. So strange is the process of its development, and so much are the houses diminished by the depth of the ravine, that the traveler can scarcely believe he is not beholding the phantoms of fairyland, or still ranging in those wonderful regions which are unlocked to the mind's eye by the wand of the god of dreams. But as he descends the western declivity of the mountain, the din of real life rises to greet his ear, and he soon penetrates into the midst of the ancient settlement, of which we have before spoken."

Men are now living in the environs of the Shawangunk whose experience there reads like a western romance. They will tell you of camping in the woods at night, sleeping on a bed of hemlock boughs with only the sky for a covering, on the very spot where populous villages are now located; where, in place of the sound of church bells, and the scream of the locomotive, their ears were greeted with only the shrill bark of the fox, the howl of the wolf, and the soughing of the wind in the tree-tops.

The mythology of the ancients clothed inanimate nature with a new and poetic interest. Every meadow had its fairy, every forest its wood-nymph, and every cascade its water-sprite; while flowery nook and woodland glade were peopled with a merry crew that danced in the light of the harvest-moon, or sported at will in the dew-bespangled grass. These creations of the fancy, while adding a new interest to rural localities, helped to lift the mind out of the prosaic ruts which a dull routine of toil induces, and gave the imagination something more agreeable to dwell upon than the humdrum cares and responsibilities of life.

In like manner it may be said that history and tradition have lent an added charm to the natural beauties of the Shawangunk region. Every lonely road has its tale of tragedy, and every mountain pass its story of encounter with wild beast or savage Indian; every lake has its legend, and every stream its store of border incident.

For untold ages before the advent of the white man the catamount here made his lair, the bear roamed in search of mast, and the deer fed on the lily pads in the upland lake. The wild Indian hunted through its fastnesses, fished from its streams, and, with stealthy and cat-like tread, followed the trail into his enemy's country.

The rocky sides of old Shawangunk have more than once been reddened with the lurid glare of burning homes; its precipices have echoed back the groans of the dying frontiersman, laid low by a shot from an ambushed enemy; the night winds have borne along its rugged outline the shrieks of women and the wails of children, mingled with the war-whoop of the savages, as the work of carnage went on.

Here, too, as we have before intimated, may be found a wealth of rare attractions to the student of geology—in fact, such as will interest all who desire to read the great lessons of creation traced by a Divine hand upon the rocky strata of the mountains, or in the fossils imbedded in the peat and marl of the lowlands. Cabinets of rare value may be collected along these hills and at the excavations of the mines, during a very brief interval of leisure.

The rocks composing the Shawangunk are mainly the shells and sandstones of the Chemung group. "Shawangunk grit" crops out on the west side of the mountain, and has been quite extensively used as millstones, locally known as "Esopus millstones." The entire mountain has been pretty thoroughly examined from presumed indications of veins of coal.

At the foot of the western slope the Bashaskill and Neversink river flow southwardly; on the east side the Shawangunk kill runs in a northerly direction, all the streams lying close under the base of the mountain. This same peculiarity is observed in the Walkill and Hudson rivers, their general course lying parallel to each other, yet flowing in opposite directions.

A NATIVE SHAWANGUNKER

The whole range is intersected by metalliferous veins. Besides, the vicinity is so full of traditions of Indians obtaining both lead and silver in abundance, and at so many points in the mountain, that it is looked upon as a bed of ores of undisputed riches. The openings to the mines were carefully concealed, as is asserted, by the Indians and early settlers, and with their death perished all knowledge of the location of the minerals. Stickney relates an account given of two men who worked a silver mine somewhere in the mountain, previous to the Revolutionary war. This mine was shown them by some Indians; they carried on operations with the utmost secrecy, working only at night, and making long and mysterious journeys to dispose of their ore. When the war broke out they joined the army, each pledging the other not to reveal the secret until the war was ended. One cold, dark night they drew a large flat stone over the mouth of the mine, strewed leaves over the place, and at the distance of thirty paces east marked three trees which stood close together.

One of the men never returned from the war; the other was absent nine years. His family meanwhile had fled for safety to a distant village, and his first duty was to look after their welfare, and provide for them another home in the forest in place of the one destroyed. When he had leisure to look after the mine he found that predatory bands of Indians had burned the marked trees, and obliterated the natural landmarks, and he was unable to locate the mouth of the mine. No one has to this day removed that stone from the entrance to this cavern of mineral treasure.

Another old gentleman related that his father once saw the mine. At his earnest and repeated solicitations, a friendly Indian chief consented to take him to it, but he must allow himself to be blindfolded. He was accordingly led for a distance into the wilderness up hill and down dale, and finally went down into the heart of the mountain, as he judged by the dripping of the water on the rocky sides of the cavern. At length the bandage was taken from his eyes, and he stood before a solid vein of silver. Though he many times searched all through the mountain, he could never afterwards find the place. Old residents say "every seven years a bright light, like a candle, rises at twelve o'clock at night above the mine, and disappears in the clouds; but no one that has ever seen it has been able in daylight to find from whence it arose."

It is related that the savage Unapois, beholding a gold ring on the hand of a white woman, demanded why she carried such a trifle. He was answered by the husband of the lady, "If you will procure me such trifles I will reward you with things suitable for you." "I know," said the Indian, "a mountain filled with such metal." "Behold," continued the other, "what I will give you for a specimen," exhibiting a fathom of red and a fathom of blue frieze, some white lead, looking-glasses, bodkins and needles, and tendering the savage an escort of two soldiers. The Indian declined the escort, but accepted the presents, and promised to give a specimen; if it gave satisfaction he might be sent back with some of the white people.

After some days the Indian returned with a lump of ore as large as his fist, which was found to be of good quality, and a considerable amount of gold was extracted from it, and made into rings and bracelets. The Indian was promised further presents if he would disclose the situation of this mountain. Unapois consented, but demanded a delay of a few days, when he could spare more time. This was acceded to, and after having received more presents he returned to his nation. He indiscreetly boasted of his presents, and declared the reason of their presentation, which led to his assassination by the sachem and others of his tribe, lest he should betray the situation of the gold mine. There was a prediction current among the Indians to the effect that after their people had passed through a period of punishment for some great offence they had committed, the Great Spirit would once more smile upon them and restore them to the land of their fathers, and they wished to reserve those mines against their return.

THE DELAWARES.

THE Indian of the Western continent belongs to the "bow and arrow" family of men. To him the chase meant everything. When the advent of Europeans drove the deer from the forests and the beaver from the natural meadows, and the pursuit of hunting was no longer profitable, the red man pined and wasted away as though his life was robbed of everything that made existence desirable. The Indian could form no higher ideal of earthly happiness; and his most blissful conception of Paradise was that of a hunting-ground abounding in game, and where the streams and lakes swarmed with fish.

A characteristic of the American Indian is a dislike of restraint. A degree of personal independence incompatible with a state of society in which each individual's actions are modified from consideration for his neighbor, has ever caused the Indian to chafe under the restrictions imposed by civilization. The greatest chief among them had no delegated authority. His power to rule was founded on public opinion, and when that was against him, he was no more than a common savage; but when largely in his favor, his power was despotic. To be foremost in danger, and bravest in battle, were requisites necessary to sustain himself in authority.

Another propensity of the Indian is a passion for war. He followed the war-path because it gratified the most deeply seated principle of action in the savage breast, a thirst for revenge; and also because that was the only means by which he might hope to satisfy his ambition, and rise to a position of authority and influence in his tribe. With the aboriginal the forgiveness of an injury was reckoned a weakness, while revenge was considered among the nobler virtues. Tales of bloody, retributive vengeance were told about their council fires, by way of inciting the young warriors to deeds of similar daring.

The Indian believed in a Great Spirit, everywhere present. He believed also in the existence of subordinate spirits, both good and bad. He belonged to a singularly superstitious race, and put the most implicit faith in dreams and omens. When disease came among them, when the chase was unsuccessful, when their crops failed or they were defeated in war, they thought the Great Spirit was displeased with them; at such times they would perform religious ceremonies with great earnestness and solemnity, by way of propitiation of his wrath.

Among them the dance was universal; but it was not for purposes of pastime, as among civilized nations. It had a deeper signification. It was a solemn ceremony, and was an outward expression of their sentiments of religion and war.

It is the logic of events that the red man yields to the conquering foot of the Saxon. The weaker race has withered from the presence of the stronger. "By the majestic rivers and in the depths of the solitary woods, the feeble son of the 'bow and arrow' will be seen no more; the cypress and hemlock sing his requiem."

The Delawares related a legend to the effect that many centuries ago their ancestors dwelt far in the western wilds. Emigrating eastwardly, after many years, they arrived on the *Namæsi Sipu* (Mississippi), where they encountered the *Mengwe* (Iroquois), who had also come from a distant country. The spies of the Delawares reported that the country on the east of the river was inhabited by a powerful nation, dwelling in large towns erected upon the principal rivers.

This people were said to be tall and robust, warlike, and of gigantic mould. They bore the name of *Alligewi* (Alleghany); their towns were defended by regular fortifications, many vestiges of which are yet apparent. The Delawares, requesting to establish themselves on their territory, were refused; but obtained leave to pass the river that they might seek a habitation farther to the eastward. The Alligewi, alarmed at their numbers, violated their word and destroyed many of the Delawares who had reached the eastern shore, and threatened a like fate to the remainder, should they attempt the passage. Roused at this act of treachery, the Delawares eagerly accepted a proposition from the Mengwe, who had hitherto been spectators of the occurrence, to unite with them for the conquest of the country.

A war of extermination was then commenced, which eventuated in the expulsion of the Alligewi, who fled from their ancient seats never to return. The devastated country was apportioned among the conquerors, the Mengwe choosing the neighborhood of the lakes, and the Delawares appropriating the territory further to the south.

For many years the conquerors lived together in much harmony. Some Delaware hunters, having penetrated far into the forest, discovered the great rivers, the Susquehanna and Delaware; and crossing the *Skeyickby* (New Jersey) country, came at last to the *Mahicannittuck* (Hudson river) Upon their return to their nation, they described the country they had visited as abounding in game, fish, fowl and fruits, but destitute of inhabitants. Summoning together their chiefs and principal men, after solemn and protracted deliberation it was concluded that this was the home destined for them by the Great Spirit; and thither the tribe went and took up their abode, making the Delaware river, to which they gave the name of Lenapewihittuck, the centre of their possessions.

The Mengwe, thus left to themselves, hovered for a time on the borders of the great lakes with their canoes, in readiness to fly should the Alligewi return. Having grown bolder, and their numbers increasing, they stretched themselves along the St. Lawrence, and became near neighbors to the Delawares on the north.

In process of time the Mengwe and the Delawares became enemies. The latter said the Mengwe were treacherous and cruel, and pursued an insidious and destructive policy towards their more generous neighbors. Not daring to engage in open warfare with the more powerful Delawares, the Mengwe resorted to artifice to involve them in a war with distant tribes. Each nation had a particular mark upon its war-clubs, which, placed beside a murdered victim, denoted the aggressor. The Mengwe killed a Cherokee warrior, and left with the dead body a war-club with the mark of the Delawares. The Cherokees, in revenge, fell upon the latter, and commenced what proved to be a long and bloody war.

The treachery of the Mengwe was at length discovered, and the Delawares turned upon their perfidious neighbors with the avowed purpose of extermination. They were the more induced to take this step, as the cannibal practices of the Mengwe[*] had reduced that nation, in the estimation of the Delawares, below the rank of human beings.

Hitherto the tribes of the Mengwe had acted each under its particular chief. Being so sorely pressed by the Delawares, they resolved to form a confederation, the better to control their forces in war, and regulate their affairs in peace. Thanwewago, a Mohawk chief, was the projector of this alliance. Under his auspices, five nations, the Mohawks, Oneidas, Onondagas, Cayugas and Senecas, formed a species of republic, governed by the united councils of their aged sachems and chiefs. To these a sixth was afterwards added, the Tuscaroras of North Carolina.

The effect of this centralization of power early manifested itself. The Iroquois confederacy became a terror to their enemies, and extended their conquests over a large part of the territory lying between the Atlantic and the Mississippi. The Delawares were frequently at war with the Dutch, and, if tradition is to be believed, the Dutch and Iroquois conspired for their destruction. However that may be, the confederated tribes, having been taught the use of fire-arms by the whites, soon asserted a supremacy over the less fortunate Delaware Indians, and the latter were reduced to the condition of a conquered people.

According to a tradition among the Delawares, their forefathers were once fishing at a place where the Mahicannittuck widens into the sea, when they beheld a white object floating upon the water. Word was sent to the village, and the people came to view the wonder. Various conjectures were made as to what it could be. Some thought it was an immense animal floating upon

---

[*] The Mengwe, or Iroquois, sometimes ate the bodies of their prisoners. It is said, too, of the Algonquins, that they drank their enemies' blood.

the water; others said it was a huge fish; others still believed it to be a large wigwam.

As the apparition moved steadily toward the land, the natives imagined they could discover signs of life in it. Their chiefs and wise men were summoned together; after mature deliberation they came to the conclusion that it was a very large wigwam, in which the Great Spirit resided, and that he was coming to visit them. This decision created a profound sensation among those simple children of the forest. The Manitou, from whom they received the choicest gifts, and who so seldom made himself visible to his creatures, was about to land upon their shores, and be seen by them and converse with them.

The sacrifice was prepared, the best food provided, and a dance ordered to honor him, and appease his anger if his mood were wrathful. Fresh runners arrived who declared their strange visitant to be an immense floating wigwam, and that it was crowded with living creatures. Later still, other messengers reported the living things were human beings, with pale faces and strange garments, and one of their number was clad in magnificent apparel. The latter they decided was the Great Manitou himself.

In due time their wonderful visitors landed. Some of the natives were overcome with fear, and were about to run away and hide themselves in the woods; but the wise men and warriors of the tribe tried to prevent such an exhibition of cowardice, and counselled that they unite in giving a fitting reception to their marvellous guests.

A large circle of their principal men was formed, towards which the man in gold lace approached, accompanied by two others of the pale faces. Salutations were given on both sides. The Indians could not conceal their wonder at the brilliant ornaments and white skin of the supposed Manitou; they were sorely puzzled when they found he did not understand the words of his children, and that he spoke in a language unintelligible to them.

While they were regarding him with a respectful gravity, a servant brought a large *hack-hack* (gourd), from which was poured a liquid which the Great Being drank, and then offered to one of the chiefs. The savage looked at it, then smelled it, and was not pleased with its pungent odor. It was then passed to the next chief, who followed the example of the first, and gave the vessel to the one next to him. In that manner it was transferred to each one in the circle, and it was about to be returned to the supposed Manitou, when a great and brave warrior conceived the act would be disrespectful to the Deity, and forthwith harangued the warriors on the impropriety of their conduct. He explained that while it would be meritorious to follow the example of the Manitou, to return what he had given them might displease him, and lead him to punish them. The speaker would, therefore, drink the contents of the cup himself, and though he perished, the sacrifice would save his nation from destruction. Having proclaimed his laudable intention, he bade his followers farewell, and drank the contents of the cup. Soon he began to exhibit signs of intoxication. While the natives were regarding him with interest, supposing him to be under the effects of the poison, he fell to the ground. His companions imagined he was dead, but he was only dead drunk.

Presently the would-be martyr exhibited signs of life; and when he had sufficiently recovered from his fit of intoxication to speak, he told the assembled chiefs that the liquor had given him the most pleasing sensations that he had ever experienced. All of them had an anxiety to feel these sensations. More of the intoxicating beverage was solicited; the cup this time was not passed without being tasted; and a general debauch followed. The supposed Manitou was Henry Hudson; and this was the first visit of the white man to the country of the Delawares.

The territory embraced between the Hudson and the head-waters of the Delaware, now included in the counties of Orange, Ulster and Sullivan, is a region of peculiar interest. Less than three centuries ago these valleys and hills swarmed with villages of the Leni-Lenape; and now not one representative of the aboriginal occupants of the soil remains among the scenes sacred to the memory of his fathers. The story of the causes that led to their extinction, and to the peopling of their *Muck-cos-quit-tais*, or "corn-planting grounds," by pale-faced usurpers, is a tale of thrilling interest, and is well worthy a niche in history.

The council seat of the Leni-Lenape or Delawares was at Minisink, near the junction of the Neversink and Delaware rivers. Here the chiefs and principal men of the nation met to decide the questions relating to the welfare of their people; here they smoked the pipe of peace, or determined the question of carrying war into the territory of their enemies.

Near Cochecton was the Indian village where the clans met, in accordance with their ancient customs, to celebrate their green-corn dances, their dog-festivals, and indulge in their favorite pastime of La Crosse. On the banks of the Hudson was the famous Danskamer, or "Devil's Dance Chamber," where burned the religious fires of the natives, that were never suffered to go out, lest the wrath of the Great Spirit should be aroused from their negligence.

When the white strangers came from over the sea, these natives shared with them their hunting-grounds, and generously set apart, for their use, fields for planting. Esopus, and other early settlements of Ulster, lay along the old Indian trail connecting the Hudson with the head waters of the Delaware, while the ancient settlement of Peenpack grew and flourished in the heart of the Delaware country. Thus the savages, thrown into frequent communion with the whites, were initiated into some of the customs of their more civilized neighbors; while the latter not infrequently adopted some of the habits of their dusky friends.

For years the hardy pioneers and their red brothers would live amicably together, fishing from the same streams, hunting through the same forests, and tilling contiguous fields of corn. Occasional broils would break out between the two races, in which the Indians were not always the aggressors. When savage ferocity was once roused, the work would be decisive and sanguinary. Without a moment's warning, in the silent, unguarded hours of slumber, the settler's home would be invaded with terrific war-whoop and murderous tomahawk, and the whole family massacred or carried away into captivity.

It is to be observed that the difficulties between the Delaware Indians and their white neighbors, which caused so much bloodshed on both sides, originated mainly from misunderstandings in regard to lands. The natives claimed, and not without reason, that they were cheated in their transactions with the Dutch; that the latter assumed possession of more land than was sold to them; and that boundaries and lines were altered, and always in favor of the whites. It cannot be denied that the Indians were not always paid the full stipulated purchase price, and were overreached by their more wily pale faces in various reprehensible ways.

Lossing, in his "Field Book of the Revolution," gives an instance in point. The natives had conveyed a territory to the "Proprietors of Pennsylvania," the boundaries of which were to extend a certain distance on the Delaware or "Great Fishkill" river, and as far back, in a northwest direction, as a man could travel in a day and a half. The Indians intended the depth of the tract should be about fifty miles, the distance a man would ordinarily walk in the specified time. But the purchasers employed the best pedestrians in the colonies, who did not stop by the way even to eat while *running* the line; the expiration of the day and a half found them eighty-five miles in the interior! The Indians boldly charged them with deception and dishonesty.

The "Proprietors" claimed that they had become the owners of the lands within the Forks of the Delaware river, by a regular form of conveyance, and that the Indians had been fully paid for them. The Delawares, on the other hand, denied the validity of the sale, and asserted that they had never received a stipulated consideration. The case was, in 1742, laid before the Six Nations for arbitration, who, after hearing both sides, decided that the disputed territory could not be sold by the Delawares, as they were a conquered people, who had lost their right in the soil; that if the lands did not belong to the white people, it was the property of the Six Nations. With two such rivals for claimants, as the scheming whites and the dreaded Iroquois, the Delawares were fain obliged to forego their claim to the disputed territory. Some years ago a quantity of old spurious coin was dug up near Otisville, on the line of the Erie railroad. It was so clumsily executed as to preclude the supposition that it was the work of a gang of counterfeiters. The more reasonable theory is that it was intended to be used to cheat the Indians as they were not the best judges of money.

Such treatment ruffled the tempers of the Delawares, and predisposed them to make other complaints. They declared that the whites had spoiled their hunting-grounds; that they had destroyed the deer with iron traps; and that the traders of Minisink always made the Indians drunk when they took their peltries there, and cheated them while they were in that condition. The period

The Delawares.

of the French and Indian war was now approaching; and had the settlers of the Shawangunk region adopted a different policy in their treatment of the Delawares, and so predisposed their dusky neighbors in their own behalf, many of the atrocities which thrilled and startled the people of that frontier would have been averted. While the Dutch and English were building up a wall of enmity between themselves and the Indians by adopting a course of treachery and artifice, the more wily French emissaries were making good use of that very circumstance to incite them against the English occupants of the territory, and so win them over to the interests of the French monarch. The results of the over-reaching policy of the Dutch and English recoiled with terrible effect on their own heads.

The defeat of Braddock, in July, 1755, on the banks of the Monongahela, was another of the causes that led the Indians of the whole territory of the Delaware to take sides with the French. That defeat, so discreditable to the military prestige of Great Britain, entirely destroyed the influence of the English with those tribes.

Once the murderous tomahawk was unburied, the whole frontier, from Virginia to the banks of the Hudson, at once felt the dire effects of savage ferocity. The following description does not overstate the reality: "The barbarous and bloody scene which is now open, is the most lamentable that has ever appeared. There may be seen horror and desolation; populous settlements deserted, villages laid in ashes, men, women and children cruelly mangled and murdered, some found in the woods, very nauseous, for want of interment, and some hacked, and covered all over with wounds."

During the winter ensuing, the enemy continued to hang on the frontiers. A chain of forts and block-houses was erected along the base of the Kittanning mountains, from the Neversink river to the Maryland line, and garrisoned by fifteen hundred volunteers and militiamen under Washington. It may not be generally known that Benjamin Franklin once engaged in a military campaign. He received the appointment of Colonel, and in the service of defending this chain of forts, he began and completed his military career, being convinced that war was not his chosen calling.

By September of 1756 it was estimated that one thousand men, women and children had been slain by the Indians, or carried into captivity. Property to an immense amount had been destroyed, and the peaceful pursuits of civilized life were suspended along the whole frontier. Although Colonel John Armstrong subsequently administered a severe chastisement upon the savages in their den at Kittanning, killing their chiefs, slaughtering their families, and reducing their towns and crops to ashes, yet scalping parties continued to penetrate into the Mamakating and Rondout Kill valleys, some of them venturing into settlements east of the Shawangunk mountains. Under these circumstances, for the settlers to remain on their farms was to court death in a hideous form. The majority of the women and children were removed to Rochester, Wawarsing, New Paltz, and other localities for protection.

The reduction of Canada by the English, and the consequent overthrow of the French power and domination on the western continent, did not afford our frontiers entire immunity from savage atrocity and outrage, as the settlers had hoped. An era of better fellowship seemed to be dawning between the two races, which for awhile seemed to promise much; but when the War for American Independence broke out, the natives again entered upon the war-path, urged thereto by British influence, and, as has been asserted, and by facts substantiated, by proffers of British gold.

The Delawares are no more seen along the rivers and valleys of the Shawangunk region. If the blood of the Leni-Lenape of the Neversink and Walkill valleys yet flows in the veins of the living, it is to be looked for in the scattered remnants of the Indian clans of the far distant west.

The Indian, like his prototype the Mastodon, who aforetime roamed through these fertile valleys, bids fair, as a race, to become extinct. Years ago, a poor, friendless Delaware came into the vicinity, the last of the tribe that was ever seen here. He was last noticed at Bridgeville, Sullivan County, where he was made the sport of a lot of vicious boys. A Mr. Rice, then an invalid, whom all supposed in an advanced stage of consumption, rescued him from his tormentors, and gave him a hat and some money. The Indian received them gratefully, and after gazing thoughtfully for some time on his benefactor, he left the neighborhood, never more to return. Some months elapsed, and the incident had nearly passed out of mind, when Mr. Rice received a letter from the Indian, in which the latter gave a minute description of his complaint, with directions for its cure. The treatment was undertaken, and the remedy proved so efficacious that Mr. Rice's health was completely restored. The grateful savage had travelled forty miles from his home in the wilderness to deposit his letter in the post-office.

Competent judges have pronounced the Delaware language the most perfect of any Indian tongue, it being distinguished, they say, by "great strength, beauty, and flexibility." The tribe have left behind them, as mementoes of their former dominion over the soil, names that they gave to mountains, streams and localities. No people, ancient or modern, bestowed more beautiful names on water-courses and valleys than did the Delawares. However long one may have been accustomed to perfect euphony and exact rythm, these appellations delight the ear as does the rich, sweet cadence of the hermit thrush that sings upon their banks—such words, for instance, as Wyoming, Mamekoting, Moyamensing and Osinsing. Their names of mountains, on the other hand, are harsh and rugged, as Shawangunk, Mohunk, Wachung, Scunnemunk, and others.

THE FIRST ESOPUS WAR.

IT is a peculiar feature of American history that many of the earlier settlements owe their establishment to the religious persecutions of the old country. Sometimes the Catholics drove the Protestants from their homes to find refuge in strange climes, as the French did the Huguenots at the Revocation of the Edict of Nantes; and again we behold a Protestant persecuting dissenters and Catholics alike, as the English did the Puritans of New England and the Romanists of Maryland. Another relic of old Europe, the outcome of the ancient feudal system, was the custom of granting large tracts to individuals called Patroons, thus establishing a system of tenantry, with the Lord of the Manor as the chief head. Both these causes, as we shall see, contributed to the settlement of Ulster county.

Holland at that time was denominated a "cage of unclean birds," because, it being a government founded on religious tolerance, all religions flocked there. Some English and French Walloons, who had found temporary refuge among the Hollanders, afterward emigrated to America, and settled at Rensselaerwyck. The management of the affairs of the Patroon of that section had been given to Brandt Van Schleetenhorst, "a person of stubborn and headstrong temper." This man was very earnest in defending what he considered the rights of his lord against the Governor of New Netherland and the West India Company. Stuyvesant claimed a jurisdiction about Fort Orange, and insisted that the Patroon was subordinate. Van Schleetenhorst denied both, and went so far as to dispute Stuyvesant's right to proclaim a fast in his jurisdiction. To insure allegiance, the Patroon pledged his tenants not to appeal from his courts to the Governor and Council; and finally, orders were issued for tenants to take the oath of allegiance to the Lord of the Manor. This bold proceeding Governor Stuyvesant was moved to call a crime. Some of the settlers sided with the Governor, and others with the doughty Van Schleetenhorst; the dispute at last ran so high that the two factions came to blows.

Among these tenants was one Thomas Chambers, an Englishman by birth, "tall, lean, with red hair, and a carpenter by trade." He was one of the Walloons that fled from his home to escape religious persecution, only to find himself involved in the troubles about the proprietary rights of the new country, a quarrel in which he had no interest; subject to the whim of his landlord or his commissary, treated as a slave, and victimized by covetous officers. He and his companions, therefore, cast about them for a new settlement, "where they could work or play, as seemed best to them." Chambers emigrated to the vicinity of Troy; but finding he was still on territory claimed by his old landlord, he removed to Esopus, having heard the land there was good, and that the savages had expressed a desire that the Christians would come among them.

Tradition says they landed at the mouth of Esopus Creek, and journeyed up until they reached the flats of Kingston. Here Chambers received a "free gift" of territory from the natives.

In 1655 a general war broke out between the Indian tribes on both sides of the Hudson, and the whites of Amsterdam and vicinity. When the news of this outbreak reached Esopus the inhabitants all fled, leaving their stock, dwellings and crops to the mercy of the savages. This action was the more necessary, as the few inhabitants were living scattered on their farms, without even a block-house for protection. During their absence their empty houses and unprotected grain was appropriated by the Indians. Albany records say the farmers returned to their homes as soon as peace was restored.

It had been the purpose of the Directors of the West India Company to construct a fort at Esopus, and orders had been issued to that effect. The orders were not obeyed, hence the unprotected state of the settlement. The savages had their wigwams all around the farms of the white people, and their maize-fields and bean-patches were near to each other. The hogs, cows and horses of the settlers roamed at will on the untilled flats, frequently destroying the crops of the Indian women. This made the Indians mad, and they complained of the depredations of the stock to the owners, but the animals still roamed.

Now and then a pig was found dead with an arrow or bullet in it. Now it was the Christian's turn to get mad. Still it might have been possible for the whites and Indians to have lived together in comparative amity, but for an additional source of trouble.

Jacob Jansen Stohl, agent for the Governor at Esopus, wrote to Stuyvesant to the following purport: "The people of Fort Orange (Albany) sell liquor to the Indians so that not only I, but all the people of the Great Esopus, daily see them drunk, from which nothing good, but the ruin of the land, must be the consequence."

In these transactions the whites were sometimes more to blame than the savages, and yet they wrote in this wise: "Christ did not forsake us; He collected us in a fold. Let us therefore not forsake one another, but let us soften our mutual sufferings."

In a letter from Thomas Chambers to Governor Stuyvesant, dated May, 1658, we find additional evidence of the baneful effects of the strong drink sold to the savages. He writes in substance: "I saw that the savages had an anker (ten-gallon keg) of brandy lying under a tree. I tasted myself and found it was pure brandy. About dusk they fired at and killed Harmen Jacobsen, who was standing in a yacht in the river; and during the night they set fire to the house of Jacob Adrijansa, and the people were compelled to flee for their lives. Once before we were driven away and expelled from our property; as long as we are under the jurisdiction of the West India Company we ask your assistance, as Esopus could feed the whole of New Netherland. I have informed myself among the Indians who killed Harmen, and they have promised to deliver the

VIEW NEAR RAMAPO STATION ON THE ERIE RAILWAY

savage in bonds. Please do not begin the war too suddenly, and not until we have constructed a stronghold for defense."

The following month Chambers again wrote:—" We have done our best to apprehend the murderer, but have been mockingly refused by the barbarians. In answer to our inquiry who sold them the brandy, the savages refer to no one in particular, but to many, now Peter, then Paul. It is evident that it is not for the sake of selling their stock of beavers alone that they keep near Fort Orange (Albany), where, as the make of the brandy keg proves, the coopers have hardly sufficient time to supply the demand by these people. The savages set fire to the cow-shed, the pig-sty, and then the dwelling-house of Jacob Adrijaensen, and not being satisfied, compelled us here to plow for them. Upon our refusal they take fire brands and hold them under the roofs of our houses, to set fire to them. The common savages do not pay any attention to their chiefs, as the latter seem to have lost their authority. We are obliged to remain in our houses, as the savages would immediately attack us when we stir about, and set everything on fire; therefore we request your favor for a succor of forty or fifty men."

In response to the above letters, at a meeting at which were present Honorable Director-General Peter Stuyvesant and three councillors, the following action was taken: They took up and seriously considered the letters from Esopus. By the first they were informed that the savages had killed Harmen Jacobsen and set fire to two houses, and behaved and acted very insolently and wantonly; by the second the savages were continuing in their intolerable insolence and boldness, forcing the people there to plow for them, etc. It was therefore resolved that the Director-General should go there forthwith, and fifty or sixty soldiers as a body-guard, to make arrangements. This Director-General was no less a personage than Peter the Headstrong, of whom Washington Irving gives the following facetious description:

"Peter Stuyvesant was the last, and, like the renowned Wouter Van Twiller, the best of our ancient Dutch governors, Wouter having surpassed all who preceded him, and Peter never having been equalled by any successor. He was of a sturdy, raw-boned make, with a pair of round shoulders that Hercules would have given his hide for, when he undertook to ease old Atlas of his load. He was, moreover, not only terrible for the force of his arm, but likewise of his voice, which sounded as if it came from a barrel; and he possessed an iron aspect that was enough of itself to make the very bowels of his adversaries quake with terror and dismay. All this martial excellence of appearance was inexpressibly heightened by an accidental advantage, that of a wooden leg; of which he was so proud that he was often heard to declare he valued it more than all his other limbs put together. Like Achilles, he was somewhat subject to extempore bursts of passion, which were rather unpleasant to his favorites and attendants, whose perceptions he was wont to quicken, after the manner of his illustrious imitator, Peter the Great, by anointing their shoulders with his walking staff." The following is embodied in the journal of Governor Stuyvesant's visit to Esopus:

"We left in the private yachts on the 28th day of May, arriving at the kill of the Esopus on the 29th. To avoid commotion among the savages, or causing them to flee at the sight of so many soldiers before they could be spoken with, I ordered the accompanying yachts to follow separately at a distance, and not to anchor near me before nightfall, nor to show too many soldiers on deck at once. I sent a barge ashore opposite to two little houses of the savages, to invite two or three of the Indians aboard. The barge presently came back with two savages, and also Thomas Chambers and another man, who were induced to come down to look for help from the good south wind and expected relief. I persuaded the savages by a little present to go inland and induce the Indian sachems to meet me at the home of Jacob Jansen Stohl the following day, his being the last dwelling in contiguity, or the day after that, assuring them that no harm should come to them or theirs. They agreed to do it, and were put on shore after I had some further talk with the two Christians, Chambers and Van Der Sluys. The other yachts arriving during the evening passed by us who were aground close to the shore. I ordered the soldiers landed with the least possible noise, without beating the drum; which being done, they were to send for me and my people on my yacht. We marched the same evening to the 'bouwery' of Thomas Chambers, that being the nearest, for the night. On the morning of the 30th, that being Ascension Day, we marched to the house of Jacob Jansen Stohl, nearest to the habitations and plantations of the savages, where we had made the appointment to meet them, and where, on Sundays and at the usual feasts, the Scriptures were read.

"When the people had assembled in the afternoon I stated to them that I had come with sixty soldiers, asking of them their opinion of what it were best to do; that I did not think the present time was favorable to involve the whole country in a general war on account of the murder, the burning of two small houses and other complaints about threats of the Indians; that now in summer, with the prospect of a good harvest, it was not the proper time to make bad worse, least of all by giving room too hastily to a blind fear; that it was not in our power to protect them and the other outlying farmers as long as they lived separately from each other, and insisted upon it contrary to the order of the Company.

"They answered they should be ruined and indigent men if they were again obliged to leave their property, which result would follow if they could get no protection against the savages. I told them they could get no protection as long as they lived separately; that it was necessary that they should remove together at a suitable place, where I could and would assist them with a few soldiers until further arrangements were made; or they might retreat with their wives, children, cattle, and most easily removed property to the Manhattans, or Fort Orange for safety; but if they could make up their minds to neither, they must not in future disturb us with complaints.

"Each was of opinion that it was dangerous to remain in their present condition; there was a good harvest in prospect, with which they hoped to sustain their families the coming winter; to abandon those fertile fields at this juncture would occasion great loss, and entail upon them and their families abject poverty. The necessity of a concentrated settlement was at length conceded, but it was thought impracticable to effect the removal of the houses and barns before harvest time, in addition to the labor of inclosing the place with palisades. They plead very earnestly that the soldiers might remain with them until after the harvest; this I peremptorily refused, and insisted that they should make up their minds without delay. To encourage them I promised to remain with the soldiers until the place was enclosed with palisades, provided they went to work immediately, before taking up anything else. Another difficulty presented itself—each one thought his place the most conveniently located for the proposed enclosure. But on the last day of May the inhabitants brought answer that they had agreed unanimously to make a concentrated settlement, and each had acquiesced in the place selected, and in the final arrangements. The grounds were staked out that same afternoon.

"In response to my request of the Indian chiefs for a conference, twelve or fifteen savages made their appearance at the house of Jacob Jansen Stohl, but only two chiefs were among them. They explained that the other sachems would not come before the next day; that they were frightened at so many soldiers, and hardly dared to appear; also that they had been informed that more soldiers were to follow.

"After assurances on my part that no harm should befall them, they became more cheerful; and the same evening about fifty savages made their appearance at the house of Stohl. After they had all gathered under a tree outside of the enclosure, about a stone's throw from the hedge, I went to them, and so soon as we had sat down, they, as is their custom, began a long speech, telling how in Kieft's time our nation had killed so many of their people, which they had put away and forgotten.

"I answered that this all happened before my time, and did not concern me; that they and the other savages had drawn it all upon themselves by killing several Christians which I would not repeat, because when peace was made the matter had all been forgotten and put away among us [their customary expression on such occasions].

"I asked them if since peace was made any harm had been done to them or theirs; they kept a profound silence. I stated to them and upbraided them for the murders, injuries, and insults during my administration, to discover the truth and authors of which I had come to Esopus at this time, yet with no desire to begin a general war, or punish any one innocent of it, if the murderer was surrendered and the damages for the burned houses paid. I added that they had invited us to settle on their lands in the Esopus, that we did not own the land, nor did we desire to until we had paid for it. I asked why they had committed the murders, burned the houses, killed the hogs, and did other injuries.

"Finally one of the sachems stood up and said that the Dutch sold the 'boison' [brandy] to the savages, and were the cause of the Indians becoming 'cacheus' [crazy] mad or drunk, and that then they had committed the outrages; that at such times they, the chiefs, could not keep in bounds the young men who were then spoiling for a fight; that the murder had not been committed by any one of their tribe, but by a Neversink savage; that the Indian who had set fire to the houses had run away and would not be here. That they were not enemies; they did not desire or intend to fight, but had no control over the young men.

"I told them if the young men had a desire to fight to come forward now; I would match them, man for man, or twenty against thirty or even forty; that now was the proper time for it; that it was not well to plague, injure or threaten the farmers, or their women and children; that if they did not cease in future, we might try to recover damages. We could kill them, capture their wives and children, and destroy their corn and beans. I would not do it because I told them I would not harm them; but I hoped they would immediately indemnify the owner of the houses, and deliver up the murderer.

"To close the conference I stated my decision: that to prevent further harm being done to my people, or the selling of more brandy to the Indians, my people should all remove to one place and live close by each other; that they might better sell me the whole country of the Swannekers [Dutch] so that the hogs of the latter could not run into the corn-fields of the savages and be killed by them. The chiefs then asked through Stohl and Chambers that I would not begin a war with them on account of the late occurrence, as it had been done while they were drunk; they promised not to do so again.

"On Monday, June 3d, the soldiers with all the inhabitants began work on the palisades. The spot marked out for a settlement has a circumference of about 210 rods,* well adapted by nature for defensive purposes; and when necessity requires it can be surrounded by water on three of its sides. To carry on the work with greater speed and order I directed a party of soldiers and experienced wood-cutters to go into the woods and help load the palisades into wagons; the others I divided again into parties of twenty men each, to sharpen the palisades and put them up. The inhabitants who were able were set to digging the moat, who continued to do so as long as the wind and the rain permitted.

"Towards evening of the 4th of June a party of forty or fifty savages came to where we were at work, so that I ordered six men from each squad to look after their arms. After work had been stopped they asked to speak to me. They informed me they had concluded to give me the land I had asked to buy to 'grease my feet,' as I had come so long a way to see them. They promised in future to do no harm to the Dutch, but would go hand in hand and arm in arm with them.

---

* Dutch rod 12 feet.

"Being in need of gunpowder, of which we had only what was in the 'bandoleers,' and lacking some plank for a guard-house, and some carpenters to aid in our work, I concluded to go in the Company's yacht to Fort Orange for the same. I arrived back at Esopus on the afternoon of the 12th, and found every body at work, and two sides of the palisades finished. About noon of the 20th the stockade was completed, it being necessary only to stop apertures where roots of trees had been in the ground; this was completed in good time the same day.

"Having accomplished the work so far I set out on my return, leaving 24 soldiers to assist in guarding the place. As they had themselves 30 fighting men, besides seven or eight carpenters, they were in my opinion capable of taking care of themselves."

But the peace begun under such favorable auspices was of short duration, as we learn by a letter from Sergeant Lawrens, the officer in charge of the military at Esopus, to Governor Stuyvesant. He wrote:—

"Send me quickly orders. The Indians are becoming savage and insolent, and have killed a fine mare belonging to Jacob Jansen. They are angry that you challenged twenty of their men to fight. Those returned from the beaver-hunt say if they had been here they would have accepted the challenge. They talk about it every day; and to-day about five hundred savages are assembled, and their numbers constantly increasing. Provide us as quickly as possible with ammunition." Ensign Dirck Smith was dispatched to the relief of the garrison with twenty-five additional troops, making the fighting strength a total of fifty men, exclusive of the citizens.

Smith was directed to make secure the enclosed place, mount a sufficient guard, and not allow any savage to pass through except upon permission of Jacob Jansen Stohl or Thomas Chambers. They were not to act "hostilely" against the Indians, but to stand strictly on the defensive. The agricultural labors were to be kept up under a guard of from twenty to twenty-five men; the laborers themselves were directed to take their arms with them, "that in case of attack they may make a better stand against the savages;" and were also instructed to keep as close together as possible.

In October of 1658 the Esopus sachems made a conveyance of the land as they had promised. They said they hoped the soldiers would now lay down their arms, that the settlers need now fear nothing. They promised they would hunt many beavers and pass right by Fort Orange with their peltries; they liked to see the plows work, but no soldiers." The following graphic account of a collision between the savages and the settlers we find in the records:

"*To the Honorable, Wise and very Valiant, His Honor Director General Peter Stuyvesant at New Amsterdam :—*

"As on the 20th, at night between 10 and 11 o'clock, some savages raised a great noise and yelling under the fort, whereupon Dirck de Goyer and two others alarmed me on the guard, I commanded the sergeant to take nine or ten men, and directed him to go out by one of the gates and return by the other one, and not to molest anybody. The sergeant sent back word that a crowd of savages was there. Jacob Jansen Stohl came to the guard, saying 'I will go, give me four or five men.' After they had returned I asked them who ordered them to fire, and they said the savages had shot first. Jacob Jansen Stohl replied violently that the dogs [Indians] had vexed us long enough; that they lie in the bushes all around; and that they have fired innumerable brand arrows into grain stacks and barns. They attempted to set fire to the barn of Hap, but the barn being covered with plank, the corn was saved; and they have killed several cattle belonging to us. One prisoner escaped from them; he gives the number of savages as four hundred. He thought the white prisoners in their hands were all alive, but badly off. He said further, if we had not some cannon here, not one of us, large or small, would have escaped."

The records say when the Dutch came to the place they fired a volley among the Indians as they lay around a fire.

One savage was knocked in the head with an axe, and was left for dead, but he presently made off. Another, while lying on the ground stupidly drunk, was hewn on the head with a cutlass, which roused him so that he fled; after which the Dutch retreated to the fort with great speed. We find the following version of the affair given by the Catskill Indians:—

Eight Esopus Indians broke off corn ears for Thomas Chambers. When they finished work the savages said, "Come, give us brandy." Chambers replied, "When it is dark." When evening was come he gave a large bottle with brandy to the Indians. They retired to a place at no great distance from the fort and sat down to drink. The eight savages drank there until midnight; by that time they were drunk, and they began to yell. At length the brandy came to an end. One Indian said, "Buy more brandy; we still have wampum." The savage who was afterwards killed went to Chambers' house to get more brandy. Chambers said, "I have given you all I had." The savage then went to where the soldiers were, taking with him the bottle which he hid under his cloak. "Have you any brandy?" said the Indian. "Yes, I have brandy," answered a soldier. "Here is wampum, give me brandy for it." "What is wampum, and what can I do with it? where is your kettle?" said the soldier. "I have no kettle, but I have a bottle here under my cloak," replied the savage. The soldier filled the bottle, but would take nothing for the brandy.

The savage came to his comrades who were lying about and crying, and asked them, "Why do you cry? I have brought brandy!" Whereupon they changed their cry, and asked if he had given all the wampum. "No, a soldier gave it to me." They replied "that is very good," and began to drink lustily from the bottle, because they had no goblet or ladle. When the bottle was passed around the savages began to wrangle and fight. Two of them presently said to each other, "We have no cause to fight, let us go away;" so they went away, leaving six. After a little time one of the remaining savages said, "Come, let us go away; I feel that we shall be killed." Said the other, "You are crazy; who should kill us? We would not kill the Dutch, and have nothing to fear from them or the other Indians." "Yes," replied he, "but I nevertheless am so heavy-hearted."

The bottle was passed twice, and the savage said again, "Come, let us go; my heart is full of fears." He went off and hid his goods in the bushes at a little distance. Coming back drunk once more they heard the bushes crackle as the Dutch came there, without knowing who it was. Then this savage went away, saying "Come, let us go, for we all shall be killed;" and the rest laid down together, whereupon the Dutch came and all of them fired into the Indians, shooting one in the head and capturing another. One drunken savage was continually moving about, whereupon the Dutch fired upon him repeatedly, nearly taking his dress from his body.

Ensign Smith knew what the consequences of this outbreak would be, and he sought to ascertain who ordered the firing contrary to his express instructions. The Dutch cast all the blame on the Indians, saying that the latter fired first. The affairs of the colony being in such an unsatisfactory state, and finding the people would not respect his authority, Smith announced his intention of leaving for New Amsterdam next day. Great excitement was manifested when this became known. The people tried to dissuade him from his purpose by representing their exposed condition, and making assurances of future obedience on their part. Smith was intractable, and continued making preparations for his departure; but by an adroit measure of Stohl and Chambers, who hired all the boats in the neighborhood, he found himself unable to carry out his resolution. It was deemed expedient, however, to acquaint the Governor of the state of affairs, and accordingly Christopher Davis was dispatched down the river in a canoe for that purpose.

Davis was escorted to the river by a company of eight soldiers and ten citizens, under Sergeant Lawrentsen, Sept. 21st, 1659. On the return of the escort to the village they fell into an ambuscade near where now stands the City Hall; the Sergeant and thirteen men surrendered without firing a shot, the rest making their escape. War now began in earnest. More than five hundred savages were in the vicinity of the fort, who kept up a constant skirmish with the settlers. By means of firebrands they set fire to the house of Jacob Gebers; numbers of barracks, stacks and barns were in like manner destroyed. One day they made a desperate assault on the palisades which came near being successful. Failing in this, the savages slaughtered all the horses, cattle and hogs they could find outside the defenses. Three weeks was a constant siege kept up so that "none dare go abroad." Unable to take the town they vented their fury on the unfortunate prisoners.

Jacob Jansen Van Stoutenburgh, Abram Vosburg, a son of Cornelius B. Sleight, and five or six other were compelled to run the gauntlet; they were next tied to stakes, and, after being beaten and cut in the most cruel manner, were burned alive. Thomas Clapboard [Chambers], William the carpenter,

Peter Hillebrants and Evert Pel's son were among the captives. These are the only names mentioned in the early records. Clapboard was taken by six warriors down the Esopus kill. At night he removed the cords by which he was bound, and successively knocked five of his captors in the head while they were asleep, killing the sixth before he could fly, and making good his escape. Another prisoner, a soldier, got home safely after a somewhat rough experience Peter Laurentsen and Peter Hillebrants were ransomed; Pel's son, then a mere youth, was adopted into the tribe and married among them. Overtures were afterwards made to the Indians by the friends of the lad for his return; but the savages answered that he "wished to stay with his squaw and pappoose, and he ought to."

News of these events filled the whole colony with fear and forebodings. Stuyvesant had only six or seven soldiers in garrison at Amsterdam, and they were sick and unqualified for duty. He then sent to Fort Orange and Rensselaerwyck for reinforcements; but the inhabitants of Fort Orange could not succor without leaving their own homes defenseless. The Governor asked for volunteers, offering Indians as prizes; only six or seven responded. He then conscripted all the garrison at Amsterdam, the Company's servants, the hands in his brewery and the clerks. The people made great opposition to this, averring that "they were not liable to go abroad and fight savages."

Notwithstanding these hindrances Governor Stuyvesant set sail October 9th with about 160 men, and reached Esopus next day. Here he found the siege had been raised thirty-six hours before, and that the savages had retreated to their homes whither the Governor's troops could not follow them, for the country was then inundated with nearly a foot of water from the frequent rains.

In the spring of 1660, there was a renewal of hostilities; an Indian castle having been plundered, and several savages taken captive, the Indians sued for peace and proposed an exchange of prisoners. Stuyvesant declined their overtures, and prosecuted the war with vigor, sending some of the captive chiefs, then in his hands, to Curaçoa, as slaves to the Dutch.

The clans now held a council. Said Sewackenamo, the Esopus chief. "What will you do?" "We will fight no more," said the warriors. "We wish to plant in peace," replied the squaws. "We will kill no more hogs." answered the young men.

Stuyvesant met their propositions with an extravagant demand for land. The fertile corn-planting grounds of the Walkill and Rondout valleys had excited the cupidity of the colonists. The savages were loth to give up so much of their territory, but they finally acceded to the Governor's demand. During the negotiations the Indians plead for the restoration of their enslaved chiefs. But in pursuance of Stuyvesant's policy, those ancient sachems had become the chattels of Dutchmen, and were toiling, under the lash, in the maize and bean-fields among the islands of the far-off Caribbean Sea; so the Governor replied that they must be considered dead. Although deeply grieved at this, the chiefs agreed to the treaty, and departed.

THE SECOND ESOPUS WAR.

SOME acts of crimination and recrimination having occurred between the Dutch settlers of Kingston and Hurley and their Indian neighbors, growing out of a misunderstanding in regard to some lands, the feud finally terminated in what is spoken of in the Documentary History of New York as the "Massacre at the Esopus." To be more certain of success the Esopus clans endeavored to get the Wappinger Indians of Duchess, and other of the neighboring clans, to join them, and succeeded partially. To lull the suspicions of the whites, a proposition for a new treaty was made only two days before the attack

On the 7th of June, 1663, a band of two hundred Indians entered the two villages in the forenoon, from different points, and dispersed themselves among the dwellings in a friendly manner, having with them a little maize and a few beans; under pretense of selling these they went about from place to place to discover the strength of the men. After they had been in Kingston about a quarter of an hour, some people on horseback rushed through the mill-gate crying out "The Indians have destroyed the New Village!" And with these words the savages immediately fired their guns, and made a general attack on the village from the rear, hewing down the whites with their axes and tomahawks. They seized what women and children they could and carried them prisoners outside the gates, plundered the houses, and set the village on fire to windward, it blowing at the time from the south. The remaining Indians commanded all the streets, firing from the corner houses which they occupied, and through the curtains outside along the highways, so that some of the inhabitants while on their way to their houses to get their arms were wounded and slain. When the flames had reached their height the wind veered to the west, otherwise the flames would have been much more destructive. So rapidly did the murderers do their work that those in different parts of the village were not aware of what was transpiring until they happened to meet the wounded in the streets. Few of the men were in the village, the rest being abroad at their field labors. Capt. Thomas Chambers, who was wounded on coming in from the fields, issued immediate orders to secure the gates, to clear the gun and drive off the savages, which was accordingly done. After the few men in the village had been collected, and by degrees others arriving from different quarters, being attracted by the columns of smoke and the firing, they mustered in the evening sixty-nine efficient men. The burnt palisades were immediately replaced with new ones, and the people distributed, during the night, along the bastions and curtains to keep watch.

In this attack on the two villages fifteen men, four women and two children were killed. Most of the women and children killed were burned to death. Of the prisoners taken by the Indians at this outbreak there were thirteen women, thirty children, and one man. At Kingston twelve houses were burned, while the New Village was entirely destroyed.

Soldiers were now sent up from New York, and the Indians were hunted like wild beasts from mountain to mountain. The force employed, including the volunteers from Esopus, numbered nearly three hundred men. Scouting parties were sent out in every direction in which it was supposed hostile Indians could be found, destroying their crops and burning their wigwams.

On the 26th of July a party of upwards of two hundred men, including forty-one Long Island Indians and seven negroes, left Kingston to attack the savages at their fort about thirty miles distant, "mostly" in a southwest direction. They had as a guide a woman who had been a prisoner of the Indians, and took with them two pieces of cannon and two wagons. The cannon and wagons they were forced to abandon before reaching the fort. They intended to surprise the Indians, but found the fort untenanted except by a solitary squaw. The next day they sent a force to surprise the savages on the mountain, but were unable to surprise any. For two days and a half the whole party then employed themselves in destroying the growing crops and old maize of the Indians, the latter of which was stored in pits. Over two hundred acres of corn, and more than one hundred pits of corn and beans, were rendered worthless by the invading forces. The natives witnessed these proceedings from their look-out stations on the Shawangunk and neighboring mountains, but made no resistance. Quinlan supposes this fort to have been on the headwaters of the Kerhonkson. After this expedition the savages proceeded to build a new fort thirty-six miles south-southwest of Kingston. The site of this fort is on the right bank of the Shawangunk kill, near the village of Bruynswick. Against this fort Capt. Kregier marched the following September, with a force of fifty-five men and an Indian guide. Kregier says in his journal, in substance:

It having rained all day the expedition must rest for the present. Asked the Sheriff and commissaries whether they could not get some horses to accompany us, so that we may be able to place the wounded on them if we should happen to have any. After great trouble obtained six horses, but received spiteful and insulting words from many of the inhabitants. One said, let those furnish horses who commenced the war. Another said, if they want anything they will have to take it by force. The third said he must first have his horse valued and have security for it.

About one o'clock on the afternoon of the 3d we started from Fort Wiltwyck; marched about three miles to the creek and lay there that night, during which we had great rain. The next morning we found such high water and swift current in the kill that it was impossible to ford it. Sent men on horseback to Fort Wiltwyck for axes and rope to cross the creek. Crossed over about two o'clock in the afternoon and marched four miles further on, where we bivouacked for the night. Set out again at daybreak, and about noon came to their first maize-field, where we discovered two squaws and a Dutch woman who had come from their new fort that morning to get corn. But as the creek lay between us and the corn-field, though we would fain have the women, we could not ford the stream without being discovered; we therefore turned in through the wood so as not to be seen.

About two o'clock in the afternoon we arrived in sight of their fort, which we discovered situated on a lofty plain. Divided our force in two, and proceeded in this disposition along the kill so as not to be seen and in order to come right under the fort. But as it was somewhat level on the left of the fort, the soldiers were seen by a squaw who was piling wood there, who thereupon set up a terrible scream. This alarmed the Indians who were working upon the fort, so we instantly fell upon them. The savages rushed through the fort towards their houses in order to secure their arms, and thus hastily picked up a few bows and arrows and some of their guns, but we were so close at their heels they were forced to leave some of them behind. We kept up a sharp fire on them and pursued them so closely that they leaped into the creek which ran in front of the lower part of their maize land. On reaching the opposite side of the kill they courageously returned our fire, so that we were obliged to send a party across to dislodge them.

In this attack the Indians lost their chief, fourteen other warriors, four women and three children, whom we saw lying on this and on the other side of the creek; but probably many others were wounded. We also took thirteen of them prisoners, besides an old man who accompanied us about half an hour, but would go no farther. *We took him aside and gave him his last meal.* We also recovered twenty-three Christian prisoners out of their hands. A captive Indian child died on the way, so that there remained eleven of them still our prisoners.

We next reviewed our men and found we had three killed, and one more wounded than we had horses. We then held a council of war; after deliberation it was determined to let the maize stand for the present. We however plundered the houses, wherein was considerable booty, such as bear and deer skins, blankets, elk hides, besides other smaller articles, many of which we were obliged to leave behind us, for we could well have filled a sloop. We destroyed as much as we could; broke the kettles into pieces, took also twenty four guns, more than half of which we smashed, and threw the barrels here and there in the stream. We found also several horns and bags of powder, and thirty-one belts and some strings of wampum. We took the best of the booty along and resolved to set off. We placed the wounded on horses and had one carried in a blanket on poles by two soldiers in turns. The first day we marched two miles from the fort.

The Christian prisoners informed us that they were removed every night into the woods, each night to a different place, through fear of the Dutch, and brought back in the morning; but on the day before we attacked them, a Mohawk visited them, who remained with them during the night. When about to convey the Christian captives again into the woods the Mohawk said to the

Esopus Indians—"What, do you carry the Christian prisoners every night into the woods?" To which they answered "Yes." Hereupon the Mohawk said "Let them remain at liberty here, for you live so far in the woods that the Dutch will not come hither, for they cannot come so far without being discovered before they reach you." So they kept the prisoners by them that night. The Mohawk departed in the morning, leaving a new blanket and two pieces of cloth, which fell to us as a booty.

Early on the morning of the 6th we resumed our journey. The same day came just beyond the Esopus kill, where we remained that night. At this place the Indian child died, which we threw into the creek. Arrived at Wiltwyck about noon of the following day.

On the 22d a detachment was sent out from Wiltwyck to guard some plowmen while they labored in the fields. About midnight the party passed along the kill where some maize lay, about two hours march from the village. On arriving there they found only a small patch of maize, as it had all been plucked by some straggling Indians or bears. Our people carried off what remained. The Indian prisoners whom we held had first informed us, to-day, that a small spot of corn had been planted there principally to supply food to stragglers who went to and fro to injure the Christians. Should they come again they'll not find any food.

About eleven o'clock on the following night, a party was sent about three miles in a northeasterly direction from Wiltwyck, having been informed there was some Indian maize at that place, to see if they could not remove it either by land or water. They returned about two o'clock in the afternoon of the next day and reported they had been on the Indians' maize plantation, but saw no Indians, nor anything to indicate they had been there for a long time, for the maize had not been hoed, and therefore had not come to its full growth, and had been much injured by wild animals. One plantation however was good, having been hoed by the Indians, but that was likewise much injured by wild beasts. They said it was beautiful maize land, suitable for a number of bouweries, and for the immediate reception of the plow. On Sunday afternoon, September 30th, powder and ball were distributed to the soldiers and friendly Indians, in the proportion of one pound of powder, one pound of lead and three pounds of biscuit for each man, who was to accompany an expedition into the Indian country. On Monday marched from Wiltwyck with 108 men and 46 Marseping Indians. About two o'clock of the following day we came to the fort of the Esopus Indians that we had attacked on the 5th of September, and there found five large pits into which they had cast their dead. The wolves had rooted up and devoured some of them. Lower down on the kill were four other pits full of dead Indians and we found further on the bodies of three Indians, with a squaw and a child, that lay unburied and almost wholly devoured by the ravens and the wolves. We pulled up the Indian fort and threw the palisades, one on the other, in sundry heaps and set them on fire, together with the wigwams around the fort, and thus the fort and houses were destroyed and burnt. About 10 o'clock we marched thence down along the creek where lay divers maize plantations, which we also destroyed and cast the maize into the creek. Several large wigwams also stood there, which we burnt. Having destroyed everything we returned to Wiltwyck, reaching there in the evening of the next day.

About noon of Sunday, October 7th, a girl was brought up from the Redoubt [Rondout], who, the day before, had arrived on the opposite bank at that place, and was immediately conveyed across the stream. The girl said she had escaped from an Indian who had taken her prisoner, and who resided in the mountain on the other side of the creek about three miles from Wiltwyck, where he had a hut, and a small patch of corn which he had pulled, and had been there about three weeks to remove the corn. She had tried to escape before, but could not find her way out of the woods, and was forced to return to the hut. Forty men were at once sent out to try and catch the Indian. They reached the hut before sunset, which they surrounded with the intention of surprising the savage, but the hut was found to be empty. They found a lot of corn near the hut, and another lot at the kill, part of which they burned, and a part they brought back with them. They remained in the hut during the night and watched there. On the 10th of that month, Louis Du Bois, the Walloon, went to fetch his oxen which had gone back of Juriaen Westphaelen's land. As he was about to drive home the oxen, three Indians, who lay in the bush with the intention of taking him prisoner, leaped forth. One of the savages shot at him with an arrow, slightly wounding him, whereupon Louis struck the Indian a heavy blow on the breast with a piece of palisade, and so escaped through the kill, and brought the news to the fort. Two detachments were instantly dispatched to attack them, but they had taken to flight and retreated into the woods.

The Indians were finally cowed. Their principal warriors had been slain, their fort and wigwams burned, and their food and peltries destroyed. A long hard winter was before them, and the ruthless white soldiers ready to swoop down upon them at any moment. Under these circumstances the Delawares sued for peace, and the truce was observed for a period of about ninety years, or until the breaking out of the French and Indian war.

When Capt. Kregier marched against the new fort his forces probably crossed the Shawangunk kill at Tuthilltown, and keeping along the high ground came in rear of the fort. A portion of the command marched down the hill directly on the fort, while the other detachment cut off their escape in the other direction. This fort stood on the brow of a hill overhanging the creek; in the side of this hill there is a living spring with the Indian path still leading to it. The old Wawarsing trail led from this fort, crossing the Shawangunk mountain near Sam's Point.

THE ESOPUS MUTINY.

AFTER the capitulation of New Amsterdam and its dependencies to the Duke of York, in 1664, some English troops were sent to garrison Esopus. They were under command of Capt. Broadhead, an arrogant, ill-tempered, overbearing officer, whom the Dutch soon came to hate with all the fervor of their natures. There was a constant collision between the English military authorities and the Dutch civil magistrates. The inhabitants drew up a formal complaint against the garrison, and among the charges were the following: —

Cornelius Barentsen Sleight is beaten in his own house by soldier George Porter, and was after this by other soldiers forced to prison, and by some soldiers at his imprisonment used very hard.

Capt. Broadhead hath beaten Tierck Clausen and without any reason brought to prison.

Capt. Broadhead, coming to the house of Lewis Du Bois, took an anker of brandy and threw it upon the ground because Du Bois refused him brandy without payment, and did likewise force the said Du Bois to give him brandy. [Broadhead afterwards said in extenuation of the act that the anker was not broken, and no brandy spilled.]

And the said Du Bois' wife coming to Broadhead's house for money, he drove her out of the house with a knife.

The soldier George Porter coming in the barn of Peter Hillebrants, and finding there Dierck Hendricks, took his sword and thrust it through Dierck's breeches.

Two soldiers coming to Miller's to steal his hens, and Miller in defending his hens, was by the soldiers beaten in his own house.

Besides all this we are threatened by Capt. Broadhead and his soldiers that they will burn down all this town and all they that are therein—" Therefore we do most humbly supplicate that you will be pleased to remonstrate and make known unto the Governor the sad condition we are in, from whom we hope to have redress."

In answer to the above "standings," Captain Broadhead replies that he will keep Cornelius Sleight in apprehension "as longe as he thincks good," and that in case the inhabitants will "fitch" him by force, that he would wait upon them.

The soldiers in their own behalf say they went to the burgher's [Sleight's] house by Broadhead's command, when they found the burgher with his piece cocked, and his hanger [sword] drawn and laid upon his arm; they disarmed him by force and brought him prisoner to the guard. But at their first arrival at the aforesaid house they "found Capt. Broadhead with his cravat torn and thrown away, and his face scratched and very much abused." [It would appear that Sleight and the English Captain had been indulging in a little scrimmage, in which the latter had got the worst of it].

Eight or nine Dutchmen went armed to the place where their comrade was confined, headed by Hendrick Yockams. Capt. Broadhead with seven men marched to them and demanded the occasion of their being in arms. Their lieutenant made answer that they would have the burgher out of the guard. Broadhead commanded them to return with their arms to their houses; their lieutenant replied they would not, but would have the prisoner out of the guard.

One of their party, by name Anthony, a Frenchman, presented his piece against our Captain, being loaded with nine small bullets, and swore if he moved a foot he would fire upon him, and would not be persuaded nor commanded, but did persist in his rebellious actions.

They sent for Capt. Thomas Chambers, who lived outside the stockade, thinking he would have headed them, but he would not; but commanded them to return with their arms to their houses. They continued under arms until about nine in the evening, threatening that they would fetch the burgher out by force that night, and villifying us with our small party of men, saying, "What is fifteen or sixteen men to seventy or eighty?" as continually they have done from the beginning.

Another of the rebellious party by name of Albert Hymons, the chief instigator of the first rising, gave out speeches in the hearing of the soldiers that "if he had been in command he would not have left one English soldier alive in the Esopus."

Tyerk Clausen says the reason why Capt. Broadhead abused him was because he would keep Christmas on the day customary with the Dutch, and not on the day according to the English observation. Capt. Broadhead acknowledged it.

De Monts swore that last New Year's Day he had some friends at his house, and Captain Broadhead quarreled with the wife of Harmen Hendricksen, and threw a glass of beer in her face.

The burghers brought into court a paper to excuse their being in arms,— "because Captain Broadhead and the soldiers threatened to burn the town, and all that was in it, and also because Captain Broadhead had committed a burgher to prison, and had misused and cut him, so that his wife and children ran about the town crying that the English had killed their father."

Jacob Johnson and Claus Clasen sworn and said the reason why Antonio Dalve presented his gun at Capt. Broadhead was because he made to him with his naked cutlass, and threatened therewith to cut him in pieces.

When Capt. Thomas Chambers commanded the Dutch to return to their homes, and they refused, he went to the English guard and told them they were a lot of stubborn rogues, and would not be commanded by him. Whereupon he said he would have nothing to do with said mutinous rogues, and returned to his own house.

The wife of Cornelius Sleight, and her daughter, complaining to the Court that Capt. Broadhead had grievously cut, beat and wounded her husband, upon which the Court dispatched a messenger to request Captain Broadhead to come to the Court and received the following answer, "That if the Commissary would speak with him they might come to him," the burghers then being in arms.

The Court thereupon ordered Captain Chambers and Evert Pelee to desire Captain Broadhead to release the said burgher, and that if Sleight had offended him, he should, according to the Governor's order, complain to the magistrates, who would see that he was punished according to his deserts. To which Broadhead made answer, "that he would keep the said Cornelius as long as he pleased, and if they would fetch him he would be ready to wait upon them."

Antonio Dalve was heard by George Hall to say, when Captain Broadhead was getting some of the young burghers to go against the Dutch at Albany, "Shall we go and fight with our friends, and leave our enemies at home?" For this seditious utterance Antonio was called to account. He said in his defence that he meant to be understood as saying "Shall we go and fight our friends [the Dutch at Albany] who sold the savages powder and ball in the last Esopus war, and leave our enemies at home? meaning the Esopus Indians."

The Court made an effort to prevail on the burghers to disperse to their homes and lay down their arms. The latter replied that the English had twice threatened to burn the town, and requested that they be empowered by their magistrates to continue under arms; but the magistrates denied the same.

The English Governor Nicolls sent up two of his privy counsellors to try the case, who, upon hearing the evidence, took four of the offending Dutch burgomasters to New York, there to receive from the Governor their final sentence.

THE WAR WITH THE JERSEYMEN.

FOR some years prior to 1700, and as late as half a century afterwards, the Minisink country was embroiled in a tedious conflict with their New Jersey neighbors, over the question of a boundary line between the colonies of New Jersey and New York.

The misunderstanding grew out of the difficulty of determining what was the "northwardmost" branch of the Delaware river. Both parties started from the same point on the Hudson river, in latitude 40 degrees. New York on the one hand contended for a line that would strike Big Minisink island, while New Jersey insisted the line should strike the Delaware river just below Cochecton, making a triangular gore several miles in width at its western extremity.

The matter was brought to the attention of the General Assembly of each colony, and considerable spirit was shown in its consideration. A committee

VIEWS OF LAKE MOHONK, ULSTER CO., N. Y.

appointed by the New York Assembly reported to the House, October 29, 1754, that they could not certainly discover what was the "Northwardmost branch of the Delaware River;" that they find Minisink, and lands to the northward thereof, have been held by New York patents for nearly seventy years, which are bounded south by New Jersey; that the patents of New Jersey, for many years after the "fixation" of said boundary, did not extend northward above said bounds, nor did they extend jurisdiction above these bounds

That of late years large bodies of Jerseyites have with violence taken possession of lands above these bounds; and that New Jersey has erected the county of Sussex in part above these bounds.

That New Jersey Justices have assumed authority over subjects holding lands under and paying a submission to New York.

Also, that New York Justices, officers, and even ministers of the Gospel in Orange county, have been seized and beaten, insulted, carried into New Jersey and held to excessive bail or confined in prisons, and prosecuted by indictments.

That people of New Jersey have from time to time taken possession of vacant lands in Orange county, etc.

New Jersey assumed and exercised the right to assess and collect taxes from people residing in the county of Orange, so that some chose to desert their possessions and move further north

Thus while the respective Colonial Assemblies were adopting active partisan measures in the controversy, it may be supposed that the people most directly interested, acting in the spirit of that semi-lawless age, did not always wait for the slow process of legislative enactment to settle their disputes, but took the details into their own hands for adjudication in their own way.

By way of more effectually opposing the incursions of the Jerseymen, the people of Orange converted their dwellings into places of defense, armed themselves for sudden attack, and formed organizations for mutual aid and succor. Col. De Key, who was also a Justice of the Peace in and for Orange county, had settled upon lands within that county under patents granted by New York, where he had lived in peaceable possession for fifty years. Having been disturbed in his lands, and threatened with personal violence and ejectment, he proceeded to the residence of James Alexander, Esq., an East New Jersey proprietor, to lay the case before him, and if possible bring about some agreement between the contending parties until the line could be definitely settled. Col. De Key was told that if he would become a Jerseyman, and fight against the New York people, he should want neither commission nor money; that if he would do neither he would be dispossessed of his plantations. Col. De Key refused to accept of the conditions, went home, and prepared for war.

Subsequently, a number of armed men from East New Jersey came to the residence of De Key, who, seeing them approach, shut himself up in the house. They drew up in battle array, cocked their guns, and presenting them towards the window where De Key stood, assured him they would shoot him through the heart; that they would starve him out, and burn the house over his head;

that if a man, woman, or child, attempted to escape, he would be shot down; that they had the strength to take all Goshen, and would do it in time. They thereupon withdrew without further violence, one of them saying—"Take care of yourself, for we will have you yet!"

Some of the patentees becoming disheartened, sold out to others at great sacrifice and removed, which served to weaken the party in possession.

Among the pioneers of Orange county was one Harmanus Van Inwegen, a bold, strong and resolute man, who had married into the Swartwout family, who were among the patentees of the disputed territory. Van Inwegen was by nature and habit well fitted for the times in which he lived, and was admirably qualified for a leader in enterprises that required daring and resolution. The better to identify his interests with the cause of the New York patentees, he was given some of the lands under controversy; the result was he soon assumed the character of a fearless and able partisan.

One day while Van Inwegen was absent from home, some Indians came and commenced abusing his family. He was immediately sent for. When the Indians saw him coming they cocked their guns, and aimed them at his breast. He rushed in among them, tumbled one redskin in one direction, and sent another flying heels over head in another direction; in short, he handled his unwelcome guests so roughly that they fled from the house.

At another time, while Van Inwegen was raking grain in his field, a New Jersey constable and three or four assistants came to arrest him, and to take possession of his grain. Not submitting quietly to the process of arrest and the confiscation of his property, the constable wounded him with his sword. Van Inwegen thereupon broke the rake in pieces over the officer's head with such effect that all attempts at arrest were abandoned.

One Major Swartwout resided on the disputed lands. The New Jersey claimants were for a long time watching for an opportunity to enter his house and get possession before he could get help from his neighbors. The Major kept several loaded guns in the house, and employed an additional number of men about the premises, all of whom were proficient in the use of fire-arms. The Major's house thus became a fortified post, with an armament not to be despised.

Major Swartwout was a large, portly man, possessed of a fine military bearing; and, when arrayed in the rich and gaudy equipments of war, appeared to a good advantage on parade. Many a time has the drill-ground at Goshen resounded to his word of command.

Notwithstanding all the precautionary measures of the Major, some Jerseymen effected an entrance into his abode during his temporary absence in 1730, drove out his family, removed his goods, and assumed possession of the premises. His wife was confined to her bed at the time by the birth of a child, and the removal was the occasion of her death.

Measures were at once determined on to reinstate the Major in his domicile. Some reinforcements having arrived from Goshen, his party ambushed on a hill in a piece of woods near the Major's home. It was arranged that Peter Gnimaer should go to the house, and at a convenient opportunity enter and ascertain the situation of affairs. If he judged the circumstances favorable for an attempt at recapture, Peter was to go into the orchard and throw up an apple as a signal. The party on the hill soon had the satisfaction of seeing Peter make the signal agreed upon. They rushed out of the woods and into the house with such impetuosity as to overpower all opposition. The usurpers were expelled, and the Major reinstated in his possessions.

The people of Orange county employed a spy to act in their interest, who was to circulate among the Jersey claimants, acquaint himself with their plans, and send back reports of their proceedings. The spy soon sent them word that on a certain day the Jerseymen intended to raid the disputed territory with a strong party, with the view of dispossessing the occupants generally.

The day came at last; and with it came the sturdy yeomanry of Orange county—fathers, brothers, sons, all—to the home of Hermanus Van Inwegen, armed, equipped, and caparisoned for war. The preparations were barely completed when the van of the Jersey company came in sight.

Major Swartwout gallantly led his little army out into the road, and formed the men in line of battle.

Jacob Cuddeback said, to Van Inwegen, "We are old men; our lives are of less consequence than those of our younger companions; let us take our places in the front of the line." This act of self-sacrifice was immediately carried into execution; even the younger men evincing no dissatisfaction at the wise arrangement. The line was formed in double column, with the two old men in front as a cover to those in rear, and the Major himself at the head of his men: with this disposition of the force, they calmly awaited the onset with breathless interest.

The Jerseymen came within gunshot and halted. Such a military array as that with which they were now confronted—at once so unexpected and so formidable—served to weaken the ardor even of Jerseymen bent on conquest. Another incident, coming also unawares, contributed to strike dismay still more deeply into the stern hearts of the invaders.

Gerardus Swartwout, a young son of the Major, who was in the line behind the old men, called out to his father in a voice loud enough to be heard by the invading party: -

"Is this all in fun, Father, or in sober earnest; are we to shoot to kill, or only aim to hit them in their legs?"

"Shoot to kill," shouted the Major in tones of thunder—"pepper every rascal of them! Down with the ruthless invaders of our soil!"

This was more than the Jerseymen could stand. Their column began to waver, when Van Inwegen called out to the Major to give the order to open the battle.

"Ready! take aim! fire!" roared the Major. The two old men in front raised their weapons at the word of command, but before they could pull trigger the Jerseymen were in full retreat for the woods. Some stray shots were sent after them by some of the young men in the rear of the line of battle, with no effect. With this the military operations of the day concluded.

Some time after this the Jerseymen made another effort to capture the Major and Captain Johannes Westbrook. They chose the Sabbath as the time when, and the door of the church as the place where, they would be the most certain of taking their prey. Somewhere between the years 1764 and 1767 one Sabbath morning, a strong party surrounded the church armed with clubs. The Major and Captain Westbrook were among the congregation of worshippers. After the services were concluded and the people were coming out of the church, both men were captured and made prisoners, but not until after a long, rough-and-tumble struggle. The Major, being reckoned the more dangerous of the two, was taken and confined for a while in a Jersey prison.

THE MASTODON.

THE Shawangunk region, even were it wanting in any other recommendation to historic mention, is remarkable as having been the home of the Mastodon. Almost under the shadow of the rock-ribbed ascents, deep in the peat and marl of the adjacent valleys, several skeletons of these huge monsters have been exhumed, some of them the largest and most complete specimens that have come to the sight of man. In a tamarack swamp near Montgomery, in 1845, a gigantic and perfect skeleton was found in a peat bog with marl beneath, where it stood in an erect position, as if the animal lost its life in search of food by getting mired. In the place where its stomach and intestines lay was found a large mass of fragments of twigs and grass, hardly fossilized at all—the remains, doubtless, of the undigested dinner of the monster. This skeleton was eleven feet high and upwards of twenty feet long, and weighed 2000 pounds. It is now in a museum in Boston. Another skeleton, scarcely less remarkable for its size and completeness, was dug up in the year 1872 in the town of Mount Hope. This weighed 1700 pounds, and is now on exhibition in New Haven, Conn. No less than nine skeletons, more or less entire, have been exhumed within the limits of Orange county.

The era and haunts of this monster mammalia furnish abundant material for consideration, and is of interest both as attracting the superficial notice of the tourist and eliciting the more profound speculations of the geologist. Whether we contemplate the antiquity of his remains entombed for unknown ages in the peat and marl of a swamp—preserved by the antiseptic property of the medium that caused his death; or whether we think of his lordly mastery over the other beasts of his time, of the majesty of his tread over valley and mountain, of his

The Mastodon.

anger when excited to fury, uttering his wrath in thunder tones there is that in the subject which clothes the locality in a new and interesting light.*

In the north part of a swamp near Crawford's, Orange county, some years since, a mastodon skeleton was found. A writer says of it: "This skeleton I examined very minutely, and found that the carcass had been deposited whole, but that the jaw-bones, two of the ribs, and a thigh-bone had been broken by some violent force while the flesh yet remained on the bones. Two other parts of skeletons were found, one at Ward's bridge, the other at Masten's meadow, in Shawangunk. In both instances the carcasses had been torn asunder, and the bones had been deposited with the flesh on, and some of the bones were fractured. That the bones were deposited with the flesh appears from the fact that they were found attached to each other, and evidently belonged to only one part of the carcass, and no other bones could be found near the spot. Great violence would be necessary to break the bones of such large animals; in the ordinary course of things no force adequate to that effect would be exerted. I think it fair reasoning, that, at the deluge, they were brought by the westerly currents to the place where they were found; that the carcasses were brought in the first violent surges, and bruised and torn asunder by the tremendous cataracts, created when the currents crossed the high mountains and ridges, and fell into the deep valleys between the Shawangunk mountain and the level countries adjacent."

At what age in the world's history the mastodon lived, how and when he died, there is no well-developed theory.

Is the death and utter annihilation of the race attributable to an overwhelming flood which submerged the earth and swept down those animals as they peacefully and unsuspiciously wandered?

Was it some unusual storm, black with fury, terrible as a tornado, and death-dealing as a sirocco, which swept the wide borders of the Shawangunk, and in one wrathful, destroying stream swept the living mastodon into utter oblivion?

Was it the common fate of nations, the destiny of every created race of animals, that by the physical law of their natures, the race started into being, grew up to physical perfection, fulfilled the purpose of their creation, and became extinct?

Was it some malignant distemper, fatal as the murrain of Egypt and widespread as the earth itself, which attacked the herd and laid the giants low? Or was it rather individual accident, numerous as the race, befalling each one, and which, amidst the throes and toils of extrication, caused them to sink deeper and deeper still in the soft and miry beds where we find their bones reposing?

When did these animals live and when did they perish, are questions no more easy of solution. Were they pre-Adamites, and did they graze upon the

---

* Eager.

meadows and slopes of Shawangunk in the sunlight of that early period, ere man had been created? Or were they ante-diluvian, and carried to a common grave by the deluge of the Scriptures? Or were they post-diluvian only, and, until a very recent period, wandered over these hills and browsed in these valleys?

A formidable objection to these animals having lived within a few hundred years is the difficulty of so enormous a creature obtaining sustenance for himself through our winters. It would seem that the mastodon lived in a palæontological period more remote, when the climate was warmer, since the allied huge animals do live in warmer latitudes. Perhaps it was the change of climate that destroyed the mastodon.

Geologists are of opinion that the mastodon flourished about the middle of the tertiary period. If so, these creatures were here ages before man was created. The period of their extinction is thought to be more doubtful, probably just before the establishing of the first human pair in the Garden of Eden.

The mastodon belongs to the graminivorous class of quadrupeds. Had he belonged to the carnivorous race, subsisting on flesh, he would have been the most destructive butcher of which we could possibly conceive

"Otisville, Otisville!" shouts the trainman from a set of stentorian lungs, opening the door of the Erie Railway passenger coach as the train slows up at a little station high up the slope of the Shawangunk, at the eastern portal of the "Pass of the Mountains.' We alighted on the platform, and the train proceeded on its way through the deep cleft in the mountain, and the rumbling was lost in the distance as it crept along the dizzy heights of the western slope.

"Will you please point the way to the swamp where the Mount Hope mastodon was found?" we said to the first man we met, who happened to be the village post-master

"Certainly; come with me. I am going that way and will show you the place."

Following his directions, after a walk of about a mile over a rough country road, we came to the place indicated. The swamp has no distinguishing features, and covers a tract of some half-dozen acres. The highway winds to one side of it, while a side-hill pasture borders the other. The mastodon's remains were found near the lower end, only a few feet from solid ground. The creature had evidently ventured into the swamp in search of food, got mired in the peat and marl, and perished there—the skeleton being preserved from decay by the antiseptic properties of those substances that were instrumental in causing its death.

There is an excavation some ten or more yards in diameter where the bones were exhumed, which is now filled with water. The circumstances under which the Mount Hope fossil was found are these:

Some years ago a family by the name of Mitchel, residing in New York city, purchased a farm in the vicinity of Otisville. The land was none of the

The Mastodon.

best; but with commendable enterprise they immediately set about improving the property. Soon a large and commodious brick house was built; fences and outbuildings repaired; and the muck and marl from the swamp a few rods from the house were drawn out and spread upon the upland.

The place for the excavation was chosen solely on the ground of convenience in getting the product to the upland; by a fortunate coincidence that was the place where the creature went into the swamp and perished. One day while the men were at work they came upon a bone. Its great size astonished them and they could not divine what sort of animal it had belonged to. Soon after they came upon more bones, similar in form to the bones of animals with which they were familiar, only they were of mammoth size. At last they came to the bones of the pelvis, which were of such huge dimensions that the whole neighborhood flocked to behold the curiosity.

The Mitchels kept at the work of digging, but they now had a double purpose in view. At first the parts of the skeleton were thrown carelessly into a heap, and left there unprotected. Now, as fast as found, they were carefully guarded, and stored away under lock and key.

As the work proceeded the water became troublesome. The owner of the farm, believing he had found a prize, arranged to have the water pumped out while the search continued. The result of their labors was the exhuming of one of the most perfect fossil remains of the extinct mastodon that has ever been found, and which weighed about seventeen hundred pounds; the skeleton when put together stood over ten feet in height, and nearly fifteen in length. Some minor parts were missing, either not having been exhumed by reason of the difficulty experienced in digging, or having been carried away as souvenirs by curious visitors before their value was known

News of the finding of this valuable geological specimen spread through the country. Inquiries poured in by every mail, and some of the leading colleges took measures to secure it for their respective cabinets. Negotiations with the college authorities reached the point which made it certain that either Yale or Princeton would carry off the prize; and the question which of the two should get it would depend on whether a Yale or a Princeton representative arrived first on the ground.

Prof. Waterhouse Hawkins, of Princeton college, took passage on a train that was scheduled to stop at Otisville, the nearest station on the Erie railroad. Prof. O. C. Marsh, of Yale college, adopted, as he said, his usual custom, and took the first and swiftest train that started in the direction he wanted to go, and did not trouble himself to inquire whether it stopped at Otisville or not. The latter found means to induce the conductor of the train to slow up at a point nearest the Mitchell farm; and when Prof. Hawkins arrived by the accommodation train some hours later, the writings were all drawn in favor of Yale, and Prof. Marsh had made all sure by a payment on the same. And that is why the Mount Hope mastodon to-day graces the Yale museum instead of the college cabinet at Princeton.

A resident of Otisville, who was personally acquainted with the conductor of the train on which the Yale professor took passage, said to him a few days afterwards:—"You had a distinguished passenger on board of your train the other day, I hear."

"Not that I know of," said the conductor.

"Didn't you slow up your train to let a gentleman off?"— mentioning the day.

"Yes, I did."

"That passenger was Prof. Marsh, of Yale college. Now tell me how you came to accommodate him so far as to let him get off between stations."

"Well, I'll tell you how that came about," replied the railway official, knocking the ashes from his Havana, and assuming an air of gravity; "you see, that fellow had some deuced good cigars with him!"

Dr. Theo. Writer, of Otisville, was present when the Professor was packing the mastodon in boxes. The Doctor had in his possession the skull of a weasel; and knowing that Prof. Marsh was an authority on skeletons, took it down to show him. "Here, Professor," said the Doctor, "here is a skull not quite so large as the one you are packing in that box, but if you will accept it with my compliments, you are welcome to it."

The Professor looked at it and instantly exclaimed, "That is a weasel's skull." And then he went on to give some facts in natural history relating to those mischievous little animals. He thanked Dr. Writer for the skull,—no gift could have pleased him better. Doubtless that weasel's skull occupies a niche in the Yale college museum to this day

CATHERINE DU BOIS.

A HEROINE OF ANCIENT WILDWYCK.

IT was early in the month of June—that season of the year in which nature assumes her holiday garb, ere the sun has parched vegetation or the heat become unbearable—that the following incidents are said to have transpired. The wheat-fields of ancient Wildwyck were undulating gracefully before the summer breeze; the rustling blades of corn gave promise of a rich and abundant harvest, and the forests were gorgeous with the blossoming laurel and May-apple.

The high stockade fence, the block-houses and bastions, and log cabins pierced with port-holes, seemed out of place in such a scene of pastoral beauty and repose. But the surrounding wilderness, melodious with wild-bird song, and fragrant with the perfume of wild flowers, was the covert of beasts of prey and lurking savages; hence the utmost circumspection was necessary to protect themselves against surprise. A guard was always stationed at the fort, and when the inhabitants went to labor in the fields they did so with their arms close at hand.

It was on the morning of the memorable 7th day of June that Lewis Du Bois arose and went about his morning duties. Returning to his log cabin for breakfast at the usual time, and the meal not being ready, acting under the impulse of the moment, he gave vent to his feelings in some unpleasant words. The gentle Catherine, who had left her beloved home in the Fatherland, where she possessed every comfort, choosing to follow the fortune of Lewis in a new and savage country, under all the privations of a backwoods life,—Catherine looked at her husband in surprise at his unwonted words; a tear started to trickle down the cheek of the young wife, as she seemed on the point of giving way to a burst of sobs, but she suddenly checked herself, and assuming the dignity of injured innocence, curtly answered him. In short this couple, on this eventful day, had their first serious misunderstanding.

The breakfast was over at last. Unlike all other meals no brisk conversation was kept up. In fact this particular breakfast was partaken of in silence, and at its close Lewis arose to go. It was his turn to labor in the field; his work lay some distance from home, and he was to take his noonday repast with him. His wife had prepared a choice venison steak, some fresh fish from the creek, a cake of the sweetest corn bread, and butter made by her own skilled hands; these she now handed him, packed carefully away in a neat little basket fashioned of white birch-bark. This she did with an averted glance, without proffering the accustomed good-bye.

Lewis was deeply pained at this; he could but think he was to blame for it all. Still his pride stood in the way of an acknowledgement on his part. Once on the threshold he was tempted to return and plead forgiveness; as he passed the little window he saw Catherine seated at the puncheon table, with her face buried in her hands. He would have gone back, but hearing his name called by other members of the working party who were awaiting him, he turned to accompany them.

During the morning Lewis felt ill at ease. His companions noted his taciturnity and vainly tried to elicit the cause. The day dragged wearily by; he longed for the hour to come when he could hasten to her side and plead forgiveness. What if something should occur, and he be not permitted to see her again! The thought startled him like a presentiment.

Notwithstanding a guard had been left at Wildwyck, so long a time had transpired since any act of atrocity had been committed, that those ordinary measures of safety that prudence would have dictated were often disregarded. On this particular morning a number of savages were noticed about the village, going from house to house ostensibly to dispose of some maize and a few beans. They had entered by all of the gates, coming in singly, or by twos and threes; and the people were unsuspectful that a large body of savages were in their very midst, ready at the favorable moment to enter upon the work of merciless slaughter and pillage.

Presently some people on horseback were seen approaching from the direction of the new village. They were enveloped in a cloud of dust, and were evidently under great excitement. As they drew nearer the people collected to learn the cause of alarm.

"Indians!" shouted the horsemen. "The Indians have burnt the new village; to arms! to arms!"

Almost instantly the war-whoop sounded, and it seemed as if Indians rose up in the fated village of Wildwyck by magic, so rapidly did they pour out of the log cabins and places of hiding. The work of shooting, tomahawking and scalping began. The screams of affrighted women and children, the shouts of the men, the groans of the dying, were soon mingled with the roaring of the flames and the dreadful sounds of carnage.

At the time of the attack Lewis was some miles away. The alarm guns were fired—the signal for every man to return to the fort. He knew some sudden and appalling danger was impending over the settlement. Then immediately followed the rattle of musketry. The fort was attacked. He saw the smoke curling up in the summer sky—the smoke of burning dwellings, and what if his own house was among those marked for destruction! Solicitude lent speed to his steps. On every hand settlers were rushing in the direction of the fort, the deepest anxiety depicted on every countenance, for all, like Lewis, had dear ones in peril.

As Lewis drew nearer the stockade he could distinguish the exultant yells of the savages—he knew the guard had been overpowered. The crackling of the flames was distinctly discernible, and the smoke and embers went up from new points as the houses were successively fired. Now he heard the piercing shriek of a female and again the wail of a child. Oh, that he had wings to fly to the rescue!

Ere he came up, breathless, with a score or more of his companions, the strife had ceased. The Indians had beheld the reinforcement coming; and securing such of the booty as they could carry away, together with a number of prisoners, they had made good their retreat. Lewis, pale and anxious, rushed in through the gate of the fort. On every side he beheld evidences of slaughter and destruction. Dwellings in flames; bodies lying about the streets, scalped and otherwise mutilated; friends gathered about the corpses of companions; others running frantically about inquiring for missing relatives, while all seemed overwhelmed with grief and terror.

With forebodings Lewis ran to the spot where his cabin stood, where he had the last glimpse of his wife at the homely breakfast table a few hours before, only to find his home a mass of ruins. He called loudly her name, but no response came. Was she taken prisoner or had she shared in the fate of many others, who met death by the flames that devoured their homes? All were too much absorbed in their own grief to heed his eager inquiries, or could not give him the desired information.

The dead had been collected, such as had not been consumed in the burning dwellings. Ten men, one woman and three children were among the victims. Bleeding, mutilated by the murderous tomahawk, the bodies were laid side by side, while sounds of bitter grief were uttered by bursting hearts. Not a soul among the living, gathered about the remains of the fallen, but had its store of grief. Such a feeling of desolation, dread, sorrow mingled with regret, as filled the hearts of the survivors of the massacre of Wildwyck, when they realized the loss of friends and homes—such anguish and utter hopelessness, can only be realized by those who have passed through the ordeal.

Among those most deeply stricken was Lewis DuBois. His house and all his earthly goods were in ashes; his wife, he at last learned, had been carried off a prisoner with other females and some children; and though he could not mourn her as dead, yet she might be reserved for a worse fate. It was not the least poignant part of his regret that the last words spoken to her—the last he might ever be permitted to speak—were those of anger; and that his last remembrance of her was her form seated at the little table sobbing at his harsh words.

But those border men were not the ones to waste precious moments in outward exhibitions of grief when duty called to act. To prepare the dead for burial, and, if possible, to rescue the prisoners, were measures immediately resolved upon. The former was a sad duty, the latter a most dangerous task. All fear was banished from those whose wives and children were in the hands of savages; they would dare anything that promised a rescue. While a few were left in charge of the fort, a band of thirty resolute men were assembled and sent in pursuit of the savages. With heavy hearts and anxious forebodings the remnant of the village saw this little band of heroes depart on their errand of difficulty and danger, following them with tearful and prayerful anxiety until they disappeared in the adjacent forest, when they betook themselves to the sad rites of the sepulture of their slain comrades.

We will next follow the adventures of the weeping captives, torn from their homes by a band of whooping savages, red with the blood of their slaughtered relatives. For the first few miles the demeanor of their savage captors was harsh and violent. They would menace them with the tomahawk by way of urging them to a more rapid movement. The Indians evidently feared pursuit, and they were anxious to put as many miles between them and their possible pursuers as they could. Once out of reach of immediate danger the party slackened their pace, and conducted the retreat more leisurely. Just before nightfall one of the prisoners gave out; she was tomahawked and scalped, and left where she fell. At last a halt was ordered, and the party prepared to bivouac for the night.

Fires were lighted, and the savages arranged themselves for the evening meal. The prisoners were permitted to remain in company, a little apart from the savages, with a single sentinel to keep watch over them. They were not a little alarmed at the noise made by the wild animals in the woods around them, but were spared the knowledge at the time that those sounds were made by beasts of prey, as they fought and feasted on the body of their lamented sister, tomahawked that afternoon.

They were here destined to have the remembrance of their misfortunes awakened anew, as the savages displayed the booty they had carried off from the fort. Mrs. B. beheld a scarlet cloak that her little boy wore when he was brained by a savage—his scream of terror was still ringing in her ears. Mrs. G. recognized a coat as belonging to her husband, who was shot down and scalped before her eyes. Catherine DuBois beheld all this with feelings of mingled emotion. As far as she knew her husband was alive. And as the occurrences of the day came up before her she thought was she not a little at fault for the misunderstanding of the morning? Might she not have been a little more patient, and not have cast back such a retort? It was their first quarrel, and now they might never meet again. Ah, those words! would they had remained unspoken!

The next morning the party again took up the line of march, following the alluvial bottoms along the banks of a stream. Towards noon a messenger arrived, and after a hurried consultation the savages divided into two parties, the larger one under the leadership of a hideously painted savage, while the smaller kept to the original course, which continued in charge of the prisoners.

Towards the close of the day a halt was called. The captives had now traversed the whole distance between the present city of Kingston and the head waters of the Shawangunk kill. The savages, probably deeming themselves safe from pursuit, had for some time omitted the precautions they observed early in their flight, but little heed being paid to their captives other than keeping them within view.

Catherine and her companions now beheld some movements of the Indians that concerned them greatly. Some of their captors had been gathering fagots and piling them into heaps—equal in number to the prisoners—while others were driving sharpened stakes into the ground near the piles of sticks. Under other circumstances these proceedings would have filled them with consternation; but these heroic women actually looked upon these preparations for their own torture with a degree of satisfaction, as they believed they beheld evidence of a speedy deliverance from their earthly troubles.

The band of Christian women bowed their heads and prayed to the Giver of all Good, that He would, in His infinite mercy, if consistent with His will, restore them to their homes and families; or if it should be theirs to suffer at the stake, that He would impart strength for the terrible ordeal that they beheld awaiting them. Then their pent-up feelings broke forth in song; and with swelling hearts, yet with voices unbroken, those captives sang Marot's beautiful French hymn, of which the following is a part:

> By Babel's stream the captives sate
> And wept for Zion's hapless fate;
> Useless their harps on willows hung,
> While foes required a sacred song.

While thus they sang the mourners viewed
Their foes by Cyrus's arm subdued,
And saw his glory rise, who spread
Their streets and fields with hosts of dead.

This was the first Christian song heard on the banks of the Shawangunk kill. Tradition says the savages were charmed with the music, and delayed the execution of the singers while they listened. Was the last stanza given above prophetic of what was then and there to take place? In answer to their prayers, God had sent them deliverance. A panic seized the red men, and they fled in dismay for the mountains. The captives, not knowing the cause of alarm, ran after them; but they presently heard the sound of well-known voices calling them back. The next moment they were clasped in the arms of their husbands and brothers.

The day was too far spent to start on the return journey, so they composed themselves for the night, with the dried leaves of the preceding autumn for couches, and the overhanging branches for shelter. The fires were lighted of the fagots gathered by the Indians, though, providentially, not for the original purpose of torture, but for warmth and comfort.

The night was sleepless. Each recounted to the others matters of interest relating to the death of friends at the village, and incidents of the captivity and pursuit. The sympathy of all was drawn out towards one of the relieving party, who, the day previous, had come upon the remains of his wife in the woods. It was she who had been tomahawked and scalped, not having the strength to keep up with the other prisoners; a pack of wolves had devoured most of the flesh, the only means of identification being her dress. The journey home was begun next morning, where a warm welcome awaited them.

GREYCOURT INN.

PASSENGERS by the Erie railway, as the train slows up at an unassuming station in southern Orange, will hear the stentorian voice of the trainman call out "Greycourt." This appellation, so rythmical, and made up of such a strange combination, at once wins the attention of the tourist; and he casts about him for some romantic incident that may have given rise to the name. He moves up to the nearest bystander, who appears to be a resident, and blandly inquires what this uncanny title means, and is answered in the prevalent dialect, "Dun-no." A second venture is met with—"Can't tell, boss· give us an easier one!" The name cannot be of Indian origin, nor does it savor of having been handed down from the broad-breeched Dutch ancestral population of the valley; yet it has an historical significance if tradition is to be believed.

It was at a time when thousands of oppressed subjects, fleeing from the intolerance and tyranny of old Europe, first sought freedom and happiness in the new land beyond the seas—the America of the west. William Bull, an Irishman, with no fortune but youth and a good constitution, imbibing the prevalent feeling among all classes, took passage in an English packet bound for New York. He counted his money—five guineas—to the skipper of the packet, and was told the amount would pay for his passage. Arrived in port he tendered his five guineas, and was gruffly told it was not enough. "But it's all I've got," said the Irishman. "Then you must be sold to pay the balance of your passage money," said the captain. All expostulation was vain; and the skipper affected to have no recollection of a previous understanding. William Bull saw he was in the captain's power; the laws of England made it obligatory on his part to render an equivalent in hard labor for the balance claimed, and he had no friend to take up his cause against the purpose of the over-reaching captain.

"Then I'll go back in the ship," said the outraged Irishman; "if I've got to be a slave, I'll be one in my own land!"

It so occurred that Daniel Cromline, who resided on the Wawayanda patent, was then in the port at which the packet had arrived. The advent of a ship in port in those days was an occasion of importance, and always drew a crowd of interested persons and curiosity seekers, and Cromline was among the number attracted thither by the novelty. The story of the Irish passenger had got abroad, and his case had excited considerable sympathy, especially as the avarice and tyranny of sea-captains was a trait by no means rare. Cromline, being in want of a "hand" at his new settlement, forthwith asked to be presented to the distressed passenger. The result of the interview was that Cromline advanced an amount covering the deficit in Bull's passage money, and took the grateful Irishman home with him.

William Bull proved to be a great accession to the working force of the new settlement in the wilderness. He was strong and willing, and of a mild and hopeful disposition. He was skillful in the use of tools, and fertile in expedients—qualities that were especially valuable where tools were scarce and the facilities limited; and where, if a much-needed article was obtained, it had to be ordered from Holland, or England, and a year was required to get it.

Daniel Cromline set to work to construct a log mansion that should be far superior to any house for miles around. As an innovation in the building art, the puncheon was discarded, and real boards, sawed by whips in a saw-pit, entered into the construction of the floors and doors, and were held in place with wooden pins. The prime workman and chief architect was William Bull, but for whose ingenuity and physical strength the edifice would have been lacking in many of its sterling excellencies.

Though William Bull had emigrated thousands of miles from the scenes of his youth, and had apparently buried himself in the heart of a vast wilderness, it must not be supposed that he had turned savage like the wild beasts and Indians by whom he was surrounded. His young and susceptible heart began to feel the promptings of the tender sentiment; and fortunately for him, Providence had provided a trim and comely lass who was to reciprocate his passion.

The youthful and imaginative reader has doubtless already pictured the long and sentimental walks of these lovers under the sombre shadows of the forest by moonlight; or the more cosy and confidential talks seated on the slab bench before the roaring fire-place after the old folks had retired, while the wolves howled without, and the panther screamed from the lonely glen; and has fancied the friends of the lady at first objecting to the match, but finally, one and all, brought over in favor of the Irishman. And so the story would read, if it were the work of fiction; but the stern logic of facts compels the statement that there were no friends to conciliate, and no old folks to propitiate, for the bride was as friendless and portionless as the groom himself.

Like her future liege lord, Sarah Wells, by the stern and exacting laws of the period, had been reduced to involuntary servitude to a landed proprietor on Long Island. By the vicissitudes of fortune her master had lost his property, and Sarah had made her way by the assistance of some friendly Indians to the neighborhood of Goshen. Here her dusky friends had built her a log hut, and supplied her for a time with venison, until chance threw her in the way of William Bull.

The marriage ceremony took place in the Cromline log palace, a local magistrate officiating. Bull was an Episcopalian; his creed required the publication of the bans three times, but this formulary was looked upon with disfavor, inasmuch as its observance would defer the wedding-day. The magistrate was equal to the emergency—he could both satisfy the scruples of William and promptly tie the nuptial knot at the same time.

So the magistrate went to the rear door of the Cromline mansion and proclaimed aloud to the trees of the forest—"If anyone has any objection to the marriage of William Bull and Sarah Wells, let him now make it known, or forever keep silent;" and having so proclaimed, shut the door and passed to the front of the house. This he did three times. The forest trees offering no objection, he commanded the high contracting parties to stand up before him; and then and there was performed the first wedding ceremony, according to the usages of civilized society, in the town of Goshen.

The wedding-feast at the Cromline cabin absorbed the talk for weeks for the entire settlement; a slab table, made like a bench, without a spread of any kind, was loaded down with refreshments. These were of a plain but substantial sort. There was the toothsome and tender venison done up in pot-roasts and tempting steaks; there was the succulent and juicy wild-turkey, hot and steaming, and served up in a dish of its own gravy; there was the rich and tempting corn, grown in the natural meadows on the "drowned lands," and made into pone, which served in lieu of wedding-cake, while metheglin was the principal beverage that washed them down. The plates on which the repast was served varied in size and pattern, some being of pewter, but more of wood; their knives were mainly butcher knives, while their forks were sharpened sticks. A dance closed the festivities, and all made merry to the sound of the fiddle. All the hunters and frontiersmen for miles around were required to make up the party. The men in deerskin breeches and rakish coon-skin caps, and the backwoods belles in garb scarcely less primitive, showed to good advantage as jigs, four-hand reels and double-shuffles were executed in true frontier style—for your sedate and spiritless modern cotillion was to them a thing unknown. The old log house still stands, almost within sound of the stir and bustle of Goshen, where this couple first set up housekeeping, and their numerous descendants to-day are among the most prosperous and influential of the valley. The annual gathering of the Bull family is now a firmly established institution.

The Cromline log mansion, after this event, speedily acquired a celebrity in border parlance. It was located on the route leading from New Windsor to New Jersey; its owner, with an eye to the main chance, entertained travelers between those points, and it soon grew to a popular inn, and a place of resort for all classes. As was meet for all inns of standing and pretension, it was in due time graced with a sign, in front. This was of an oval shape, painted and decorated on either side, and suspended by hinges from a cross-piece on the top of a pole some twenty feet high that stood apart from the building. On one side of this sign, out of customary deference to the King—for this was before the Revolution—was painted the arms of royalty; on the other, in gaudy colors, was represented a goose, because of the proximity of Goose Pond swamp. That old house was privileged to behold many a jovial revel, of a different sort from the wedding-feast of Mr. and Mrs. William Bull. During the wild days of Indian warfare many a redskin passed beneath the sign of the Old Goose for his drink of fire-water. And during the trying times of the Revolutionary struggle, it was the resort of Whigs, Tories, Cowboys, and marauders of every sort, who needed the stimulus of brandy to nerve them to their work. That house stood for 116 years; when decay and the march of improvement consigned it, notwithstanding all its associations, to the doom of demolition.

During the War of Independence, the sign with its opprobrious English coat-of-arms,* came to be the butt of endless jokes and gibes. But the landlord did not choose to abate the nuisance The painting finally became weather-beaten; the gaudy colors faded; the coat-of-arms turned to an uncertain grey, and was derisively dubbed "Grey Coat." This was gradually metamorphosed into "Greycourt,"† a name which the locality still retains.

---

* A crown-stone had been obtained from England at a great outlay for the "old jail" at Goshen. But such was the feeling against everything that savored of Great Britain that Gabriel Wisner, with the approval of the people, demolished the offending crown-stone with a hammer.

† It may interest the reader to trace the transition from primitive "Duck Cedar" into classic "Tuxedo."

MINISINK BATTLE.

BRANT and his fighting men were the scourge of the Shawangunk region during the entire War of the Revolution. His name was a terror to the inhabitants of that locality; and deeds of blood and cruelty, performed by him and under his direction, are told to this day that are too harrowing for belief.

Historians differ as to whether Col. Joseph Brant was a half-breed or a pure-blood Mohawk. The traits of character developed in his career would seem to indicate the latter as being nearer the truth. He had one sister, Molly, who became the leman of Sir William Johnson. Brant was placed, through the influence of Sir William, at a school in Lebanon, Connecticut, where the lad was educated for the Christian ministry. It would appear, however, he adopted an entirely different mode of life. At the age of twenty he became the secretary and agent of Sir William, through whose influence he was induced to espouse the cause of Great Britain in the revolutionary trouble that was brewing. Through the same influence he was created a Colonel of the British army; and by reason of his birth was a warrior-chief of the Iroquois. Having had the advantages of a liberal education, he became, in consequence, an influential personage among them, and was treated with much consideration by the British monarch. He organized and sent forth the predatory bands of Indians which devastated the frontier from the Water-Gap to the Mohawk river. Some of these irruptions he commanded in person, particularly those which visited Wawarsing (Ulster county) and Minisink. In 1780 he boasted that the Esopus border was his old fighting ground.

His personal appearance is thus described: " He was good looking, of fierce aspect, tall, and rather spare, and well-spoken. He wore moccasins elegantly trimmed with beads, leggings, and a breech-cloth of superfine blue, a short, green coat with two silver epaulets, and a small, round laced hat. By his side was an elegant, silver-mounted cutlass; and his blanket of blue cloth (purposely dropped in the chair on which he sat, to display his epaulets) was gorgeously adorned with a border of red."

Brant has been denounced as an inhuman wretch. Even an English author attributes to him the atrocities of Wyoming. Although in battle he generally gave full scope to the murderous propensities of his followers, it cannot be denied he endeavored to mitigate the horrors of war whenever he could do so without destroying his influence with his own race.

During the summer of 1779, Brant with about three hundred Iroquois warriors set out from Niagara. About the middle of July they appeared on the heights on the west of Minisink, like a dark cloud hanging on the mountain tops, ready to break upon the plain below. Just before daylight, on the morn-

4

ing of the 20th, the inhabitants of the valley were awakened from their slumbers by the crackling of the flames of their dwellings. Cries of dismay, the shrieks of the victims of the tomahawk and scalping knife, and the war-whoop of the savages, broke upon the morning air in all their terror. Some managed to escape to the woods with their wives and children, and some to the blockhouses. The savages and Tories plundered, burned and killed as they were disposed.

After destroying twenty-one dwellings and barns, together with the old Mamachamack church and a grist-mill, and killing an unknown number of patriots, the enemy disappeared loaded with spoil. They did not attack any of the block-houses, for which the red men entertained a wholesome fear.

On the evening of the same day Col. Tusten, of Goshen, received intelligence by an express of the events of the morning. He immediately issued orders to the officers of his command to meet him the following morning (the 21st) with as many volunteers as they could raise. One hundred and forty-nine men were at the place of rendezvous at the appointed time.

A council of war was held to consider the expediency of pursuit. Col. Tusten was opposed to risking an encounter with the noted Mohawk chief, especially as his followers outnumbered the Goshen militia, two to one. Besides the militiamen were not well supplied with arms and ammunition, and the Colonel counseled that they wait for reinforcements which were certain to arrive. Others, however, were for immediate pursuit. They affected to hold the Indians in contempt; and declared that they would not fight, and that a recapture of the plunder was an easy achievement. The counsels of reckless bravery, untempered by reason and intelligence, are not always wisest to follow. The deliberations were cut short by Major Meeker, who, mounting his horse and flourishing his sword, vauntingly called out—"Let the brave men follow me; the cowards may stay behind!"

This appeal decided the question; it silenced the prudent. The line of march was immediately taken up, following the old Cochecton trail seventeen miles, where they encamped at Skinner's mill.

The pursuit was commenced some time in the night. Tradition and the testimony of old papers show that the party reached the house of James Finch, at what is now Finchville, where they took breakfast. Mr. Finch slaughtered a hog, which he roasted and served up to his guests. The patriots partook of a hurried meal, gathered up the fragments of the hog into their knapsacks, and continued their march over the mountain. They told Mr. Finch not to accompany them, but to stay and have dinner ready for them on their return, as they would be gone but a few hours. Their way led them along the depression where the present highway is laid, past the burial ground where the dead of the settlement were formerly buried; and from the summit of the pass nearly half of their number took their last view of the eastern slopes.

Crossing the mountain, they reached the house of Major Decker, then pushed on over an Indian trail seventeen miles further. How many of our strongest men, in these effeminate days, could endure such a tramp, encumbered with guns and knapsacks?

On the morning of the 22nd they were joined by a small reinforcement of the Warwick regiment under Col. Hathorn, who, as the senior of Tusten, took the command. At Halfway brook they came upon the Indian encampment of the previous night, and another council was held. Colonels Hathorn, Tusten and others were opposed to advancing further, as the number of Indian fires, and the extent of ground the enemy had occupied, were conclusive evidence of the superiority of Brant's force. A scene similar to that which had broken up the former council was here enacted, with the same results. The voice of prudence had less influence than the voice of bravado. It is said that the officer to whose tauntings this last rash act is attributed made quite a display of his bravery while on the march, but, with his company, was only *within hearing* while the engagement lasted, and could not be induced to go to the relief of his countrymen.

It was evident that Brant was not far in advance, and it was important to know whether he intended to cross the Delaware at the usual fording-place. Captains Tyler and Cuddeback, both of whom had some knowledge of the woods, were sent forward with a small scouting party to reconnoitre Brant's movements. What they saw led them to think Brant had already crossed, as there were savages and plunder on the opposite shore, and an Indian was then passing over, mounted on a horse that had been stolen from Major Decker. The two scouts fired at this fellow, and, it is said, wounded him fatally. But they were immediately shot at by some savages in their rear, and Capt. Tyler fell dead. Cuddeback succeeded in reaching the main body of the militiamen, and reported what he had seen and heard. Tyler's death caused a profound sensation among his fellow soldiers, but it only served to add fierceness to their determination.

After leaving the mouth of the Halfway brook * (now Barryville) it is believed that Brant followed the river bank to the Lackawaxen ford, to which he had sent his plunder in advance. Hathorn resolved to intercept him at the crossing, and to do so attempted to reach the ford first by a rapid march over the high ground east of the river. As they approached the ground on which the battle was fought, Brant was seen deliberately marching toward the ford. Owing to intervening woods and hills, the belligerents lost sight of each other, when Brant wheeled to the right and passed up a ravine known as Dry brook, over which Hathorn's route lay. By this stratagem, Brant was enabled to throw himself into Hathorn's rear, cutting off a portion of Hathorn's command, deliberately selecting his ground for a battle, and forming an ambuscade.

The battle-ground, says Quinlan, is situated on the crest of a hill, half a mile northeasterly from the Dry brook at its nearest point, three miles distant

---

* We follow the description given by Quinlan, in his admirable History of Sullivan, as the best yet given of the battle.

from Barryville and one from Lackawaxen. The hill has an altitude of twenty-five or thirty feet above its base, and two hundred above the Delaware, and descends east, west and south, while there is a nearly level plateau extending toward the north. This level ground is rimmed (particularly on the south side) with an irregular and broken ground of rocks. On that part of the ground nearest the river the Americans were hemmed in, and caught like rats in a trap.

The battle commenced at nine in the morning. Before a gun was fired, Brant appeared in full view of the Americans, told them his force was superior to theirs, and demanded their surrender, promising them protection. While engaged in parley, he was shot at by one of the militiamen, the ball passing through Brant's belt. The warrior thereupon withdrew and joined his men.

The battle opened and the forces were soon engaged in deadly conflict. Above the din of the strife, the voice of Brant was heard, in tones never to be forgotten by those who survived, giving orders for the return of those who were on the opposite side of the river.

A part of the Americans kept the savages in check on the north side of the battle-ground, while others threw up hastily a breastwork of stones about one hundred and fifty feet from the ledge which terminated the southern extremity of the plateau. Confined to about an acre of ground, screened by trees, rocks, flat stones turned on their edges, or whatever opportunity offered or exigency demanded, were ninety brave men, who, without water, and surrounded by a host of howling savages, fought from ten o'clock to near sundown on a sultry July day.

The disposition of the militia, and the effectual manner in which every assailable point was defended, reflects credit on the mind that controlled them. By direction of Hathorn there was no useless firing. Ammunition was short, and it was necessary to husband it carefully. A gun discharged in any quarter revealed the position of its possessor, and left him exposed until he could reload. With the exceptions indicated, every man fought in the Indian mode, each for himself, firing as opportunity offered, and engaging in individual conflicts according to the barbarian custom.

The annals of modern times contain no record of a more stubborn and heroic defense. In vain Brant sought for hours to break through the line. He was repelled at every point.

What the fifty men were doing all that eventful day, who were separated from their companions during the morning, no one can now tell. We will put a charitable interpretation on their conduct, and suppose they were driven away by superior numbers. Their movements are veiled in oblivion, and there let them remain.

As the day drew to a close, Brant became disheartened. The position of the brave patriots seemed to be impregnable, and it is said he was about to order a retreat when the death of a militiaman opened the way into the American lines. This faithful soldier had been stationed behind a rock on the north-

Minisink Battle. 53

west side, where he had remained all day, and kept the savages in check. Brant saw the advantage his death afforded, and, with the Indians near him, rushed into the midst of the Goshen militia. The latter seeing the savages swarming into the centre of the hard-fought field, became demoralized, and sought safety by flight. Many of them were killed or wounded in the attempt. Some incidents of the battle are worth repeating.

Brant killed Wisner with his own hand. Some years afterward he was heard to say that after the battle was over, he found Wisner on the field so badly wounded that he could not live nor be removed; that if he was left alone on the battle-field wild beasts would devour him; that he was in full possession of all his faculties; that for a man to be eaten by wild beasts while alive was terrible; that to save Wisner from such a fate, he engaged him in conversation, and shot him dead.

Captain Benjamin Vail was wounded in battle, and after the fight was over, was found seated upon a rock, bleeding. He was killed while in this situation, and by a Tory.

Doctor Tusten was behind a rock attending to the necessities of the wounded when the retreat commenced. There were seventeen disabled men under his care, who appealed for protection and mercy. But the savages fell upon them, and all, including the Doctor, fell victims to the tomahawk and scalping knife.

Several attempted to escape by swimming the Delaware, and were shot. Of those engaged in the battle, thirty escaped, and forty-five, it is known, were killed. The remainder were taken prisoners, or perished while fugitives in the wilderness.

Major Wood, of the militia, though not a Mason, accidentally gave the Masonic sign of distress. This was observed by Brant, who interposed to save Wood's life, giving him his own blanket to protect him from the night air while sleeping. Discovering subsequently that Wood was not one of the Brotherhood, he denounced the deception as dishonorable, but spared his life. The blanket was accidentally damaged while in the prisoner's possession, which made Brant very angry.

One of the militiamen attempted to escape with the others, but was so far exhausted that he was forced to turn aside and rest. In a little while he saw several Indians, one after the other, pass by in pursuit of the militia, but managed to keep himself out of their sight. Presently a large and powerful Indian discovered him, when, raising his gun, he fired his last shot and fled. The savage did not pursue; he was probably disabled by the shot if not killed.

Samuel Helm was stationed behind a tree, when he discovered the head of an Indian thrust from behind a neighboring trunk, as if looking for a patriot to shoot at. Helm fired and the savage fell; but Helm was immediately hit in the thigh by a ball from another Indian whom he had not seen. Helm dropped to the earth, but the savage did not immediately rush up to take his scalp, being anxious first to discover the result of his shot. This gave Helm a chance to reload which he did behind a natural breast-work which screened him from view. After dodging about a little the Indian made a dash for his scalp, but received a bullet instead, which put an end to his life. Helm said that the consternation of the Indian, on being confronted with the muzzle of his gun, was truly ridiculous.

In April of the following year, Brant started from Niagara with another force to invade the frontier. At Tioga Point he detailed eleven of his warriors to go to Minisink for prisoners and scalps. With the remainder of his force, he started to invest the fort at Scoharie. Here he captured some prisoners who made him believe that the place was garrisoned by several hundred men— a bit of strategy that foiled even the wily Indian chieftain. Brant turned back, and shaped his course down the Delaware. One day his command was startled by the death-yell, which rang through the woods like the scream of a demon. They paused, waiting for an explanation of this unexpected signal, when, presently, two of the eleven Indians who had been sent to the Minisink emerged from the woods, bearing the moccasins of their nine companions. They informed their chief that they had been to Minisink, where they had captured, one after the other, five lusty men, and had brought them as far as Tioga Point and encamped for the night. Here, while the eleven Indians were asleep, the prisoners had freed themselves from the cords which bound them, when each took a hatchet, and with surprising celerity brained nine of their captors. The other two savages, aroused by the noise of the blows, sprang to their feet and fled; but as they ran, one of them received the blade of a hatchet between his shoulders. Thus was the death of the slain heroes of Minisink avenged.

For forty-three years the bones of those heroes slain on the banks of the Delaware were allowed to molder on the battle-ground. But one attempt had been made to gather them, and that was by the widows of the slaughtered men, of whom there were thirty-three in the Presbyterian congregation of Goshen. These heroic ladies set out for the battle-field on horseback; but, finding the journey too hazardous, they hired a man to perform the pious duty, who proved unfaithful and never returned.

In 1822, the citizens of Goshen were led to perform a long-neglected duty by an address of Dr. D. R. Arnell at the annual meeting of the Orange County Medical Society, in which he gave a brief biography of Dr. Tusten. A committee was appointed to collect the remains and ascertain the names of the fallen.

The committee at once set upon the duty before them. The first day they traveled forty miles through the wilderness. At Halfway-brook, six miles from the battle-ground, the party left their horses. The vicinity was an unbroken wilderness, with no trace of improvement of any kind, and the danger of attempting to ride was so great that they chose to clamber over the rough ground on foot.

The committee were astonished at the route taken by the little army; the descents were frightful and the country rugged beyond conception. The majority of the bones were found on the spot where the battle was fought and near a small marsh or pond a few rods east. This fact shows that the militia, made reckless by thirst, went for water and were killed. Some were found at a distance of several miles. They were the remains probably of wounded men, who had wandered away and finally died of their wounds and hunger. Wild beasts may have removed others. The skeleton of one man was found in the crevice of a rock where he had probably crept and died. The whole number of bones collected by the Committee was about three hundred; other bones were subsequently found by hunters and brought in

It may be suggested that all of the bones collected may not have been the remains of the white soldiers; that it would be impossible to distinguish, so long afterwards, the skeleton of a white man from that of an Indian. It should be borne in mind that it was the rule of Indian warfare, when successful, to gather up and carry off all their slain. On this occasion the survivors saw the Indians engaged in this very duty.

The gathered remains were taken to Goshen, where they were buried with imposing ceremonies in the presence of fifteen thousand persons, including the military of the county, and a corps of Cadets from West Point under the command of Major Worth.

This monument gradually fell into decay and no measures were taken to preserve it. In 1860, Merrit H. Cook, M. D., a resident of Orange county, bequeathed four thousand dollars for a new one, which was dedicated on the 83d anniversary of the battle, on which occasion John C. Dimmick, a native of Bloomingburgh, officiated as orator of the day. Mrs. Abigail Mitchell, a daughter of Captain Bezaleel Tyler (slain at the battle of Minisink), was present, and witnessed the ceremonies. She was five years old at the time of the battle, and had resided the greater part of her life at Cochecton. On the 22d of July, 1879, the one hundredth anniversary of the Minisink battle, a large and enthusiastic gathering was held on the battle-ground. Although the approach to the place was rough and exceedingly difficult, it being necessary to cut a road through the woods for the occasion, upwards of two thousand persons were present at the ceremony. A monument was set upon the ground sacred to the blood of the slain heroes, and dedicated in commemoration of their services.

MONUMENT ON MINISINK BATTLE-GROUND.

It was on one pleasant morning in June that we left the hotel at Lackawaxen before the people were astir, and crossing the Delaware and Hudson aqueduct, began the winding ascent of the mountain. After a brisk walk of about two miles we came to the residence of Mr. Horace E. Twichell, to whom we had a letter of introduction. That gentleman kindly volunteered to go with us to the battle-ground, which lies partly on his premises, and locate the points of interest.

The battle-field comprises several acres of table-land, bordered by an abrupt descent on all sides except a narrow neck at its northern extremity. It is thickly strewn with pieces of slate rock, which the brave heroes turned to good account in standing upon their edges, and lying behind their friendly shelter during the engagement. Some of these stones still remain in the position in which they were then left.

On the neck of land there is a huge boulder. Behind this natural rampart, a hunter had taken his position on the day of the fight, and while his comrades loaded the guns for him, he so effectually swept the only available approach to the battle-ground, as to keep the whole force of Indians at bay during the entire contest. At length the hunter was killed, and the Indians, taking advantage of the circumstance, rushed in and the battle became a rout.

A few yards from this rock, screened on all sides by the contour of the ground and the protecting ledge, the spot was pointed out where for years lay the skeletons of the brave Dr. Tusten and his seventeen slain companions, who were all tomahawked and scalped after the battle was over. Further on stands an old pine tree, on which are the initials "J. B.," believed to have been cut in the bark by the Indian fighter, Joseph Brant.

An incident of the battle was related to me while rambling over the field. A soldier was assisting a wounded comrade to escape. The Indians were heard in close pursuit, and the wounded man soon saw that all efforts on his part were fruitless. So taking his pocket-book and papers he handed them to his companion, with the request that he give them to his wife at Goshen, and bade him leave him to his fate. The man made good his escape, and delivered the package and money as directed.

Mother McCowan, still living at Handsome Eddy, used to see the skeletons around the spring to the east of the battle-ground, and remembers seeing some of the soldiers that were engaged in the battle.

Mr. Isaac Mills, about forty years ago, found a skeleton about three-fourths of a mile from the battle-field. Judge Thomas H. Ridgeway, of Lackawaxen, informed us that he remembers going to pick huckleberries on the mountain seventy years ago, when the skeletons of the slain Minisink heroes lay thickly scattered about among the bushes, and distinctly recalls his childish fears of the bones.

Near the foot of the monument, entirely covered up with loose slate, was found the skeleton of a man. This was probably the work of the Indians, who, for some reason, gave this man a sepulture.

The round stone on the top of the monument is a white flint boulder, found in the Delaware river near the spot where the Indian was shot by the scouts previous to the battle.

BRANT AND THE SCHOOL-GIRLS.

THE name of Brant was sufficient to strike the hearts of the early pioneers with terror. Fears of an attack from the Mohawk chief and his red warriors kept the settlements in a continual ferment. Stories of pillage and murder, carried on under Brant's direction, were passed from lip to lip—some doubtless without foundation, others greatly exaggerated—still the chieftain had committed deeds of blood sufficient to merit the reputation he bore.

As might be expected, there were many false alarms, on which occasions the women and children would take refuge in the nearest block-house, while the men would arm themselves and prepare for defense. The young people were particularly alert, and at the least unusual noise in the woods would sound the alarm. A young man in Sullivan county ran breathless into the nearest village declaring that his father's house was surrounded by more than twenty savages. The men turned out with their guns; but on reaching the scene of the supposed danger, they discovered the enemy to be only a number of hoot-owls.

The dread of Indians overcame all other fear. It is related of Mrs. Overton, of Mamakating valley, that, during the temporary absence of her husband, the young mother would abandon her log-cabin at night, and taking her children with her, sleep in the woods or in a rye-field. Tradition says that her youngest child was but a few weeks old and very cross and troublesome; but it was observed that at such times it was very quiet.

But if the people were sometimes needlessly alarmed, at other times it would have been greatly to their advantage to have been more on their guard. The day before the massacre at Minisink, the notorious Brant, with a body of Tories and Indians, attacked the settlement in the present town of Deerpark. Such of the inhabitants as were warned of their danger in time, fled to the blockhouse for shelter. Others were surprised in their homes and in the field, and were either captured or slain.

Some savages entered James Swartwont's blacksmith shop. In the shop were Mr. Swartwont and a negro who assisted at the forge. Swartwont directed the negro to stay in the shop as the Indians would not be likely to molest him, while Swartwont crawled up the forge chimney and concealed himself there. Scarcely had he done so when the savages rushed into the shop, and appeared much disappointed at finding no one but the negro present. They, however, contented themselves with rummaging about the shop, tumbling everything over, and making havoc of whatever came in their way. Presently one of them, spying the bellows handle, caught hold of it. Finding it would move, he began to operate the handle, which of course made the sparks fly. He now began blowing at a furious rate, and the other savages gathered round to see the operation. Swartwout, being directly over the fire, was nearly suffocated by the heat and smoke. The negro, apprehensive that Swartwout could not much longer retain his position, called upon the savage to desist, crying out with a voice of authority—"Stop, or you will spoil that thing." The Indian respected the caution, and ceased to blow.

Not far away, near the fort of the Shawangunk, was the log school-house. The savages raided the settlement while the school was in session. While the fathers and mothers were fleeing for their own safety, they thought of their children, a mile or more away, and hoped the school-house might escape the attention of the savages. But in this they were doomed to disappointment. The

BRANT AND THE SCHOOL-GIRLS.

Indians entered, killed and scalped the teacher, Jeremiah Van Anken, in the presence of the scholars. Some of the larger boys shared the same fate, being cut down with the tomahawk; others succeeded in escaping to the woods. The girls stood by the slain body of their teacher, not knowing where to turn or what to do.

Presently an Indian came along, and dashed some black paint on their aprons, bidding them hold up the mark when they saw the Indians coming, and that would save them; and with the yell of a savage he sprang into the woods. This Indian was none other than Brant; and as the savages ran about from place to place, murdering and scalping such as came in their way, on seeing the black mark they left the children undisturbed. The girls induced the boys to come out of the woods, and the children arranged themselves in rows, the girls with the marked aprons standing in front. As the Indians passed and repassed they would hold up the palladium of safety, and were suffered to remain unharmed.

Major John Decker resided in the Mamakating valley, and tradition says the Indians raided it for the purpose of obtaining his scalp, for which the British had offered a handsome reward. He was Major of the Goshen Regiment of Foot of Orange county.

The Major's house was constructed of wood, with logs laid up by way of fortification, and was closed by a heavy gate. It was the month of July. The men were at work in the harvest field, and no one was in the house except the aged mother and a child. The Major's wife and a colored woman were at a spring washing.

A Tory entered and told the mother they were going to burn down the house, and proceeded to build a fire in the middle of the floor. Two pails of water stood in the kitchen; the old lady poured this on the fire and extinguished it. The Indians told her not to do that again or they would kill her. Mrs. Decker attempted to run across the fields to another fort, but Brant sent a savage to bring her back; coolly informing her that his object in having her brought back was that she might see her husband's house burn down; at the same time assuring her that she would not be harmed.

"Can I save anything?" cried the terrified woman.

"Yes, anything you can," was the response of the Mohawk chief.

Mrs. Decker rushed into the burning dwelling, caught up two beds and bedding, one after the other, and, with the assistance of some young Indians that Brant sent to help her, brought them to a place of safety. That night the family of Major Decker slept on the banks of the Neversink, with no other covering than the canopy of heaven.

The Major was absent that day at a funeral; it was on his return that he had seen from afar the smoke of his burning dwelling. He put spurs to his horse, and presently met a party of Indians in the road. The Major rode directly through the party without being fired at. Then, probably through fear of encountering a larger force, he wheeled about and rode back again, when he was fired upon and wounded. His horse becoming unmanageable, he rode into a tree-top, closely pursued by the savages. Here he left his horse and took refuge in a cave, at a place near where the Erie railroad now passes. The Indians followed to the opening in the rock, but did not find the object of their search. That night he made his way on foot through the mountains to Finchville, where he found his son, who was one of the lads that had escaped slaughter at the school-house.

This son, on running away from the Indians at the time of the attack, found a child a year and a half old, which had been lost by its mother in the confusion. He took up the little child, found his father's cow by following the sound of the bell, gave the little one some milk, and restored it unharmed to its mother.

CLAUDIUS SMITH; OR THE ORANGE COUNTY TORIES.

THERE is much in the career of Claudius Smith to interest the student of human nature. Whether we regard his deeds of violence as but the legitimate working of his evil propensities, in defiance of God and man, or whether we deem him in a measure fortified in his attitude toward the Whigs by his sense of loyalty to the king, we cannot deny that he displayed qualities of leadership worthy of a better cause. Had he shown a like energy and prowess at the head of a few thousand troops, his praises would have been sounded on every lip. We leave for others to draw the line between the bandit chief, whom all abhor, and the lordly conqueror, whom all affect to honor.

Claudius Smith is described as having been a man of large stature and of commanding presence; possessed of powerful nerve and keen penetration; cautious and wily; in short, he was admirably formed by nature for a bandit chieftai

Claudius early manifested a thieving propensity, in which it is said he was encouraged by his father. The boy, on one occasion, having stolen some iron wedges, on which were stamped the owner's initials, his father assisted him to grind the letters out. His mother, who appears to have been of a different mould, was shocked at the depravity manifested by her son; and she once said to him as though with the voice of prophecy—"Claudius, some day you will die like a trooper's horse with your shoes on," meaning that he would come to his death by violent means. These words of his mother seemed to rankle in the heart of Claudius; and at a subsequent period of his life he publicly recalled them under circumstances that indicated an infernal depravity, deep and ingrained, in his nature.

The topography of the country in which he resided, and the times in which he flourished, were eminently favorable for the development of those qualities which made his name such a terror to the Shawangunk region. The town of Monroe, Orange county, is entitled to the distinction of having been the residence of Claudius Smith. This and the adjoining towns abound in wild mountains with almost impregnable fastnesses, favorable alike for marauding incursions and the secreting of booty. From these inaccessible mountain haunts the robbers would swoop down upon the unsuspecting and defenceless residents of the valley, murder and plunder to their hearts' content, and escape to their retreats before assistance could be obtained. Besides, the British forces located at Stony Point and Fort Lee furnished a cover for the marauders to whose protection they could fly when hard pressed, and likewise a favorable market for stolen property; and we may add, the British frequently were known to instigate these expeditions by the offer of reward.

Under such conditions, Claudius Smith, who, had circumstances been

Claudius Smith; or the Orange County Tories

otherwise, might have developed into a respected citizen, speedily acquired a local reputation as unenviable as that of Robin Hood. His name is first met with in public records as being in jail at Kingston, "charged with stealing oxen belonging to the continent." From Kingston he was transferred to the jail at Goshen, where he soon found means to escape. He had sons old enough to join him in his plundering expeditions, and one of them, after the death of Claudius, assumed command of the gang.

The active and influential Whigs of the vicinity were the especial objects against which the Tory bandits directed their attacks. Claudius had made public threats against Col. Jesse Woodhull, Samuel Strong, Cole Curtis and others. From some act of personal kindness shown him by Col. Woodhull he revoked his threat against that gentleman, but carried it out against Major Strong. The Colonel was in such continual dread of his enemy that he did not sleep in his own house for months before the threat was revoked.

The Colonel had a valuable blooded mare which the freebooting Tory had set envious eyes upon, and had given out that he would steal it. For better security Woodhull had the animal placed in the cellar of his dwelling. One evening Claudius, having secreted himself in a straw barrack near the house for the purpose, seized a favorable opportunity to dart into the cellar while the family were at tea, and took the animal out. He had not left the yard with his stolen property before he was discovered by the inmates of the house. A gentleman at the table sprang up with his gun, and was about to fire upon the retreating robber when the Colonel stopped him, observing, "Don't shoot; he'll kill me if you miss him."

On another occasion Claudius made a forcible entry into the Colonel's house during the absence of the latter from home. Mrs. Woodhull possessed a valuable set of silver, and it was that which excited the cupidity of the Tory chief and his gang. While the robbers were engaged in breaking down the door, the heroic lady had hurriedly secreted the silver in the cradle, and placing her child into it was apparently endeavoring to calm the little one to sleep. Claudius searched thoroughly for the missing plate; not finding it, he was content to leave, taking with him some articles of minor value only. Mrs. Woodhull had some difficulty in quieting the child, who was old enough to talk a little, and who inquired of her mother if she thought they would steal her calico frock.

It was that same night that the gang attacked the house of Major Strong. They came to the Major's house about midnight when that gentleman was in bed. They broke open and entered the outer door of the house; they next removed a panel from the door leading to another room out of which opened a bedroom, where the Major lodged. The latter had come out of his sleeping apartment with a pistol and a gun; he was fired at by the miscreants, who held the muzzles of their guns through the broken panel, but was unhurt by the discharge. He was preparing to return their fire when his assailants called upon him to deliver up his arms, when he should have quarter. Setting down his gun against the wall, he approached the door to open it; but as he advanced they perfidiously fired upon him a second time, killing him instantly, two balls entering his body.

Other incidents are given of Claudius Smith's career which would disprove the accepted opinion that he was lost to the common dictates of humanity. It is claimed in his behalf that the poor man found in him a friend; that he was ever ready to share his meal and purse with any who stood in need; and furthermore, that what he stole from the affluent he frequently bestowed upon the indigent.

Col. McClaughry was taken prisoner at the fall of Fort Montgomery in 1777, and confined in British dungeons and prison ships for a long time. During much of his confinement he was absolutely suffering for the necessaries of life. To ameliorate his condition his wife proposed to send him some home comforts, and applied to Abimal Young for a small loan for that purpose, who she knew had plenty of specie by him. The old miserly fellow surlily and peremptorily refused the loan, and the poor woman went home discomfited.

The incident came to the ears of Claudius. "The old miser," exclaimed the Tory chief; "I'll teach him to be a little more liberal. If he won't lend Mrs. McClaughry of his own will, I'll take the money from him and send it to the Colonel myself."

Tradition says that shortly after this, one dark night, Claudius with a few trusty followers actually invested the house of Young to force that gentleman to produce the desired money. The old man refused to yield to their demands. Claudius knew there was money secreted somewhere about the house, but a diligent search failed to reveal it. They threatened to no purpose. They next took Young out into the yard and told him they would swing him up to the well-pole if he did not divulge the place of its concealment; he persisted in his refusal to tell, whereupon the bandits put a rope around his neck and suspended him from the well-pole.

Letting him down after he had hung a sufficient time, as they judged, he soon revived, and they again demanded his money. The old man was still stubborn; he refused to reveal the place where it was kept, and again he was dangling in the air. This was done three times. The robbers were getting impatient; and the third time they let the old man hang so long that he was nearly dead when let down. When he finally revived they renewed their demand, but he had not changed his determination in the least. It was evident to them that he would sooner part with his life than his money. They returned to the house, made another search, and were rewarded by finding some money, together with a number of mortgages, deeds and other papers, which they carried off. To the credit of Claudius be it said, a part of the booty went to minister to the comfort of Mrs. McClaughry's imprisoned husband.

When Claudius Smith was about to suffer the penalty of death for his crimes, while he stood at the scaffold at Goshen with the noose about his neck, Abimal Young made his way to the platform and inquired of Smith where those papers were that he and his followers stole from him the night they hung him up to the well-pole, averring that they could be of no use to him now. To which request the hardened man retorted, "Mr. Young, this is no place to talk about papers; meet me in the next world and I will tell you all about them."

An old resident of Orange county, still referred to as Judge Bodle, on one occasion met Claudius in the road in a lonely locality. Each knew the other, as they were neighbors; the Judge saw that escape was impossible, so he approached the noted bandit with a bold front. The meeting was seemingly a friendly one, Claudius evidently enjoying the discomfiture of the Judge. He inquired of the latter the news from the river, and continued: "Mr. Bodle, you seem weary with walking; go to my dwelling-house yonder and ask my wife to get you a breakfast, and tell her I sent you." It is not related whether the Judge accepted the invitation or not; probably he made the speediest time possible to a place of safety as soon as he was out of sight of his would-be entertainer.

The atrocities of the Tory gang at last became so daring and formidable that, after the assassination of Major Strong, Gov. Clinton, October 31, 1778, offered a large reward for the apprehension of Smith and his two sons, Richard and James. On being apprised of the Governor's proclamation, he fled to Long Island for safety. What is worthy of remark, both Gov. Clinton and Claudius Smith—the executive and the outlaw—were residents of southern Orange county, and may have been personally known to each other.

The determination of Claudius to go to Long Island for greater security was most unfortunate for himself. One Major John Brush made up a party, and during a dark night visited the house in which the Tory chief was stopping, seized him while he was in bed and carried him across the sound into Connecticut. He was next conveyed under a strong escort to Fishkill Landing, where he was met by Col. Isaac Nicoll, sheriff of Orange county; and from thence, under guard of Col. Woodhull's troop of light-horse, was taken to Goshen. Here he was heavily ironed and placed in jail to await his trial. He was tried on the 13th of January, 1779, on three indictments for burglary and robbery, and found guilty on each of them, and nine days thereafter was publicly executed in Goshen.

During the period of his incarceration at that place, both before his trial and while he was awaiting execution, Claudius Smith lived in hopes his men would undertake his rescue. Even when he was being led to the scaffold he was observed to cast furtive glances over his shoulder towards Slate hill, where about a mile away was a cave which was said to be a rendezvous of the robber gang. But he was so strongly guarded that no attempt at rescue was made, and would doubtless have failed if undertaken. One of the guard was stationed at all times at the "grief-hole" opening into his cell, with a loaded musket, with orders to shoot him dead if any attempt was made on the jail by his friends outside.

The fated hour arrived, and Claudius was led out of his gloomy prison and permitted to take his last look upon earth. He walked up the steps of the scaffold with a firm tread. He had dressed himself with scrupulous neatness, in black broadcloth with silver buttons, and white stockings. This was in the days of public executions; and he looked from the scaffold into the faces of thousands who had gathered there to see him die. He smiled grimly as he spoke to several men in the crowd below whom he knew.

Before the final adjustment of the noose Claudius stooped to remove his shoes. When asked why he did so he repeated the words of his mother that he would die with his shoes on, and added that he "wanted to make her out a liar." He was interred near the scaffold. Years afterwards a gentleman by the name of Wood, as he stood conversing with an acquaintance on the village green at Goshen, happening to press upon the greensward with his cane at a certain spot, found it would easily pierce the soil as though there was some sort of hollow underneath. A slight examination of the place showed it to be a shallow grave, and that the bones of a human skeleton lay entombed there. Further inquiry proved the remains to be those of the noted bandit chief, Claudius Smith.

Scores of people were attracted to the place, and some of the more curious carried away portions of the skeleton as souvenirs. Orrin Ensign, the village blacksmith, made some of the bones into knife-handles; doubtless some of them are still doing duty in that capacity. It is even believed by many of the people of Goshen that the skull of Claudius Smith is embedded in the masonry over the front door of the present court-house in that place.

Some of Smith's associates were even greater criminals than himself. His son James was hung at Goshen soon after his own execution; his eldest son, William, was subsequently shot in the mountains, and the body never was buried but became the food of wolves and crows, where the bones lay bleaching for years afterward.

The following facts, gathered from a newspaper printed in 1779, will serve to give a little more of the history of this family:

"We hear from Goshen that a horrible murder was committed near the Sterling Iron Works on the night of Saturday, the 26th of March, by a party of villains, five or six in number, the principal of whom was Richard Smith, the oldest surviving son of the late Claudius Smith, of infamous memory. These bloody miscreants it seems that night intended to murder two men who had shown some activity in apprehending those robbers who infested the neighborhood.

"They first went to the house of John Clark, near the iron works, whom they dragged from his house and then shot him. Some remains of life being observed in him, one of them said '*He is not dead enough yet*,' and shot him through the arm again, and then left him. He lived some hours after, and gave some account of their names and behavior. They then went to the house of a neighbor, who, hearing some noise they made on approaching, got up and stood on his defense, with his gun loaded and bayonet fixed, in a corner of his little log cabin. They burst open the door, but seeing him stand with his gun,

ROCK RIFT ON THE DELAWARE DIVISION ERIE RAILWAY, NEAR PORT JERVIS, N. Y.

they were afraid to enter, and thought proper to march off. The following was pinned to Clark's coat:—

"'A WARNING TO THE REBELS.—You are hereby warned at your peril to desist from hanging any more friends to government as you did Claudius Smith. You are likewise warned to use James Smith, James Fluelling, and William Cole well, and ease them of their irons, for we are determined to hang six for one, for the blood of the innocent cries aloud for vengeance. Your noted friend Captain Williams and his crew of robbers and murderers we have got in our power, and the blood of Claudius Smith shall be repaid. There are particular companies of us that belong to Col. Butler's army, Indians as well as white men, and particularly numbers from New York, that are resolved to be avenged on you for your cruelty and murder. We are to remind you that you are the beginners and aggressors, for by your cruel oppressions and bloody actions you drive us to it. This is the first, and we are determined to pursue in on your heads and leaders to the last *till the whole of you are murdered.*'"

But this son of Claudius did not possess the qualities of leadership displayed by his father, and the clan was finally broken up by the people of Monroe, assisted by some troops from Washington's army. Richard Smith took refuge in Canada; others fled to parts unknown, and thus ended the highwayman's profession in Orange county. Many localities of the vicinity will long be remembered from their association with the deeds of blood and crime that made the clan famous. Their retreats in the mountains can be readily found to this day by the curious.

That the Tories buried much valuable booty in these mountains may be inferred from the circumstance that about the year 1805 some of Smith's descendants came from Canada, and searched for the property according to directions that had been handed down to them. They found a lot of muskets, but nothing else. About the year 1824, descendants of Edward Roblin, another of the gang, came from Canada with written directions, and explored the country with no better results. Search was made in a certain spring where it was said valuable silver plate had been secreted, but nothing of value was found. Perhaps the other members of the band found the depository, and, unknown to Smith and Roblin, appropriated the property.

EDWARD ROBLIN.

MORE than a century ago there lived near the base of the Shawangunk mountain, in Orange county, a well-to-do farmer by the name of Price. One day a boy came to him seeking employment. Mr. Price eyed the lad circumspectly over the rim of his gold spectacles, asked him a few questions, and was so well pleased with his ready answers and intelligent ways that he consented to take him on trial. The boy proved to be an industrious and trustworthy hand, and remained with Mr. Price until he had grown up into a tall, fine-looking young man. That lad was Edward Roblin.

Now it so happened that Mr. Price had a comely daughter named Zadie, a year or two younger than Edward. Inasmuch as the young people were thrown much into each other's company, with few other associates of their own age, it was but natural that the childlike friendship of youth should ripen and develop into a more tender and enduring affection as they grew to maturity.

Mr. Price was not a very observing man, or he was too much absorbed in money-making, or else the young people maintained a very discreet behavior during their courtship; certain it is, that the first intimation the old man had of the state of affairs, was when young Edward one day approached him and formally asked the hand of his daughter in marriage.

This revelation fell upon the father like a thunderbolt. He flew into a towering passion; sent his daughter up stairs, and forbade their speaking to one another again. In vain the young man pleaded his cause; he had served him long and faithfully, almost as many years as Jacob had served of old. The father was immovable. "You can't have my daughter, and that's the end of it," and he sent the young man from his presence.

In one important matter the father failed to exhibit the wise foresight for which he was noted—he did not discharge the young man; in fact he could not well manage the farm without him. It must not be thought strange, therefore, that the young people found means to communicate with each other, and to carry on a sort of clandestine courtship.

One morning Edward was not found at his chores. And he was always so punctual. Mr. Price went to his room and knocked. No response. He opened the door. The room was empty, nor did the bed bear evidence of having been slept in the night before.

"A pretty how-d'ye-do, I do declare," and the old man flew quickly to the door of his daughter's apartment. He did not stop to knock. The door yielded to his touch. Her room, too, was without an occupant, the bed carefully made, and the pillows in place. The truth now broke in upon the mind of the old man.

"It's fully twenty miles to the Dominie's, and, by my troth, I'll be there, too!" ejaculated he.

He hastened to a local magistrate, where he swore out a warrant on a false accusation against young Roblin for debt. He next secured the attendance of a constable, and thus equipped the two went flying over the country behind Mr. Price's fleetest horse. Arrived at the house of the Dominie they did not stop for ceremony; there was no time for that; but they burst unannounced into the room just as the young couple were standing up before the minister.

"Ha, my pretty birds, but I've caught you finely!" And while the father took charge of the young lady, the constable took charge of the young man, leaving the Dominie to muse at his leisure on the mutability of human affairs, and mourn over his loss of a marriage fee. Zadie, disconsolate and inconsolable, was taken back to her home; while Edward, without friends and in the clutches of the law, was thrown into prison along with felons of the basest sort. In vain he protested he was under no pecuniary obligation to Mr. Price; that the money paid to him by that gentleman, on which the charge for his arrest was based, was for services well and faithfully rendered. The word of Mr. Price was sufficient to deprive Edward of his liberty, whether by just cause or otherwise was then nothing to the question; while his influence was such that he could get the trial postponed for an indefinite period. Meanwhile Edward's incarceration was an insurmountable barrier to his love-making for the present; at the same time the old man chuckled at the success of his scheme to get Edward effectually out of the way, while he proceeded to mature his plan of marrying Zadie more to his wishes.

To while away the dull hours of his imprisonment Edward learned to play the fiddle. He soon became so skillful in the use of the instrument that he found in it a new language in which to express his disappointment, and merge his never-dying affection for his sweetheart into sounds of melancholy melody that were wafted far beyond the limits of his prison bars. His story of romantic incident had got abroad; and love-lorn damsels would come with slippered feet to listen to his tale of disappointment, as he drew it out in languishing harmonies. Not unfrequently whole bevies of Goshen maidens would gather under his window of a pleasant summer evening, and, casting anxious glances upward at the barred window, heave a sigh of pity in his behalf.

Months rolled by. Edward was still in prison. No trial had been accorded him, with no immediate prospect of any. All this while he had received no word, no token from Zadie. The vigilance of a father was never relaxed, and no love epistles could pass between them.

Driven to desperation by the entreaties and commands of her tyrant father, Zadie at last married a man she abhorred, much older than herself, but who had the reputation of being wealthy. As soon as this was consummated, the father with a malicious pleasure took means to have it speedily communicated to the ears of young Roblin. The strains of the fiddle were now more melancholy and grief-laden than ever; and one of the fair listeners under Edward's window was moved to tears, so great a sorrow did the doleful vibrations convey.

The jail-keeper had a pretty daughter. It was a part of her duty to take food to the prisoners. It may have been the result of accident, or sheer advertence on her part, but the fullest plate and the choicest slice was apt to be handed in at the "grief-hole" of Edward's cell. The jailer himself often condescended to speak a kindly word to him. An interest now began to be awakened in the minds of outsiders for his release; even Mr. Price himself could now have no reason for desiring a continuance of his imprisonment. But young Edward did not wait for the slow process of law to relieve him from his confinement.

One morning as the jailer was making his accustomed rounds he was surprised to find the cell of Edward tenantless. An inspection of his dwelling revealed the fact that his daughter's room was likewise unoccupied. Just then word came to him from the stable boy that the stall of his favorite chestnut gelding was empty. Putting this and that together, the poor jailer was lost in imagining all sorts of evils; in short he was so bewildered he knew not which way to turn; his grief at the loss of his chestnut gelding was the most bitter of all; and to satisfy himself he made a visit in person to the stable, and found it was but too true—his favorite was gone, the stall was empty, with the exception of a limb from a chestnut tree in the yard, which limb was tied to the manger in lieu of the horse. To this limb was attached a note addressed to himself in the following words:

MY DEAR FATHER-IN-LAW—As you will be when you read this,—pardon the liberty I take in exchanging horses with you. I acknowledge this is a horse of another color, still there is not much difference; as yours was a chestnut horse the exchange is but fair, for this is a horse chestnut. It is the best legacy I can leave you at present, coupled with the best wishes of

EDWARD ROBLIN.

All the village dames suddenly discovered that the jailer's daughter was a shiftless minx. Nothing more was heard of her or of her husband until Edward turned up with the Tory gang of Claudius Smith. Edward was second in enterprise and daring to none but his chief.

The husband of Zadie Price turned out to be a poor, miserable fellow, whose reputed wealth was only pretension. Zadie soon returned to her father's home, rapidly went into a decline, and in a few years died of a broken heart.

LIEUTENANT BURT.

PERHAPS the most severe chastisement ever meted out to the Tories and their Indian allies in the region of which we write, was on an occasion in which Lieutenant James Burt took an active part. Lieutenant Burt was a resident of the town of Warwick, Orange county; and was an active Whig, bold, aggressive, and vigilant in defending the neighborhood against the attacks of the Tory outlaws.

In the village of Warwick resided a silversmith by the name of Johnson. He lived in a stone house, and from the nature of his business, having at times considerable silver plate and money about him, he kept his apartments carefully secured and guarded. The promise of so much rich booty excited the cupidity of his Tory neighbors, and they resolved to attack and rob the house on the first favorable opportunity. Accordingly, one dark, rainy night, a party of eleven Tories surrounded his house, some of Johnson's nearest neighbors being with the gang.

Johnson's household consisted of two sisters and two negro boys, none of them being of any assistance in defending the place. He made a stubborn resistance; but the robbers broke open the house, and one of them dealing a heavy sword-cut on Johnson's shoulder, which disabled him, the ruffians were free to ransack the house at their will.

One of the negro boys and a Mr. Coe had been out that night eeling. Coming home just as the Tories were at the height of their pillaging, the latter, supposing the settlers had mustered to attack them, became frightened and fled, taking with them all the valuables of the house.

Lieutenant Burt was immediately apprised of the occurrence; and though the night was dark, and the rain falling in torrents, he immediately started to warn out his company. His way led him through a piece of woods; and while passing through he thought he heard three guns snap. Burt drew up his musket to fire, proposing to shoot at random in the direction of the sound; but as he feared the flash of his gun would expose his position, he refrained and passed on.

He warned out his company, and before morning they were in full pursuit of the Tory gang. Coming upon some Continental troops in the mountains, the latter were induced to join in the pursuit, the regular troops following one side of the range and the volunteers the other.

Lieutenant Burt's company suddenly came upon the robbers while the latter were encamped and eating their breakfast. They at once opened fire upon the robbers, and killed five out of the eleven. The other six started to run, when another of the gang was brought down by a shot in the leg, and secured. The other five made their escape and fled toward New Jersey, closely followed by their pursuers. A number of stolen articles were found at this place.

The whole population along the route of retreat was alarmed and everybody joined in the pursuit of the fugitives. Three more were shot during the chase; the other two made their way to Hackensack, where each stole a horse and continued their flight. They were again pursued, the farmers tendering the troops the use of their horses for the purpose; at last one was shot and killed, and the other wounded and captured.

Lieutenant Burt had told the story of his hearing the snapping of guns in the woods, but his companions were inclined to discredit his story, and jeered him not a little at his groundless alarm. To convince them he was not mistaken, Burt led them to the spot where he heard the guns snap. It was found the robbers had been seated on a log within a few yards where the Lieutenant passed, as was shown by a number of stolen articles they had left there. The rain had wet the priming of their guns, to which circumstance he probably owed his providential escape.

THE DUBOIS HOMESTEAD.

AN early settler and patentee of Orange county, and one who figured quite largely in events pertaining to the frontier history of what is now Montgomery township, was Henry Wileman, an Irishman by birth, and a man of many sterling qualities. He was the proprietor of a tract of 3000 acres granted him in 1709; the estate was located on the east bank of the Walkill, below the village of Walden. His name appears on the records as a member of St. Andrew's church, as early as 1733. A church edifice constructed of logs, that had been built on his land for the use of the society, was standing in 1775.

Wileman was a free-liver, noble, and generous to a fault. He built his log palace on the site where afterward stood the DuBois homestead, of Revolutionary fame. It was a beautiful location: the soil was fine, and the patentee of 3000 acres entertained right royally. His convivial propensities frequently carried him to excess, and, if tradition is to be credited, the revelries in the Wileman log house were notorious through the country round.

In process of time Henry Wileman died, and it was meet that he should be buried as became a patentee of 3000 acres. It does not appear that he ever married; or that any relative had ever followed him to this distant clime. But the rich, when they die, never lack for mourners, or at least those who outwardly affect great sorrow for their death. So it came to pass that the friends of Wileman arranged to have the burial take place with all the pomp and splendor and outward tokens of regard for his memory that should characterize the funeral solemnities of a great man, according to the notions and customs of those early times

It was then the prevailing usage to furnish liquor on all such occasions. No funeral was complete without it. They would sooner think of doing without the sermon than without the rum. As Wileman died possessed of his thousands of acres, it would be a lasting disgrace to limit the supply of liquor when celebrating his obsequies. The cellar was stored with the choicest wines; what could be more appropriate, or what could better voice the public sorrow, than that these wines should be drawn forth and made to do duty in assisting in the giving of suitable honors to the memory of their late owner!

In short, the people, young and old, were urged to drink. If any were backward, they were chided for their lack of respect for the memory of the departed, whose obsequies they were then observing; and the wine was handed round when they could not well help themselves.

At length the hour came in which the funeral cortege was to move from the late residence of the deceased to his place of sepulchre. This was before the day of black caparisoned steeds and heavily draped catafalques. The procession was more primitive in its make-up. All being ready, the bearers of the remains of the deceased, the bier carriers, mourners, friends and neighbors in attendance, started on foot to the little burial-place behind the log church, where the open grave awaited its tenant.

But the people had undertaken a greater task than they could accomplish. Overcome by the intensity of their sorrow, or by their too frequent and long-continued libations of the contents of the wine-cellar, the friends, mourners, and finally the bearers, one by one fell out by the way, either to sink insensible into the highway, or to make their way homeward as best they could.

In short, the corpse was let down in the road before they had proceeded half way to the grave, and there abandoned.

Among that number there was one sober enough to realize that the dead ought not to be left unburied, and that it savored too much of irreverence to leave the corpse unattended in the middle of the road. To convey the remains to the churchyard by his own unaided strength was simply impossible; it was no less impracticable to carry the coffin back to the house, and await a more favorable opportunity to complete the burial. Here was a quandary that would have puzzled the brain even of a soberer man. At last he hit upon a way out of the difficulty, and put the plan into immediate execution. He procured a shovel, and proceeded to dig a grave in the road by the side of the coffin; when he had dug to a sufficient depth he rolled the coffin over into it, and there covered up the mortal remains of the free and noble-hearted Irishman, the patentee of 3000 acres. With no monument to mark his last resting-place, this was all the sepulchre that was accorded him for many a long year.

By an alteration in the road the grave was thrown into an adjoining field; and when Mr. Peter Neaflie afterward excavated a cellar for a dwelling, he unexpectedly came upon the coffin and bones of Henry Wileman, and gave them a respectable burial.

The farm on which these occurrences took place was the property, at the time of the Revolution, of Peter DuBois, a British Tory and a refugee. In 1782 it was occupied by a detachment of the American army from the cantonment at New Windsor, sent here to protect some government property.

One cold, stormy night, late in October of that year, John McLean, afterward Commissary General of New York for a number of years, was sent from this encampment with papers for the Commander-in-Chief at Newburgh. At a point in the Shawangunk road where it crosses the Stony brook, McLean was waylaid, seized, taken from his horse, gagged, tied to a tree, and the papers removed from his custody. In this position he was left by the robbers to the chances of liberation by a possible traveler. He was relieved from his uncomfortable position early the next morning by a horseman who chanced that way, but he nearly perished from cold during the night. This accident, by bringing him into notice, contributed not a little to his subsequent political preferment. His horse was never recovered, but the government remunerated him for his loss. It is believed the marauders were some of the notorious gang of Claudius Smith.

MASSACRE AT FANTINEKILL.

THE following incidents occurred (says the Bevier pamphlet) in the midst of a settlement of the descendants of the French Huguenots, and bring to view the distinguishing traits of that people. They were bold, persevering and resolute, and were firm believers in the doctrine of a particular Providence, which they did not forget to invoke in every time of need. The three families, to whom this narrative especially relates, lived at Fantinekill, near to each other, and about three-fourths of a mile northeast of Ellenville.

A young negro, known as Robert, lived at Widow Isaac Bevier's. He heard an unusual tramping around the house, just at the dawn of day, like that of horses. He got up and listened, and found that the noise was made by Indians.

He opened the door, and stepping back for a little start, jumped out and ran. In his flight he received a wound on his head from a tomahawk, and a ball was fired through the elbow of his roundabout, but did not hurt him. The Indians sang out in their own tongues, "Run, you black! run, you black!" It does not appear that he was pursued by them. He made his escape over the lowland to Napanock, stopping by the way at a stack to staunch the blood that was flowing profusely from his wound. The Indians immediately commenced the attack; the widow's sons were both killed, the house was set on fire, and the women driven into the cellar. The daughter Magdalene took the Dutch family Bible with her. When the flames reached them there, they chose rather to deliver themselves up to the savages than to suffer a horrible death by fire. They made their way through the cellar window, the mother in advance. The Indians were ready to receive their unfortunate and unoffending victims. What tongue can describe the feelings of mother and daughter at that moment? Sentence was immediately pronounced against the mother—death by the ruthless tomahawk—whilst the daughter was detained as a prisoner. It is said that a young Indian brave took a sudden fancy for her, and interposed in her behalf. The afflicted girl, as soon as she knew the decision of their captors, threw an apron over her head so as not to see her mother killed ! All this while she had retained the Dutch Bible in her arms; this was now wrested from her and stamped in the mud.

When the Indians left the place they took her a short distance into the woods, and sent her back with a war-club, and a letter written by the Tories to Capt. Andrew Bevier, at Napanock. In the letter the Tories invited the old Captain to dine with them next day at Lackawack. There was an allusion in it to the club—that so they meant to serve him. This club was stained with fresh blood, and adhering to it were some locks of human hair. On the girl's return she recovered her invaluable treasure—her Dutch Bible; some of the leaves were soiled by the mud, but not materially. It is still preserved as a precious relic in the family of her relatives.

This widow Bevier had a daughter by the name of Catherine, that had been lately married to Abram Jansen, whose father lived about four miles southwest of Fantinekill. The elder Jansen was strongly suspected of being a Tory, and of communicating with and assisting the Indians, the following being some of the circumstances on which this suspicion rested: 1. His premises, although on the outposts and unguarded, were not molested. 2. The prints of Indian moccasins were seen about his house. 3. His daughter, who was at a neighbor's house, was importuned to return home the night before Fantinekill was burned. 4. It was so managed that his daughter-in-law was absent from her mother's house on a visit to Jacob Bevier's at Napanock. 5. By the death of his daughter-in-law's family, his son fell heir to the estate at Fantinekill.

The family of Michael Sock were all killed. As none survived to tell the tale, no particulars can be given here. There were a father, a mother, two grown-up sons and two small children in the household. A young man, either a Sock or a Bevier, had run some distance from the house into a piece of plowed ground, where a desperate contest had evidently taken place between him and an Indian. A large space had been trodden down, and the scalped and mangled corpse of the young man lay upon it — he had several wounds from a tomahawk on his arms. A few days before there had been a training day at Napanock, and this same young man had loudly boasted that he was not afraid of Indians.

At the house of Jesse Bevier, the savages and their accompanying Tories met with a warm reception. The first salute that Uncle Jesse received was when the blocks in the window were stove in, and two or three balls were fired just above his head as he lay in bed. He sprang up and seized an axe, with which he prevented them from entering the window, at the same time calling to his sons David and John, who immediately responded. A desperate action ensued, for this family were all famous marksmen. This was especially true of David, who had some choice powder for his own use, which his mother brought forward in the course of the conflict. He declined to use it, saying that common powder was good enough to shoot Indians with. They had the powder loose in basins on a table for the sake of convenience, and measured the charges in their hands. The women assisted in loading, it being common to have a double stock of arms. But the enemy approached from a point against which this little band of Huguenot heroes could not bring their guns to bear, and found means to set fire to the old log house.

Their situation now became critical. Every drop of liquid in the house was applied to retard the progress of the flames. The women took milk, and even swill, in their mouths and forced it through the cracks of the logs, hoping in this way to protract their existence until relief could come from Napanock. At this awful crisis, when death in its most awful form was staring them in the face, that pious mother proposed that they should suspend hostilities and unite in petitions to the throne of grace for help David replied that "she must do the praying while they continued to fight." So that mother prayed, and the prayer was answered in an unexpected manner.

In the course of the morning, after the battle commenced at Fantinekill, Jesse Bevier's dog, without any sign or motion from his master, nor having been trained to any thing of the kind, ran to Napanock, to the house of Lewis Bevier, his master's brother. He approached Lewis, and jumping up against his breast looked him in the face, then ran to the gate which led to his master's, looking back to see if he was coming; this he did several times. Lewis could distinctly hear the firing at Fantinekill, and could easily divine what was going on. So, taking his arms, he hastened to the house of a neighbor, and told him the dog had come to call him, and that he was resolved to go to his brother's relief, although the Indians were expected there every minute, and it was almost certain death to go alone, yet "it was too much for flesh and blood to stand."

Standing by, in hearing of the conversation, was the neighbor's son, Conradt, a stalwart youth who was extremely fleet of foot, and who boasted that no Indian could outrun him. This young man's patriotism was kindled by the remarks of Lewis, and volunteering his services, the two set out over the lowlands for Fantinekill. When they came near, the Indian sentry on the hill fired an alarm. The Indians and Tories, not knowing how large a company was coming, immediately withdrew from the vicinity of the house and the two men rushed in. The flames at this moment had extended to the curtains of the bed. The door was now thrown open, and the women rushed down the hill to the spring after water, while the men stood at the door with guns to protect them.

Among the women who went to the spring was Jesse Bevier's daughter, Catherine. While at the spring she heard the groans of the dying in the swampy grounds near by. Among them she recognized some Tories—she could distinguish them by their striped pantaloons, and by the streaks which the sweat made in their painted faces. The fire was happily extinguished, and this family saved from an awful catastrophe.

Colonel Cortland's regiment had been lying in the vicinity of Napanock for some time preceding this event, but their time of service had expired a few days before the attack on Fantinekill; and it is supposed that the Tories had made this fact known to the Indians. But the soldiers, having received some money, had got into a frolic at a tavern at Wawarsing, and were there on the morning of the alarm. They were mustered with all possible speed, and when they came to Napanock, were joined by Capt. Andries Bevier's company, and the united forces marched to the scene of action. When they came to the Napanock creek, the Indian yells and war-whoops were heard on the western hills, and the savages fired upon them as they were crossing the stream, and continued to fire upon them as they passed on toward Fantinekill. Their fire was returned by the regiment, but it is not known that any loss was sustained on either side at this stage of the action. The Indians bore off west, setting fire to the woods as they went to avoid pursuit.

When the war-whoop was heard on the hills west of Napanock, and the soldiers were seen leaving the place to go to Fantinekill, the women, children, and invalids made a precipitate flight to the Shawangunk mountain, expecting the Indians would enter Napanock and burn the place, which they could have done with ease. Two sons of Andries Bevier, aged twelve and fourteen, ran across the mountain, through the burnt woods, barefooted, a distance not less than five miles. They first came to the residence of a Mr. Manse, on the east side of the mountain, then passed on to Shawangunk village, and gave the alarm. Several members of Jacob Bevier's family also made their way through the woods; but some of the neighbors missed their way, got lost, and were all night in the mountain, which was full of people from both sides, with horns, looking for them. The small children, and those of the inhabitants that were feeble and infirm, went only to the base of the declivity, and secreted themselves among the scraggy rocks, especially along the sides of a noted defile known as "Louis Ravine." In their flight they were joined by the young black, Robert, who escaped from Fantinekill.

In fording the Rondout creek, a child of Andrew Bevier came near being swept down with the current. He was caught by a friendly hand and helped ashore. When they arrived at the foot of the mountain an invalid soldier climbed a tree to see if Napanock was on fire. When he heard the sound of musketry he said he could distinguish the firing of Cortland's regiment from that of the Indians, because the former "fired by platoons." Towards night the men came to look for their families; but the women and children who were in hiding, apprehending they might be Tories, gave no heed to their calls until they were certain they were friends.

Mr. Jacob Bevier, of Napanock, was sick and unable to be moved. All the family had fled across the mountain except an insane brother, who was sitting on the fence unconscious of his danger, and a daughter who had resolved to remain with her father. Jacob expostulated with her, saying that if the Indians came, she could not save him, and in that case both must inevitably fall before the tomahawk and scalping-knife. Every feeling of humanity and affection rose in opposition to the disinterested exhortations of a tender father; but his sound reasoning and the instinct of self-preservation at length prevailed, and she made her way for Old Shawangunk, and being more fortunate in finding the path, she arrived first at the place of destination.

The noble conduct of Capt. Kortright on this occasion is worthy of record. As soon as he heard of the affair at Fantinekill, without awaiting orders from his superior officer, he directed his sergeant to order out his company, in all about seventy men, armed and equipped, with provisions for two days, and to report at his house next morning at daylight. The summons was promptly obeyed, and the company was marched to Grahamsville with a view of intercepting the Indians on their return from Fantinekill. He selected a suitable place, arranged his men in order, and awaited the arrival of the Indians. But, as usual, the savages discovered him first; and instead of coming by the usual route, they passed by in the rear of his men. The first intimation that Kortright had of the presence of the Indians was a volley delivered into his midst from an unseen enemy. One rifle ball struck within six inches of the old Captain's head; but the savages kept at a safe distance, knowing they had an old Indian fighter to grapple with.

One of the soldiers named Johannis Vernooey declared that he was hit by a ball. The others, thinking it was only the result of fright, sang out, "Where has it hit you, Honsum? Where has it hit you, Honsum?" At last it was discovered that the strap which held the buckle to his knee was actually cut off by a bullet. The Indians soon made their way off, filling the woods with their yells and war-whoops, without once coming into view. As an eye-witness of the affair expressed himself, "You can't see an Indian in the woods."

Bevier affirms that six of the persons who perished at Fantinckill were buried in one grave near the place where they lived and died. The loss of the enemy is not known. The only house that stood where the village of Ellenville is now located, was burned. It was owned by John Bodley, and its occupants had a narrow escape. They, in common with other families scattered along the valley, fled to the mountain and secreted themselves.

BURNING OF WAWARSING.

THIS last attempt of the savages, under the command and by direction of British authority, to exterminate the inhabitants of this frontier, occurred on the 12th of August, 1781, and was the most extensive invasion since the commencement of the war. This expedition was fitted out at one of the northern British posts, and put under the command of a white man by the name of Caldwell, with explicit directions to commence his assault at Captain Andrew Bevier's at Napanock; and to kill or capture all the inhabitants, and destroy or carry off all the property along the Kingston road to the half-way house kept by the Widow Hasbrouck, twelve miles northeast of Napanock— "if he thought he could get back alive." Caldwell was told if he did not carry out his instructions, he should be tried for his life on his return. Such is the language of the Bevier pamphlet. These allegations, were they not backed by testimony not to be controverted, would appear to be the creation of some fertile brain to vivify a page of fiction. We leave for other hands the task of attempting to excuse or palliate the crime of authorizing the slaughter of helpless women and children, for a crime it was, though sanctioned by the Crown of England.

It may be well here to state that it was the practice along the frontiers to keep out spies or scouts on the side exposed to savage inroads, who were to

Burning of Wawarsing.

patrol the woods and give notice to the settlements in order that they might not be taken by surprise. Philip Hine was one of those chosen to perform this duty. In providing himself with a supply of provisions, he had occasion to purchase some meat of Jeremiah Kettle, who resided in the vicinity of Newtown. Kettle made particular inquiries of Mr. Hine as to where he was going, the nature of his business, and the purpose for which he wanted the meat, to which the latter made honest replies, not suspecting his interlocutor was a Tory, who would find means of communicating the information to the Indians.

Hine, accompanied by another spy named Silas Bouck, started on his migratory errand. When they reached the Neversink river, twenty miles or more southwest of Napanock, they discovered a body of four or five hundred Indians and Tories, evidently bound on an expedition against some of the frontier settlements. The scouts watched their progress secretly until certain that their place of destination was Wawarsing; they then took a circuitous route, and struck the road far in advance of the point where they had seen the enemy. The Indians had been apprised by the Tory, Kettle, that spies were out, and were on the alert. Discovering some footmarks where Hine and his companion had crossed a stream of water, runners were immediately sent in pursuit, who overtook them within half an hour after the latter had entered the road. But there seems to have been a providence in this apparent misfortune, and the perfidiousness of Jeremiah Kettle was made the means of saving many precious lives.

The prisoners were required under pain of death to give a correct account of the fortifications and other means of defense along the frontier. Among other things they informed their captors that there was a cannon at Capt. Bevier's, in Napanock. On account of this intelligence the enemy did not carry out their instructions and commence their attack at that place. Some of the Indians had probably witnessed the destructive power of grapeshot and cannon-balls in the war of 1755, and had a wholesome fear of that engine of destruction. But they would not have been injured in this case, for the old cannon lay on the woodpile without a carriage, and was useless for purposes of defense. Nevertheless the dismantled field-piece intimidated an enemy five hundred strong, and saved Napanock from attack.

The inhabitants of Napanock never lost sight of their gratitude to that old cannon. It was given a carriage, and restored to a condition becoming an "arm of war." After peace was declared, at each recurring Independence Day, the old nine-pounder was brought out where its presence was sure to evoke great enthusiasm, and patriotic hearts beat faster as they voted it the position of honor in the procession. Blooming maidens crowned it with wreaths, as did their daughters for successive generations after them. Fourth of July orations bestowed upon it the meed of unbounded praise. And often as the sterling patriots met to live over again in memory the struggle of the Revolution, and to march to the sound of fife and drum, around the liberty pole on the hill at Capt. Simon Bevier's, amid the strains of martial music was heard the roar of the ancient nine-pounder, multiplied into a score of voices in the echoes that were hurled back from the sides of old Shawangunk, as though the grim old mountain itself had joined in sounding the pæans of liberty.

After the captors of Hine and Bouck had obtained all the information they wished, the prisoners were taken apart from each other, tied to trees, and left in that situation until the Indians returned. Here they were compelled to remain for the most part of three days and nights, without anything to eat or drink, and liable to attack in their defenseless condition from wild beasts. In addition to their physical sufferings were added their well-founded apprehensions that their wives and children would fall a prey to the scalping-knife, and also that they themselves might meet with a like fate if the enemy were in an irritable mood on their return.

It had been the intention of the enemy to detach one hundred of their number, under the command of Shanks Ben, who were to proceed through the forest from the Delaware river to Newtown, to commence the work of death there, and meet their comrades at some place in the valley of the Rondout. But by an accident which occurred in drying some damaged powder, several of their number were burned, among them Shanks Ben, so that he was unable to enter upon that service. It is said they made the proposition to Silas Bouck that if he would perform that duty, they would grant him his liberty the moment he came to Newtown; but the noble-hearted patriot rejected the proposal with disdain!

After securing their prisoners, as above stated, the enemy set forward. On that ever-memorable Sabbath, the 12th of August, 1781, at the dawn of the morning, they arrived at the old stone fort at Wawarsing, which was situated near the old church. Having taken the spies, no notice had been received at the fort of their approach, and most of its occupants were yet in their beds. Two men had gone out of the fort that morning, Mr. Johannis Hornbeck and a colored man named Flink. Catherine Vernooey was also about leaving the fort to go and milk, when she saw the Indians coming. She returned to the fort, closed the door, and called Chambers to assist her in getting the huge brace against it. Chambers was stationed on the sentry-box at the time, but being somewhat deranged, he did not fire his gun. Fortunately, however, he sung out "vyand, vyand,"--enemy, enemy. No sooner had the door been secured than the Indians came against it with all their might, in order to burst it in. Had not the door been secured at that instant, the enemy would inevitably have gained admittance to the fort, and the fate of its inmates would then have been sealed.

The negro, Flink, soon discovered the Indians approaching the fort. He concealed himself until he saw they did not obtain an entrance; then leaving his milk-pail, he made his way with all possible speed to Napanock, to apprise the people there of the arrival of the enemy. Mr. Hornbeck, the other individual who had left the fort, was on his way to see his corn-field, and heard the alarm when about a mile away. Being a large fleshy man, unable to travel fast on foot, he caught a horse and rode with all speed to Rochester. When

Burning of Wawarsing.

he arrived there, so overcome was he by excitement and fatigue, that ne fell upon the floor as one dead. He recovered sufficiently to be able to return home in the afternoon in company with the troops that were sent in pursuit of the Indians.

The stone fort at Wawarsing was now the scene of active operations. The men leaped excitedly from their beds, and, without much regard to dress, seized their guns, which were always at hand, and commenced the defense. John Griffin was the first who fired, the shot bringing one of the sons of the forest to the ground. Another Indian came to remove his fallen comrade, and just as he stooped over, Cornelius Vernooey gave him a charge of duck-shot that he had intended for a wild duck that came in his mill-pond. The other savages hurried them away, and it is probable that both of them were killed. The Indians did not fancy the reception they met with here, so they dispersed to the more defenseless parts of the neighborhood, to plunder and fire the buildings.

Peter Vernooey lived about one-fourth of a mile south-east of the fort. The Indians made an attack upon his house, but were bravely repulsed by the garrison, which consisted of three men. On the first advance of the Indians, Vernooey shot one from a window in the south-east side of the house. One of the men went into the garret, and discovered some savages behind a ledge of rocks to the north-east of the dwelling, watching for an opportunity to fire when any one came before the port-holes. While he was preparing to shoot at them, he saw the flash of their priming—he drew his head back suddenly, and a ball just grazed his face. An old hat hanging up in the garret, which the Indians supposed contained a man's head, was found to be full of bullet-holes.

The conduct of the women of this household was worthy the daughters of liberty. It appears there were three—Mrs. Peter Vernooey, and two of her relatives from Lackawack. One of them loaded the guns for the men, while the others stood with axes to guard the windows, which were fortified with blocks of hard wood. Mrs. Vernooey had a family of small children. They were lying in a bunk, and became very uproarious at the unusual proceedings about them; but the heroic matron addressed them in language so decided and unequivocal that they instantly became quiet.

At Cornelius Bevier's the enemy found none to oppose them. They entered the house, built a fire on the floor with some of the furniture, and then left the premises, taking along a colored woman and two deformed colored boys a short distance, until they supposed the flames had obtained sufficient headway, when they let them return home. The woman and boys went to work and succeeded in saving the house. At no time did the Indians appear to wish to kill the blacks. This was probably because they were slaves, and no bounty was paid by the British for their scalps. The Indians regarded the negroes as belonging to a race inferior to themselves.

The next assault was made at Cornelius Depuy's, where a few neighbors were assembled, as the custom was, for mutual safety and defense. The enemy advanced from the hills south-east of the house. The person acting as commander of this little garrison gave the order not to fire until the Indians came quite near; but a lad of sixteen was too full of enthusiasm and patriotic fire to await the word of command. He had his old Holland gun well primed, which he leveled at one of the redskins, and brought him to the ground at the first discharge. The enemy thereupon fled. A few shots were sent after them, with what effect is not known.

The enemy made their next attack at the stone house of John Kettle, in the defense of which the noble conduct of Captain Gerard Hardenburgh is deserving of particular notice. At the time of the alarm Capt. Hardenburgh was at the house of a relative one mile east of Kettle's with six of his men. Notwithstanding the risk, he determined to go to the relief of his countrymen. When he came in sight of Kettle's he saw a number of Indians in advance in the road. To offer battle with his insignificant force in the open field, would be an act of madness.

There was no time to be lost, however, and all depended on the decision of the moment. His active and fertile mind instantly devised a stratagem that suited his purpose to perfection. He turned aside into the woods with his little band of heroes, so that their number could not be observed by the enemy, took off his hat, shouted with all his might, and advanced towards Kettle's house. The Indians did not know what to make of this manoeuvre. It might mean that a company of Tories had come from Newtown to their assistance, and it might be that troops were marching up from Pine Bush to the relief of the settlement; the savages took the safe course and skulked in every direction. This gave the Captain time to reach the house. At that moment the Indians, who had discovered the ruse, poured a shower of bullets at them; but the brave heroes escaped unhurt. The besieged broke holes through the rear of the house with an axe, and also through the roof, for port-holes, through which they poured an effective fire upon their assailants. Hardenburgh found the house occupied by three soldiers and a son of John Kettle. The Indians made repeated assaults in force on this fortress, but were as often driven back with loss. Thirteen of their number were left dead on the field. John Kettle was at Herhonkson at the time of the attack. Jacobus Bruyn had removed with his family over the Shawangunk mountain through fear of the Indians, and Kettle had gone up to Bruyn's premises to see that all was well. He started to go to the fort at Pine Bush, but was met in the road by an advance-guard of the savages, and shot. His was not the only scalp the Indians secured in this expedition.

While these events were transpiring at Wawarsing, the forts at Napanock and Pine Bush were the scenes of intense interest and suspense. When the firing ceased for a moment, the affrighted inhabitants were ready to conclude that the beleaguered garrison had been overpowered, and that the savages were engaged in mangling and scalping the bodies of their friends and brethren. Then again would be heard the report of one of the Holland guns, which could be plainly distinguished from the sharp crack of the light arms of the Indians, telling that the patriots yet lived, and were waging a heroic defense for their homes. The rattle of musketry in the first attack on Wawarsing was heard at Pine Bush; and as it was unlawful to fire a gun on the Sabbath, except in self-defense, or as an alarm, it was known that the place was attacked. Alarm guns were immediately fired at Pine Bush, at Millhook, and so along the frontier towards Kingston.

Colonel John Cantine, of Marbletown, was then first in command at Pine Bush. Capt. Burnet, of Little Britain, and Capt. Benjamin Kortright, of Rochester—both brave and resolute officers—had their companies ready at an early hour, anxious to proceed to the scene of conflict; but Colonel Cantine made no move to that effect. When the flames of the burning buildings were seen ascending in the lower part of Wawarsing, the captains addressed him as follows:—" How can you remain here, when, in all probability, the Indians are murdering our friends at Wawarsing?" There, and not till then, did he put the troops in motion to go to their relief. He sent a guard in advance; and when they arrived at the site of the Middleport school-house, the guard returned and told the Colonel that the Indians were at Herhonkson. Cantine immediately wheeled about, and with a few others, marched back to the fort. Captains Burnet and Kortright advanced with their companies to the summit of the hill, south-west of the school-house, in order to confront the enemy if they should advance, at the same time making the greatest possible show of numbers by deploying their men along the brow of the hill, then wheeling suddenly and marching again to the summit, where they might be seen by the enemy. The Indians not making their appearance, and apprehensive that they might take a circuitous route and pass them unnoticed, Burnet and Kortright returned to Pine Bush. At their suggestion Colonel Cantine ordered out a guard some distance from the fort on each side to watch the movements of the enemy and protect the women and children below the fort.

As already stated, the negro Flink escaped from the Wawarsing fort as the Indians attacked the place, and ran with all speed to Napanock. Capt. Pierson was in command at that place; and although suffering from indisposition, he left his bed, stepped out in front of the fort, and called for volunteers. He said he did not want a man to go that would not face the enemy, and fight like a hero. He was solicited by the women and others to remain for their protection, but he replied that he was bound by his official oath to go where the enemy was. Conradt Bevier and Jacobus DeWitt, and some ten or twelve others, tendered their services, and the little band set forward. When they came to the school-house, half a mile from the fort at Napanock, they found it in flames —no doubt fired by the Indians. They carried water in their hats and saved the building. They then cautiously advanced over the lowland until they came in sight of Wawarsing. At this time, an Indian sentinel who had been stationed on a hill to give notice of the arrival of reinforcements to the garrison, fired off his gun, which caused the Indians to withdraw farther from the fort.

Those within now made signals for Captain Pierson and his men to approach and enter. To do this the relief party were obliged to pass over an open space exposed to the shots of the enemy; but the undertaking was accomplished in perfect safety. Encouraged by this addition to their numbers, the besieged came out, and fought the Indians from behind trees, buildings, and whatever objects afforded protection, after the Indian fashion.

In the meantime the Indians entered the church, and amused themselves by throwing their tomahawk at the numbers, which, according to the custom of the times, were placed on the panels of the pulpit to designate the psalm or hymn to be sung. These figures served as targets to throw at. With such force were the missiles sent that two or three tomahawks were driven entirely through the panels. This injury was never repaired, but was suffered to remain as a memorial of the past. Two Indians were standing in the church-door, and Wm. Bodly and Conradt Bevier crept along the fence in the bush to get a shot at them. Bevier leveled his piece and pulled the trigger, but it unfortunately snapped. The Indian looked around as though he heard it. Bevier made a second attempt, and again it snapped. Bodly then fired, and both ran for the fort about one-fourth of a mile away. The Indians sent some shots after them, one of the balls cutting a limb from an apple-tree under which Bevier was passing. Bodly's shot struck in the door-post, just grazing the crown of the Indian's head. Long after the war a man by the name of DeWitt was in the western part of New York and spoke with the Indian who met with so narrow an escape at the church-door. The Indian, on learning that DeWitt was from Wawarsing, enquired if he knew who it was that shot at him while standing in the church-door. DeWitt told him it was William Bodly. The Indian answered—"It was a good shot. If I ever meet that man I will treat him well." This incident illustrates a trait in the character of a "warrior."

Towards noon, when most of the Indians were in the lower part of the town, Cornelius Bevier went to water his cattle, accompanied by Jacobus DeWitt. They had ascended the hill toward the old burying-ground, when they discovered two Indians walking directly from them in Indian file. Bevier thought he could shoot them both at once, but just as he got ready to fire, one of them stepped aside. He shot one of the Indians and then both men ran for the fort. In passing under an apple-tree, DeWitt stumbled and fell; just at the instant a shot from the surviving Indian passed over his head. DeWitt ever afterward felt he owed his escape to an interposition of Providence. The Indian's body was subsequently found near the place. He had put on new moccasins and other extra apparel during the period intervening between the time of his receiving the fatal wound and the moment of his death, as though preparing himself for the final change that was to transport him to the happy hunting-grounds.

The people at the fort saw an Indian going with a firebrand to set fire to a dwelling-house occupied by some of the Hornbeck family. Benjamin Hornbeck loaded one of the long Holland guns, and tried the effect of a shot upon the miscreant. The ball struck a stone on the hill, and bounded against the Indian who immediately dropped the firebrand, gave a tremendous leap, and ran like a deer for the woods. This single shot was the means of saving that house from the general conflagration of that eventful day.

The old neighborhood of Wawarsing on that Sabbath morning must have been a scene of sublime grandeur. Thirteen substantial dwelling-houses, with their outbuildings, fourteen barns with barracks, stacks of hay and grain, and one grist-mill, were all enveloped in flames—no one being able to offer any resistance to their raging fury. The houses were stored with the articles requisite for the comforts and conveniences of civilized life—the products of the industry of many years; and the barns had just been filled with a plenteous harvest. The Indians remained all that day in the vicinity, pillaging the houses, driving off the stock, and securing whatever plunder they thought would be of service to them. Between sixty and seventy horses, most of them very fine, and a great number of cattle, sheep and hogs, were driven off. The Indians took some ground plaster as far as Grahamsville, supposing it to be flour, and attempted to make bread of it. At Esquire Hardenburgh's they fared sumptuously. They took some huckleberry pies, of which there was a goodly stock on hand, broke them up in tubs of sweet milk, and then devoured them. Had not the Indians devoted so much of their attention to plunder, they might have secured more scalps. Some of the inhabitants who had concealed themselves in the bushes along the fences, met with narrow escapes when the Indians came to drive the cattle from the fields; they threw little sticks and stones to drive the animals away from their places of concealment.

When the Indians were preparing to leave the place a personage of no ordinary rank and pretension was seen emerging from the woods into the highway near the old church. His appearance was truly imposing. He was mounted on a superb horse that had been stolen from Esquire Hardenburgh, and was arrayed in gorgeous apparel, according to Indian notions. He had silver bands about his arms, and over forty silver brooches were suspended about the person of his majesty. He was discovered by some soldiers who were watching to get a parting shot at the enemy as they were leaving the town, and one of them named Mack fired upon the chief. The latter was seen to reel in his saddle, but some other Indians turned his horse into the woods, and he was lost to view for a time. Afterwards Cornelius found his corpse in the woods near the place where he was shot, with the ornaments and trinkets still upon him. It is probable that the loss of this chief did much to intimidate the Indians and hasten their retreat.

In the course of Sunday afternoon, Capt. Pawling came up with some State troops from Hurley in time to relieve some of the inhabitants. There was a cabin in the woods situated in advance of the others, in which lived a man and his wife. At the first appearance of the foe, they fled into their castle, and gave battle to a party of savages who came up to attack them. The house was well supplied with arms, and while his wife loaded the guns he poured such a destructive fire into the midst of his foes, that they soon recoiled with loss.

Baffled in their attempts to force an entrance, they collected a heap of combustibles and set fire to the premises. The savages then retired a short distance to watch the result. The man ran out with a couple of buckets, procured water, and with it extinguished the flames. The Indians ran down upon him, but not being quick enough to prevent his gaining the door, they hurled their tomahawks at his head—happily without effect. Pawling's force being augmented by Col. Cantine's troops of Rochester and those of the garrison at Wawarsing, the little army amounted to about four hundred men. They lodged at the Wawarsing stone fort Sunday night and early the next morning set out in pursuit of the enemy.

When they came to Grahamsville they saw where the Indians had lodged the night before, and where they had attempted to make bread out of ground plaster. Towards night the pursuers arrived at Peenpack, along the Delaware, when the advance-guard returned and informed the officers that they had come to a fire of small sticks, and that the sticks were not burned through. This was evidence that the Indians could not be far in advance. It having been proposed to double the advance-guard, Captain Kortright offered to go with his whole company. While a consultation was going on among the officers, a gun in the hands of Dr. Vanderlyn, of Kingston, was discharged. The report alarmed the enemy; the Indians of the party instantly fled in small squads, leaving their white commander Caldwell alone with the Tories and the scouts, Hine and Bouck, whom they had released on their return march and were conducting to Niagara. At this place large packages of spoils, including quantities of clothing, were left by the Indians in the confusion of their hasty flight; but they were not found by the whites until several months afterwards. A council of war was held to determine whether to advance or retreat, at which it was resolved to give up the pursuit and return home. Capt. Hardenburgh and some others were anxious to pursue, but Col. Cantine opposed it. Capt. Hardenburgh, vexed at what he considered Cantine's somewhat questionable prudence, observed to his Colonel that "he could not die before his time;" to which the latter replied that if the Indians held a tomahawk above his head his time would be then and there.

A German by the name of Vrooman deserted the Indians on Honk hill, while Wawarsing was in flames. He had been with them three years; and becoming tired of his allegiance, he left his gun at a distance and approached the troops, making signs of peace. Some of the soldiers wished to kill him, but this was not permitted. From this man much of the matter embraced in this narrative was obtained. Vrooman said the invading horde was a party from Niagara, and that they consumed more than a month on their journey to Wawarsing. During this time they were so much distressed for want of provisions that they ate up their pack-horses and dogs. He reported that the garrison at Niagara was in a melancholy situation for want of provisions, and that the Tories there most bitterly execrated the day that they were deluded by a tyrant's emissaries to take up arms against their native country. It is said that the efficiency of the Indians at the descent upon Wawarsing was greatly impaired by reason of their previous privations, and from eating the soft corn they had taken from the corn-fields at Wawarsing. The squaws met them, on their return to Niagara, with parched corn.

The commander of the expedition, Caldwell, was now in a sore strait. He had failed in the main object of his expedition—the taking of prisoners and scalps. He was forsaken by his Indian guides, while hundreds of miles of trackless forest intervened between him and his base of supplies; and he was menaced by a foe greatly outnumbering his own force who were close at his heels, exasperated beyond measure at his work of devastation, and anxious to wreak vengeance upon the destroyer of their homes. Had Cantine advanced instead of retreating, Caldwell's diminished forces would have fallen an easy prey, and a large portion of the spoils would have been recovered.

Caldwell was now in a measure dependent upon the magnanimity of the scouts, Philip Hine and Silas Bouck. The latter agreed to pilot the party through to Niagara on condition that Caldwell would do all in his power to save him from running the gauntlet when they arrived at the fort. When they reached that post, Hine proposed allegiance to the British Crown; and was permitted to have some liberty, and went on an expedition with the British troops against Troy. It does not appear that he participated in any engagement against the Americans. One tradition is that he came back after peace was restored; another says that he escaped under pretense of going on a hunting expedition. At all events he lived to return to his friends who had mourned him as dead.

Silas Bouck, his brother scout, was taken to Montreal, put into a log jail, in company with two other prisoners, and furnished with a scanty supply of provisions, even those being of the filthiest and meanest kind. In this extremity the three prisoners set about devising some means of escape.

They succeeded in raising up one of the boards of the floor, and with the help of an old knife dug a hole under the side of the building. In the day time they lay still; at night they dug, carefully concealing the dirt under the floor, and replacing the board before morning. Having some reason to apprehend the time of execution was at hand, and a dark night favoring, they made their exit through the subterraneous passage, and entered the St. Lawrence. Bouck was ahead. They had not gone far before one of his companions cried out that he was sinking. But no assistance could be afforded—each had work for himself. When nearing the opposite side a similar cry was heard from the other. Before reaching the shore Bouck too began to grow weak, and he feared he should meet the fate of his companions. He thought he might touch the bottom, but was afraid to try. At last he attempted and found it was not beyond his depth; and after reaching the beach he made his way into the wilderness without knowing where he was going.

At length morning came. The sun rose, and by that he shaped his course with more certainty. Never were the benignant rays of that luminary more welcome to a traveler than on this occasion. Soon hunger began to torture Hine's already emaciated frame. He saw a rattlesnake in his path. Fortunately he had preserved his pocket-knife, with which he cut a crotched stick and put it over the neck of the snake, and then cut off its head. This snake he dressed and ate raw. This appeased the appetite for a while, when hunger again began to pinch him hard.

As he was pursuing his journey he came in sight of a small house. He watched it closely, and ascertained that its occupants consisted of two persons only—a man and his wife. He resolved to wait until the man should leave the house, when he would rush in, kill the woman, get some provisions and be off. He did not have to wait long for the opportunity. The moment he entered the door the woman cried out—"You are a deserter!" Some bread and meat lay on the table, which she told him to take and be off or he was a dead man; for there was a large body of Indians near by, and that her husband had gone to them. He took the bread and meat and fled with all haste into the woods, and crawled into a hollow log. He had been there but a short time when he heard the Indians traversing the forest in search of him. In the night he came out of the log, and resumed his journey. After enduring a degree of suffering seldom equalled, he arrived at Catskill, on the Hudson, about fourteen months after he was taken prisoner.

The freemen of Rochester, Ulster county, were assembled at a public-house to transact some business of a patriotic nature. The long and bloody war with Great Britain was drawing to a happy termination, and every patriot's pulse beat high with the prospect of domestic peace and national glory. While in the midst of their rejoicing, a person was discovered in the distance having the appearance of a way-worn traveler. As the stranger approached some one hinted that his step was like the stride of Silas Bouck. They had long supposed him dead—still he might be alive. They were not long in suspense. The joyful news resounded through the assembly that Bouck was coming, and with one simultaneous rush they ran to meet him. They could scarcely believe the evidence of their own eyes. They caught him up, and carried him into the house, while the air resounded with their shouts of joy. It was a reunion such as is seldom witnessed. After the trials of a protracted and bloody war, they were now to enjoy, in common, the dearly bought boon of liberty.

On the return of the Indians to Niagara it was ascertained that eighteen of their number were missing. One of the absent Indians, however, returned late in the fall, having driven a cow all the way, and lived on the milk.

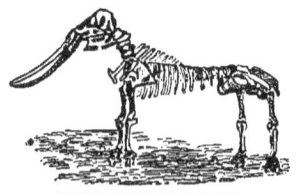

MOUNT HOPE MASTODON.

KORTRIGHT'S EXPEDITION.

DURING the Revolution three men were living, with their families, in the vicinity of Pine Bush, in the town of Rochester, named Shurker, Miller, and Baker. Shurker had been suspected of being a Tory. A Whig neighbor had once intimated as much to him, personally; but Shurker denied the charge, and made the strongest attestations of fidelity to the cause of liberty. This conversation was overheard by the Tories, and by them communicated to the Indians. Living thus on the outpost, these people had the strongest temptations to keep the good will of the enemy, in order to save their lives and property, though at heart they were Whigs.

One morning, at early dawn, the alarm of "Indians" was heard at the military posts at Pine Bush. The report of firearms rent the air; and in the twilight, flames were seen ascending from the doomed buildings in awful grandeur to the heavens, telling, in unequivocal terms, that the destroyers were there. Capt. Benjamin Kortright, who knew not what fear was, marshalled his band and marched to the scene of action. When they came in sight, they saw the enemy were already retiring. They halted a moment to extinguish the flames of a burning building, where they found Shurker with his brains dashed out. While the whites were at this place the Indians fired a volley on the hill near by. After putting out the fire, they pursued the enemy. When they came on the hill, they found Miller, literally perforated with bullet holes. It is remarkable that the women and children were not molested on this occasion; the most reasonable explanation is that a large proportion of the enemy were Tories; and that there may have been some ties of relationship or affinity that restrained them in this instance from their usual barbarity.

Capt. Kortright continued the pursuit until they came to Vernooey creek; then their provisions being exhausted, they returned to Pine Bush. On their way they buried the unfortunate Shurker and Miller, who fell martyrs to the cause of liberty. The fate of Baker is wrapped in impenetrable mystery. Nothing more was ever heard of him. He was the bravest and most muscular man of the three. It is probable he was reserved by the Indians as the object on which to wreak their vengeance in return for the three savages killed by Anderson.

At the time of this massacre a body of three hundred troops were stationed at the Fort on Honk hill. The officer in command, on being informed of the above facts, resolved to fit out an expedition to waylay the Indians on their return at the Chestnut woods, now known as Grahamsville, about thirteen miles from Napanock. The officer called out for volunteers, and John Graham stepped from the ranks. He was asked how many men he would have, to which he answered that he would take no more than "his honor" gave him, which was a sergeant's guard, and consisted of eighteen men and a sergeant and corporal. He was offered more men, but refused to take them. One of Graham's party was Abraham Van Campen, a noted hunter and expert Indian fighter. The others were from the old settlements east of the Shawangunk mountain, and unused to border warfare.

Graham's company marched on immediately, and reached the Chestnut woods in advance of the enemy He selected his position where the Chestnut brook enters the Papacton creek. At this place the hills form a triangle, and there is a space of nearly level ground at the junction of the streams. Here he resolved to remain and surprise the Indians if they came that way, in the meantime dispatching Van Campen to procure some fresh venison. Before he returned, the Indians came, discovered the plot of the whites, and made their dispositions for attack.

One Indian only was sent forward in the regular path in front of the little garrison; all the rest had approached unobserved, and occupied elevations on every side, where they were securely posted behind tree-trunks, with their fingers on the triggers of their guns awaiting the signal of death from their leader. Graham had just been very deliberately taking a drink from a rivulet near his camp; and as he rose, he saw an Indian in the path and directed his men to fire. Just as they aimed, the Indian fell upon his face, and the balls whistled harmlessly over his head. The next instant he was again upon his feet, and disappeared among the bushes as a murderous volley was poured into Graham's men from every side. Only two men, beside Van Campen, escaped, who made the best of their way back to the fort to carry the news of the massacre. Never was a flock of wild birds more effectually and skillfully taken in a fowler's net. History does not record the name of the leader of the Indians, but the generalship exhibited in the affair leaves little doubt that he was the celebrated Colonel Brant.

It was thought necessary to send a force of three hundred men to bury the dead. When the detachment arrived the bodies were falling to pieces from putrefaction, and were so offensive that the work of burial was with difficulty performed. They found them all scalped, and divested of every article that could be of any use; but their persons were not mangled as was frequently the case, with the exception of Graham's, which some declare was disemboweled. The bodies were buried in trenches on the spot where they fell. The troops had considerable sport with one of the men who escaped. During his hasty flight, in jumping across a brook, his bayonet had stuck into the ground, and he had left his gun, not taking time to pull it out. It was found to be loaded and all the cartridges were in the box; so it was evident that he had not once fired his piece.

Some years since a party came to the Chestnut woods to ascertain the precise spot where the unfortunate slain were laid. They did not succeed, though some were then living who could point to the exact location. Quinlan says that the burial-place of Graham and his men is a short distance back of the old school-house near the junction of Chestnut brook and the Papacton. A lad named Paul Benson, in company with two other boys, were constructing a dam across the brook, when they dug up some bones. These they took to Neil Benson, who pronounced them human bones, and ordered the boys to take them back. This so terrified them that they ran off, leaving the bones with Mr. Benson. Quinlan adds that a log, that was cut on the battle-ground, when sawed into lumber, was found to contain eight bullets.

ANDERSON AND OSTERHOUT.

JUST before the beginning of the Revolution, there was a tavern kept at Lackawack by a widow lady. This was frequented by Indians as well as white men. The widow had a son by her first husband, whose name was Caleb Osterhout. Either Caleb or a friend of his, George Anderson, had at one time offended the Indians by advising her not to sell them any more liquor, and the latter determined on revenge. Awaiting a favorable opportunity when these men were both at this tavern over night, some Indians entered, took them prisoners, and carried them off in triumph. While the struggle was going on, the woman fled from the house with no other covering than her night clothes; she was out all night in the woods and in a shower of rain. The next day she made her way to Wawarsing and gave the alarm, when a party was sent off in pursuit.

George Anderson could understand the Indian dialect, and he gathered from their conversation that they had determined to scalp Osterhout, as he was in poor health and not able to travel fast. They said his scalp would fetch more than he would be worth alive. Anderson made known this decision to his companion, and endeavored to nerve him to the point of making a desperate effort to escape. That night, providentially, an opportunity offered. The Indians had partaken of their supper, secured the prisoners for the night, and had lain down by the side of the camp-fire. A knife had been accidentally dropped by the savages, which Anderson surreptitiously covered with leaves. The knife was missed, and search was made for it; but not finding it readily the search was given up. Fatigued by the day's march, the Indians were soon wrapped in a deep sleep.

This was their opportunity. By the faint light of the flickering embers, Anderson found the knife and cut the thongs that bound his fellow-prisoner, and was in turn freed from his fastenings; the next thing was to dispatch the Indians, and each took a hatchet and prepared for the work. Anderson commenced, but he was in such haste that he only partially stunned his first victim, who rose up and fell into the fire. His next blow killed the second Indian instantly. Osterhout had failed in his attempt upon the third Indian, and Anderson crossed over to the other side of the fire and dispatched him. In the meantime Osterhout had pulled the first Indian out of the fire, instead of killing him. His conduct can only be explained in that he was, for the moment, unnerved and excited by the circumstances in which they were situated.

Two squaws were with the Indians; they were awakened by the noise, ran off and made the woods resound with their frantic yells.

One tradition of this event says, it was agreed between Osterhout and Anderson that the former should kill the squaws and the latter the Indians. Could this have been effected, it would have rendered the position of the white men more secure. As it was, they were well aware the squaws would waste no time in informing other Indians who were lurking in the vicinity. They would soon be upon their track like veritable bloodhounds; and should they be so unfortunate as to fall into the hands of the savages after having murdered three of their number, they were well aware that the most fearful torture that savage ingenuity could invent would speedily be visited upon them.

Incited by this reflection to the most strenuous efforts, and encouraged by what they had already accomplished, they speedily made their preparations for returning home. They first appropriated the provisions of the slaughtered Indians, and other articles that might prove useful to them in their journey. As their route lay through an unbroken wilderness, traversed by bands of hostile Indians, the utmost circumspection was necessary on the part of the escaping captives.

Osterhout was naturally a timid man, and of weak constitution, and was totally unfitted for such rough experience as they were undergoing. Their escape depended mostly on Anderson's vigilance and perseverance. Their movements were necessarily slow, each day's journey being limited by Osterhout's rapidly failing strength. Their scanty supply of provisions was soon exhausted, and hunger added its tortures to their sufferings. They had arms and ammunition, but they dare not fire at any game for fear of being heard by Indians. One day they came upon a horse which had been turned into the woods; this animal they killed with a spear, and cutting the flesh from the thighs devoured it raw. They were obliged to avoid the usual route, and often found it necessary to secrete themselves during the day and travel only at night, in order to escape the vigilance of the Indians. On one occasion they were so hard pressed that Anderson was obliged to swim a river with his companion on his back.

After untold suffering they came to a stockade fort at Honk hill, at which lived a man named Timmerman. When provisions were set before them Osterhout was fed like a child. Anderson had self-control sufficient to care for himself. Osterhout survived the shock but a short time, when he was numbered with his fathers.

The conduct of George Anderson subsequent to this event became very eccentric. The strength and vigor of his intellect seemed to have vanished; we can no longer contemplate him as the brave and undaunted hero. This was no doubt the result of physical disease, brought on by the excessive fatigue and hardship of his captivity and escape. He appeared to be constantly apprehensive of some imminent danger, the result of a mental derangement. He left Wawarsing, wandered on the Shawangunk mountain, and took up his abode in a cavern in the eastern slope. From this lonely retreat he would sally forth in the night, and indulge in petty thieving, by which means he supplied his physical necessities. He became a pest to the people, but they forbore to punish him out of consideration for his misfortunes, as they were aware he was not morally responsible for his acts.

POLLY TIDD.

ON one of the roads leading from Pecksville to Stormville, in Duchess county, there is yet standing an unpretentious dwelling-house in which, many years ago, lived a family whose history is associated with a startling tragedy. The incidents are but faintly outlined in the memories of even the oldest inhabitants of the neighborhood; still there are a few who have a distinct recollection of hearing the older settlers tell of the lonely life and eccentricities of Polly Tidd, the last survivor of this unfortunate family.

In this house, some years prior to the Revolution, there lived a well-to-do farmer by the name of Solomon Tidd. His family consisted of a wife, two daughters nearly grown, and an only son about ten years of age. One day in early autumn, Solomon and his wife drove down to Fishkill village to dispose of some farm produce, and to make some necessary purchases for the family, leaving the boy and his sisters at home. On their return from the village, while passing through a piece of woods about a mile from the house, their old horse, "Roan," began to prick up his ears, and to accelerate his pace in a way that he had not been known to do in years. "Some painter or bear, likely, snooping in the bushes, for there can't be no Ingins about," said Solomon, by way of accounting for the strange behavior of their family horse.

"Hark, did not some one call?" cried out Mrs. Tidd, who was not a little frightened at the idea of the possible proximity of a panther or bear.

"Seems to me I did hear sunthin," answered Solomon, "but guess I must have been mistaken. Old Roan thinks there's some varmint around that he don't like, though, and I don't care how soon we get out of this. So do your best, Roan"—continued the old man to his usually sedate roadster, who had quickened his pace into a gallop.

"Where are the children," cried Mrs. Tidd in alarm as she entered the door, breathless from her breakneck ride, only to find the house empty, and no one within call. "Could it be they'd be foolish enough to come down the road to meet us, and got caught by a painter?" And the good old lady shuddered at the thought.

"No, I guess not," said her husband, yet there was a tremor in his voice that showed he, too, had misgivings.

"And Harry was so anxious for his new shoes and the girls for their plaid frocks! I wonder why they're not here," soliloquized Mrs. Tidd. And then glancing at the table. "Well I declare if they haven't eat up all my fruit-cake, and broke open my best jar of presarves! 'Pears like as though they'd had the whole neighborhood to dinner. But where on 'arth are they gone to? They wouldn't have started for wintergreens up in the back pasture, would they?" But the father was too much absorbed in his own thoughts to give heed to her queries.

As hour after hour passed, and the missing ones were not found, the parents became seriously alarmed. Word was sent to their neighbors, none of whom had seen the children, and the whole settlement volunteered to search for them. Night closed in, but no tidings. Torches were now procured, and their gleaming could be seen along the mountain side borne in the hands of sympathizing friends, whose voices sounded strangely upon the night air as they hallooed the names of the wanderers, and shouted to one another as they prosecuted their search. Morning came and the news spread far and wide. Men and boys of neighboring towns assembled, and that day hundreds were engaged in beating the woods for miles in every direction. But all was of no avail; it became evident that further search was useless.

The mother became almost frantic at her loss. Indeed it seemed for awhile that her reason would be dethroned; but in time the more violent paroxysms of her grief wore away, and she fell into a state of settled melancholy. Years passed, and Solomon Tidd and his wife were laid to rest in the graveyard on the mountain side, in utter ignorance to the last of the nature of the calamity that had rendered them childless.

When Solomon and his wife had been gone from home about an hour on the day of the children's disappearance, a gentle tap was heard at the door. Polly, the elder of the girls, was about to open it, when her sister Esther stopped her, and asked "Who's there?" "A friend," was the response. Esther quickly detected a peculiar accent in the voice, and would have bolted the door; but her purpose was diverted by the more persistent Polly, when they were confronted by two Indians. The latter entered and asked for food; when the frightened children set before them the best the house afforded. While eating, the savages enquired in broken English where their father and mother were; and the girls, unused to the arts of diplomacy, gave honest answers to their questions. At this the Indians were observed to exchange significant glances; and as they rose to go, informed the children that they were to accompany them. The lad, terrified beyond measure, set up a cry; when he received a blow from the larger Indian that sent him reeling to the floor. The savage then brandished a knife and said, "Me kill, if you don't stop noise!"

The Indians now manifested the utmost haste. They fairly urged their captives into a run across the open field opposite the house, nor did they slacken their pace until they gained the covert of the woods. The path along which they were going led not far from the highway. Presently they heard the rumble of a wagon, and the children recognized the voice of their father as he encouraged his frightened horse. At this juncture the lad essayed to cry out "Father!" but the word was broken off in mid-utterance by a blow on the head from the nearest Indian, which stretched the little fellow apparently lifeless upon the ground. When the sound of the wheels died away some leaves were hastily strewn over the lad, and the flight down the mountain path resumed. Presently the noise of rapid footsteps was heard behind them, and the party turned to behold the boy, who had recovered consciousness and kicked away the leaves; and, terrified at being left alone in the woods, had unwittingly run into the power of the worst enemy that he could have encountered. No harm was offered the lad, but he was given to understand if he made another outcry he should be killed.

Being so far from the river, the Indians knew their own safety depended on the speed of their flight. One savage in advance, the other in the rear, with the captives in single file between—the strength of the children was tested to the utmost. It became evident as they progressed that the boy could not keep pace with them; and he was taken aside, his brains dashed out with a tomahawk, the body thrown into a cleft of rocks for the wolves and ravens to devour, and the flight resumed.

In due time the savages with their captives reached their village at the base of the Shawangunk mountain. Here Polly and Esther were formally adopted into two Indian families that had each been recently bereaved of a daughter, and they were set at work gathering corn, collecting fuel, and other menial drudgery of the Indian women. In this way a year or more passed; and the girls were blooming into womanhood. The fair face of Esther had attracted the notice of a young brave, and he sought her hand in marriage after the manner of court ship in vogue with his tribe. On two successive evenings he presented himself at the wigwam where Esther lived, partook of the food offered by her hands, and reclined on the couch of skins. But Esther, while she extended the usual courtesy required by the rules of Indian hospitality, was so far unversed in savage wooing as not to understand how she was to signify her acceptance. The succeeding day Esther was set at work to gather sticks, a hint designed to intimidate her to accept his matrimonial advances, though she understood not its purport. That evening her swarthy suitor again presented himself at her door, dressed in his best deerskins, and received as before the hospitality of her wigwam. Her non-compliance with Indian custom was interpreted as a rejection of his suit, and the savage departed next morning crest-fallen.

This was an affront to the tribe that must not be allowed to go unpunished. A captive white woman had refused the hand of one of their bravest warriors! Esther was told to array herself in her best apparel, and innocent of giving any intentional offense, and with not the faintest suspicion of the fate that awaited her, she was led a short distance into the forest where she found the village assembled. There she was tied to a stake, the wood she had gathered on the previous day was piled about her, and she was told that she must die.

"Let me first speak to my sister," were the last audible words she uttered; but the request was not granted, for Polly had been taken away so that the screams of her ill-fated relative could not reach her.

Some months afterward a young warrior by the name of Wawonda came to the wigwam where Polly lived as a suitor for her hand. She received him with respectful cordiality, and the next evening he came again, remaining a guest as before, and departing with the dawn. That day Polly was set at work gathering sticks. As she was thus engaged a friendly squaw approached and inquired if she knew what she was gathering those sticks for. She replied she did not. "Did not Wawonda visit the wigwam of the pale-face last night?" "He did," was the reply. "And did he not come the night before?" "Yes," was Polly's answer. "Well," continued the woman, "Wawonda wants pale-face to keep his wigwam and dry his venison. He will come again to night. If pale-face accepts him all will be well; if not, to-morrow these sticks will be used to burn her at the stake as was burned her sister Esther for refusing Wanoni!" When Wawonda presented himself for the third time at the wigwam of the captive, he was accepted as an acknowledged suitor according to the custom of the tribe, and thus was Polly duly installed at the head of the domestic affairs of Wawonda's household.

Years rolled by. Polly had heard naught of her relatives since the day of her capture. Though living in sight of her native mountains she was for a long time too closely watched for a successful attempt at escape. Two half-breed boys were added to her household, and her time was too fully occupied to think of aught else. As the white settlers increased in number, the game in the forest diminished, and notwithstanding Wawonda's skill in hunting, the family was often pinched for food. Polly, therefore, found it necessary, inasmuch as her liege lord felt it was beneath his dignity to engage in manual labor, to go among the white families and do their washing. In this way her rounds took her into the vicinity of Newburgh, and now for the first time she seriously considered the purpose of again visiting the scenes of her early home. At the first opportunity she fled with her two boys across the river, and once more stood at the threshold where she had been born and reared, and where she had taken her last look of her parents.

But the place had changed, and new faces were at the door. She inquired after her parents by name, and was told they had died of broken hearts years before. She sought out the companions of her childhood, but they had grown out of her remembrance; and her most intimate friends could not recognize in her the fresh, romping girl they had known in former years, such ravages a life of drudgery among the Indians had wrought in her frame. She half regretted leaving her home in the wilderness, and but for the interference of friends would in all probability have returned to her bondage. Wawonda, it is said, used to come down to the river at Newburgh, and sit for hours gazing over at the mountains where his white squaw and half-breed boys resided, but he never dared venture into their vicinity. As Polly's identity was established beyond cavil, the property of her father was placed in her possession, which was sufficient, with judicious economy, to provide for her wants.

The two boys grew up tall and slender, but both died before reaching manhood. Polly lived to a good old age, and often related, to groups of eager friends, the story of her captivity among the Delaware Indians.

CAPTIVITY OF MRS. COLEMAN.

DURING the perilous times of the French and Indian war the settlements east of the Shawangunk were not exempt from visits of scalping parties of Indian hostiles. It was at this stormy period that two brothers by the name of Coleman occupied a double log house with their families a short distance south-east of the present village of Burlingham.

On a Sabbath afternoon one of the brothers went into the woods to search for a span of horses that had strayed from home. While there he was sur

DEATH OF COLEMAN.

prised by a war-party of Indians lying in ambush, and was shot and scalped. The savages then proceeded to the house, where the other brother was sick, and confined to his bed. There was a crevice between the logs next the bed on which the sick man lay, through which the Indians could insert the muzzles of their guns. The first intimation of danger the family had, was the startling report of fire-arms, the belching flames of gunpowder from the walls of their cabin and the piercing death-shriek of the brother as the fatal bullet penetrated his brain. The next moment the painted demons burst into the house, dragged the corpse from the bed to the door and tore away the scalp with savage exultation. The women and children looked on, paralyzed with horror, and in momentary expectation of meeting a like fate. The savages chose to spare their lives, however, and took them all prisoners.

One of the women had a child about two weeks old. Being feeble and unable to walk, she was placed astride an old horse, and her feet were tied under him with a rope. They then gave her the child to carry in her arms. Next setting fire to the building they hurried off in a north-west direction over the Shawangunk mountain. The babe was restless, and cried; and the savages, fearing its wailing would guide the whites who might be upon their track, told the mother she must keep it still or they would kill it. The mother did all she could to calm the little one, but it would not be quieted. Then one of the savages rushed up to her side, tore the infant from her arms, and taking it by the heels knocked out its brains against a tree before her eyes, and threw it as far from the path as his strength would allow. There the body was left to be torn and devoured by wild beasts.

The party passed over the mountain, reaching the Mamakating valley a little after dusk. Here they rested a short interval; as soon as the moon rose they resumed their journey, traveling the remainder of that night, and a part of the next day. The journey through that night was gloomy and fearful. Even the little children, after the brutal murder of the babe, dare make no complaints. Like wandering ghosts in the uncertain light they pursued the broken path before them, occasionally startled by the howl of a wolf or the scream of a panther, their distress heightened and made more unbearable by the uncertainty of the fate that awaited them.

Day came at last to the weary and hapless wanderers, but it brought no revival of their drooping hearts. Their natural protectors, so recently murdered by the ruthless savage, and themselves prisoners entirely at his mercy—the condition of those widows and orphans was not calculated to revive the spirits. As the day advanced their physical sufferings increased, as, foot-sore and exhausted, they were urged at an accelerated pace by their inhuman captors.

The report of the tragedy soon spread throughout the neighboring settlements, and before Monday morning quite a number of the brave and sympathizing settlers had gathered about the Coleman cabin. The mangled bodies of the brothers, one of which had been brought in from the woods, where it had been found, and the charred embers of the log dwelling, all bore unmistakable evidence of the tragic event. The men were all armed with rifles and hunting-knives, and knew how to use them effectively; for the necessities of border life had skilled them in the use of those weapons.

At the first streak of dawn the party set out upon the trail. No time was lost in a useless discussion of the probable results of the pursuit. It was enough that two of their friends had been murdered, and several women and helpless children carried off into captivity, by a savage and relentless foe. Little difficulty was experienced in following the trail, the impressions made by the feet of the horse being quite distinct. When they came upon the remains of the babe, and discovered the brutal manner in which it had been killed, their

HAHN HOUSE, MONTICELLO, N.Y. HENRY HAHN, PROPRIETOR.

KINGSTON IN 1695.

1. Blockhouse. 2. Church and Burial Place. 3. House where the Governor is entertained. 4. Part separated and fortified. 5, 5, Town Gates

horror and indignation knew no bounds; they pressed forward with the greater energy with the stern purpose of wreaking vengeance on the marauders.

So rapidly did they march that they traveled as far that day as the Indians did in a night and day, encumbered as they were with women and children; towards night they found they were close upon the savages. The latter became aware that they were pursued, while the captives were ignorant of the proximity of their friends. They were then probably on the "barrens" of one of the Delaware river towns. The Indians were not in a condition for a fight and were aware that their enemies outnumbered them; so they sought to escape by stratagem.

The nature of the ground at this point being such that the horse's hoofs would leave no impression, they turned at right angles from the path and secreted themselves, with the captives in a thicket. This was the first intimation the prisoners had that succor was near; but they were informed they would suffer instant death if they made the least noise. Presently they heard the sounds of their friends following in the path they had just left. Nearer and nearer they came, until the individual voices of their neighbors could be distinguished. But the poor children and their mothers did not dare even to look in the direction from whence the sounds came, for a savage stood over each of the trembling and anxious captives with a weapon upraised, ready to deal the fatal blow if an alarm was made. Would that a kind Providence might interpose, and prevent their passing on without discovering that the path had been abandoned. Now that help was so near, the hearts of the poor captives were wellnigh bursting at the suspense. They could hardly suppress a cry that they knew would bring their friends instantly to their side; but they knew it was in the power of the savages to strike every captive dead before relief could come. Gradually the voices grew more and more indistinct, then entirely ceased, and hope gradually died in the breasts of the prisoners, for the chance of liberation had passed.

After the whites had gone by, Mrs. Coleman, for the first time, was taken from the horse, on which she had been tied for twenty-four hours. The party remained in their place of concealment until the next morning; then the feeble and bereaved mother was again placed in her former position, and the journey resumed.

From Sunday afternoon until Tuesday forenoon the party did not partake of a morsel of food. The Indians had brought no provision with them, and were afraid to fire their guns, fearing to expose their position to the whites. Before noon on Tuesday a deer was shot, and their appetite appeased. During their flight they came successively to the Neversink and the Delaware rivers; in crossing these streams the Indians would drive the horse, with Mrs. Coleman on his back, in advance of the others, to measure the depth. But the grief of the poor woman at the death of her husband and child, her anxiety for her remaining children and her present fatigue and sufferings, rendered her in a measure insensible to the danger of being submerged.

On Thursday evening they arrived at an Indian village some fifty miles beyond the Delaware river. Their journey over mountains, and through the trackless woods was terminated, but not so their sufferings. After the customary rejoicing at the success and safe return of the warriors, a large fire was kindled, and the people of the village assembled. The captive white children were stripped naked, and then compelled to run around the fire, the savages following them with whips, which they applied to their naked bodies without mercy. When the children screamed with pain and affright, their tormentors would exhibit the greatest satisfaction, and yell and laugh until the woods rang with hideous mirth. In this cruel amusement the Indian boys participated with evident relish.

While this was going on it seemed to Mrs. Coleman that her heart would break. She was unable longer to endure the agonizing screams of her own children, as they were pursued and lashed about the fire. She knew she was powerless to do them any good, so she resolved to flee to some secluded spot, where, out of reach of the Indians, she could quietly lie down and die. Stealing away softly and quietly until out of their sight, she ran as fast as her limbs would carry her. Presently she discovered a light in the distance, and by an unaccountable impulse, she resolved to go to it, not caring whether she lived or died. Here she found an old squaw who occupied a wigwam by herself. This squaw had lived among the white people, could speak their language tolerably well, and was known as Peter Nell—a name probably a corruption of Petronella, given her in baptism by the Moravians. To her Mrs. Coleman applied in her extremity. The womanly heart of the squaw was touched. She received her white sister kindly; assured her that the Indians should do her no further harm; and making her a bed of leaves and bear-skins, bade her rest until she could prepare some proper nourishment.

This kind-hearted daughter of the forest presently came with a dish of venison soup prepared after the manner of the white people, which proved very refreshing to the sick and exhausted captive. The latter remained with her benefactor until her health was completely restored, when the squaw rendered her still further service by assisting her to return to her friends in Orange county.

The fate of the other captives is unknown. It was many years afterwards reported that two of them escaped, but of this there is no certainty.

PHEBE REYNOLDS AND THE TORIES.

MAN is largely a creature of circumstances. Whatever may be his natural endowments we cannot shut our eyes to the fact that his character is moulded by his surroundings. The girl that has been reared in luxury and ease, the subject of assiduous care as though she were a tender and volatile plant, will acquire a softness and effeminacy that will lead her to lose self-control upon the slightest occasion. Her less-favored sister, born with like endowments, but who has been brought up amid the hardships and dangers of frontier life, when her fortitude is put to the test, will be found capable of performing acts of heroism that will put many of the lords of creation to shame. Among all the heroines of the border, whose deeds of hardihood and self-denial have been put on record, there will be found not one excelling in the sublimer virtues the subject of this sketch.

Phebe Reynolds was the daughter of Henry Reynolds, and one of a large family of children. They were residing, at the time of the Revolution, in a log cabin in the present town of Monroe, within the region of country infested by the notorious Claudius Smith band of outlaws. One night the gang surrounded Reynolds's cabin with purpose to effect an entrance, but found the windows and doors securely barred and bolted. They next mounted the roof, and two or three essayed to drop down the wide-mouthed chimney; one of the family poured the contents of a feather-bed upon the fire, and the robbers were forced to beat a retreat to escape suffocation.

Some time afterward a second attempt was made with a different result. Benjamin Kelley and Philip Roblin, both of whom were near neighbors of Reynolds, together with several others, went to Reynolds's house one dark night, and knocked for admission, representing themselves to be a detachment of the American army in search of deserters. After hurriedly dressing himself Reynolds opened the door, and then went to the fire-place to procure a light. While his back was turned to his visitors one of them struck him with the flat side of his sword, and told him to make haste. This at once revealed the character of his guests. He made a rush for the door, but just outside stumbled over a log, and fell headlong. Ere he could recover himself the gang were upon him, and he was dragged back into the house.

When the struggle began, Reynolds called loudly for his son, then a mere lad, to come to his assistance. When the boy came into the room, one of the men seized him, set him down upon the floor, and told him if he moved even so much as to turn his head right or left, he would cut it off. This so terrified the boy that he sat as motionless as if he had been carved in stone. Mrs. Reynolds, accompanied by some of the other children, now came into the apartment; when she saw her husband in the hands of ruffians, she fell upon the floor in convulsions; and it is believed she remained unconscious through most of the ensuing strife.

After binding Reynolds, and wounding him with their knives and swords, they, in the presence of his family, proceeded to hang him on the trammel-pole of his fire-place. Having accomplished this, the members of the gang dispersed through the several rooms and commenced plundering, leaving him, as they supposed, in the throes of death.

At this time Phebe Reynolds was twelve years old, but large and robust for one of her age. She had become inured to the dangers and terrors of border life, and was resolute and fearless, particularly when her blood was up. Taking advantage of their temporary absence, Phebe caught up a knife and hastily cut the rope by which her father was suspended. She also threw the noose from his neck and managed to get him upon a bed.

HANGING OF REYNOLDS.

It was not long before the ruffians discovered what had been done, and again they gathered in the room to murder Reynolds. The girl boldly confronted them with her knife, like a lioness at bay. They commanded her to go away, threatening her with instant death if she refused. She declared she did not wish to live if they murdered her father. They then menaced her with swords and knives; still she stood her ground courageously. Finding them determined to murder her father, she sprang upon the bed, clasped her hands tightly around him, and attempted thus to shield him from their bloody instruments. One of the men then took the rope and cruelly beat the girl; but she did not even moan, or wince, although she was marked from head to foot with broad, angry stripes.

Finding this to be of no avail, the marauders forcibly tore her away, and once more Mr. Reynolds was left hanging to the trammel-pole, while they resumed their work of plundering the house.

Again did the heroic daughter cut the rope, and was leading her father to another room, when his strength gave out, and he sank upon the floor. Again did the wretches discover what had been done, and they attacked him with their knives and swords as he lay upon the floor, and once more the brave daughter threw herself upon him, and endeavored to protect him; receiving on her own person many of the blows that were intended for him. In short, her clothing was saturated with the blood flowing from numerous cuts in her forehead and breast. Finally the robbers threw Mr. Reynolds into an old chest, and, shutting down the lid, they left the place, first destroying his private papers and setting fire to the house. They also rolled a large stone against the door, which opened outward, and told them they would shoot the first one that dared to raise the latch, with the design that the whole family should be burned up with the house.

Phebe now made her way to the chest, and, raising the lid, found her father, stiff and rigid, and apparently dead. With such help as her mother and the lad could give, the body of her father was lifted from the chest, and while this was being done, a low moan escaped his lips. She immediately pried open his teeth with a pewter spoon, and gave him a few drops of water. This seemed to revive him, and she gave him more while she proceeded to staunch the blood that was flowing from his wounds.

While thus occupied her mother was moaning and wandering aimlessly from room to room, and presently she noticed that a bed, a hogshead of flax, and some other inflammable material were on fire. The mother, appalled at this discovery, cried out, "Oh, Phebe, the house is on fire in three places!" "Why don't you put it out?" demanded the daughter. "Oh, I can't," was the dismayed reply, "if it burns down over our heads!" "Then come and take care of father and let me do it." The brave girl promptly dashed water on the burning beds, threw a drenched rug over the flax, and went back to her father.

While engaged in dressing his wounds, she told the lad to go out and alarm the neighborhood; but the boy did not dare to leave the house. She then, after doing all she could for the safety and comfort of her father, set out upon the errand herself. Although her person was covered with cuts and wounds, her clothing saturated with her own blood, and she had passed through a scene of terror such as few could have had the fortitude to face, yet she was so cool and collected that she noticed the crowing of cocks in the neighborhood as she passed along the road, and knew that morning was near.

The alarm spread from house to house. A body of men immediately assembled, and shortly after sunrise started in pursuit of the ruffians. The latter were followed into their retreat in the mountains with such energy that they were taken by surprise and four or five of them were killed. One of the killed was Kelley, the leader of the gang, who resided within a mile of Reynolds's house, and had passed for a Whig. He was shot by a young man named June, who knew Kelley personally. It appears that June had been informed the robbers were at a certain place playing cards. When he approached their hiding place they heard him coming, and rose to their feet. As they did so, he fired into their midst: the shot mortally wounded Kelley, whose body was afterward found at a sulphur spring to which he had wandered and died. The remains were partially covered up with leaves and brush, and near by was the wedding suit of Henry Reynolds, tied up with a bark string. This suit Mr. Reynolds had preserved over fourteen years; yet he expressed a wish never to wear or see the clothes again since they had been on the back of a Tory. Only two of the ruffians escaped, and they were afterwards arrested in New Jersey. Reynolds would not consent to appear against them, probably on account of his Quaker principles.

While some of the neighbors were pursuing the marauders, others, including the physicians of the town, were attending to the injuries of the family. Reynolds, it was found, had been cut and stabbed in more than thirty places. An ear had been so nearly severed that it hung down on his shoulder. It was replaced as well as circumstances would admit, but the wound healed in such a way as to disfigure him for life. One of his hands was cut so badly that he never afterwards fully recovered its use.

For weeks Reynolds was on the brink of the grave; but he possessed a strong constitution, fortified by a life of temperance and regular habits, and he was once more restored to health. His wounds so completely covered his person that, as he lay bandaged, he more resembled an Egyptian mummy than anything else. His neighbors were very kind to him; they cut his wheat, gathered his hay, and even provided for his family.

When the physicians turned their attention to Phebe, it was found that the wounds on her forehead and breast were of a serious nature, and that her body and limbs were badly bruised and lacerated. Whenever she came within her father's sight, her bruised and bandaged appearance so affected him, that the physicians directed that she should not be allowed to come in his room; and instead of exacting fees for their attendance, the physicians filled Phebe's hands with coin.

Soon after this event Henry Reynolds removed to Sullivan county, where he lived to a good old age, greatly respected by all who knew him. There are people still living in Fallsburg and Neversink who have heard the facts related by Henry Reynolds himself as he exhibited his scars. Phebe became the wife of Jeremiah Drake, of Neversink Flats, and died in November, 1853; her remains repose in the little burial-ground, near those of her husband. Her posterity are among the most highly honored residents of the Neversink valley. One hundred years after the marriage of Henry Reynolds, says Quinlan, it is estimated that his descendants numbered upwards of one thousand.

MISS LAND'S MIDNIGHT JOURNEY.

ON the east bank of the Delaware river, near the Falls of Cochecton, during the Revolution and for some time thereafter, there stood a log house, a fair representative of the rude cabins of the frontier. This was the residence of Bryant Kane, whose family consisted of a wife and several children. Kane was thought to entertain sentiments favorable to the King, for which he incurred the ill-will and suspicion of his neighbors; the feeling became so strong against him that he was forced to leave the neighborhood, information having reached him that Captain Tyler, who was killed subsequently at the battle of Minisink, had issued orders for his arrest.

Before leaving home Kane engaged a man named Flowers to stay with his family and manage the farm; and, confident that no harm could befall them, and that the feuds and vindictiveness of partisan warfare would not be visited upon innocent women and children, he did not take his family with him. But Bryant Kane was never suffered to look upon their faces again.

On the opposite bank of the river resided Robert Land, also a Tory, and, like Kane, a refugee from his home. It was known that Indians and scouts were in the neighborhood, and their presence was a source of uneasiness. One day in the month of April the wife of Robert Land, and her son, a lad of nineteen years, fearing a visit from the Indians, drove their cattle to a place of concealment in the mountains. Here they remained all night to guard them, leaving three other brothers and two sisters at home.

When the family had retired, and all were asleep, one of the daughters was disturbed by some one in her room. She awoke to find an Indian standing by her bed, drawing a spear point gently across the sole of her foot. The fellow spoke kindly to her in his broken Indian accent, and told her to get up and run to the neighbors and let them know the Indians had come. He had found means to enter her sleeping apartment without alarming the other members of the family, and had chosen this novel method of awakening her. Whether her nocturnal visitor really intended to befriend the settlers by putting them on their guard is not known; but without further explanation he left the house as mysteriously as he came.

Miss Land arose, dressed herself, and silently left the house. Singularly enough she did not alarm her brothers and sisters, who were still wrapped in slumber. She drew her shawl closer about her head, for the night was chilly, and hurried down to the river side. Her way led down the bank through a ravine, over which a clump of hemlocks cast a deep gloom. Her fancy half pictured a wild beast or Indian warrior crouching under the shadow. She then sought for the dug-out, and, having found it, boldly pushed for the opposite shore. The wind sighed dismally through the evergreens; an owl, in a dry tree that hung over the river, was sounding its boding cry; the night was dark and the waters swollen. Miss Land thought she never before undertook so lonely a journey.

She pointed the canoe's head to the river path that led up to Kane's house; she knew the spot by a large hemlock that stood at the brink and leaned over the river. She was soon winding up the zigzag path; she had so often passed over it that she knew its every crook and irregularity.

As she came into the clearing all was silent, save the low moaning of the wind among the pines, and the cry of the owl down by the river bank. The girdled trees, denuded of their limbs and blackened by fire, stood around like grim and ghostly sentinels. Approaching the house, no sign of life was visible. She thought of the probability that Indians might be lurking at that moment in the shadows of the charred stumps, ready at the signal to startle the night air with the war-whoop, and slaughter the sleeping inmates.

Her feelings served to quicken her pace. Once at the door of the Kane cabin she endeavored to attract the attention of those within. She rapped on the door; then went to Mrs. Kane's bedroom window, but could get no response. She next tried to open the door; it yielded, and with palpitating heart she entered the house. She called the members of the family by name, but received no answer. All was still as the house of death.

Presently she stumbled over some object upon the floor. Stooping down she found it to be the prostrate body of a woman, and was horrified to find her apparel wet with blood.

Miss Land fled from the house; she was too much frightened to shriek. She quickly aroused the family of Nicholas Conklin, the nearest neighbor of the Kane's and told them what she had discovered. It was deemed prudent not to venture abroad before morning.

At the break of day Mr. Conklin and some neighbors went to the Kane cabin, where they found that the entire family, including Mr. Flowers, had been murdered and scalped. Mrs. Kane had evidently been scalped while alive, for she had died while attempting to dress herself, and a portion of her dress was drawn over her mutilated head.

After gazing at the horrid scene, the party accompanied Miss Land home. Her mother and brother John were still absent; while her little brother Abel had been taken from the house by Indians during the night. Not long after this Mrs. Land and John returned, and were informed of what had taken place. They thought it very strange that their family should be made a target for both parties. John resolved on an attempt to recover his missing brother; so, hastily collecting a few of his neighbors, among them some friendly Indians living in the vicinity, he set out upon the trail of the marauders, which led toward the Mohawk country.

After a brief but rapid march they overtook the retreating party, and found them posted for battle. John was not disposed to fight; he only wanted a parley with a view to releasing his brother. An explanation took place, the result of which was that Abel was restored to his friends after first being compelled to run the gauntlet. In executing this feat his speed astonished everybody present. He received only a few blows, and such was the admiration of the Indians for the spirit and dexterity he exhibited, that he was suffered to pass through unharmed. The two parties then separated; John and his companions to their homes, and the Indians, who proved to be a wandering party of Mohawks, to their own country

Three years subsequent to the murder of Bryant Kane's family at the Falls of Cochecton, Col. Bryant, with a party of Tories and Indians, made a descent on Harpersfield, in Delaware county. They captured several of the patriots of the settlement, including Mr. Freegift Patchin, whom they took to Niagara. Some time after the Revolutionary war, Patchin published a narrative of his captivity, in which he says one of his captors was Barney Kane, a Tory. This is thought to be the Bryant Kane whose family was murdered on the banks of the Delaware.

During the journey from Harpersfield to Niagara, Patchin says Kane boasted that he had killed a Major Hopkins, on an Island in Lake George. A party of pleasure had gone to this island on a sailing excursion, and having delayed their departure until too late to return home, determined to spend the night on the island. Kane and his party, perceiving that they were defenseless, proceeded to the place as soon as it was night, and attacked them as they were sleeping around a fire. Several of the Americans were killed, among them a woman. This woman had a babe which was not injured in the least. "This," said Kane, "we put to the breast of its dead mother, and in that manner we left it. Major Hopkins was wounded, only his thigh-bone being broken. He started up, when I struck him with the butt of my gun on the side of his head. He fell over but caught on one hand. I then knocked him the other way, but he caught on the other hand. A third blow, and I laid him dead. These were all scalped except the infant. In the morning a party of Whigs went over and brought away the dead, together with one they found alive, though scalped, and the babe which was hanging and sobbing at the breast of its lifeless mother."

Whether the massacre of Bryant Kane's family so wrought upon a nature not originally bad as to convert him into a fiend, or whether his own crimes against his Whig neighbors led to the slaughter of his wife and children, is not known. The feelings which prompted and the motives which actuated the commission of the bloody deeds by the early settlers against their neighbors, will never be unveiled until the day of final reckoning.

After the declaration of peace, Bryant Kane wandered from place to place in the valley of the Delaware. His property was confiscated; and having lost both family and fortune, he sought for consolation in the intoxicating cup, and finally left the country. The time and manner of his death no one can tell.

John Land became so obnoxious to the Whigs that he was arrested and sent to the "New Jersey log jail." From this he escaped; but was soon retaken, wounded in his head with a sword, and hanged until his life was nearly gone. He was informed that next time he would be hanged in earnest, and after being heavily ironed was once more cast into prison. Subsequently a Whig named Harvey became responsible for his good conduct, and he was permitted to enjoy the liberties of the town. He lived with Harvey until 1783, when he returned to Cochecton. He became a respectable citizen of the United States, although he was stigmatized until the day of his death as "John Land, the Tory."

THE TORIES AFTER THE REVOLUTION.

THE bitter animosity engendered during the Revolutionary war between the Whigs and Tories did not subside immediately after the treaty of peace in 1783. The few of the latter who remained in the country were ever after subjected to social ostracism, and were most fortunate if they escaped personal violence. The patriotic inhabitants of the frontier could not so soon forget the manner in which their babes had been taken from the cradle and from the breasts of their mothers, and their brains dashed out, by the hated and despised

Tories; nor could they blot from their memory the fact that those foes to their country, while professing friendship to the Whigs, acted as spies for the enemy, and secretly joined the predatory bands of Indians in their incursions against their nearest neighbors of the settlements, and shared in the booty while they excelled their savage allies in deeds of inhumanity. Indeed, this anti-Tory feeling only died out when the last patriot of the Revolution expired. That there would be numerous collisions between the two factions was to be expected, as that would be no more than the legitimate result of such bitter personal resentment; nor could the wranglings cease except with the death of the parties.

At a militia training in Rochester, about the year 1783, several individuals who were known to be Tories attended. The patriots regarded them with undisguised hatred, and were indignant at their presumption in being present, and only waited the slightest pretext to gratify their ill-feeling by a pitched battle. They did not hesitate to call them Tories to their very faces and hard words passed on both sides. At last a Whig gave a Tory a kick, which was repaid with interest by a blow. Others fell in on both sides, and a general and desperate skirmish ensued. As nothing but fists and clubbed muskets were used, the fight was long and obstinate, but attended with no fatal results. When the affray was over, the Tories bent their steps homeward, meeting a Whig on their way, on whom they administered some retaliatory vengeance. Bruised and bloody, he presented himself before the other Whigs and related what had occurred, adding that the Tories were loading their pieces with balls. The Whigs then charged their guns likewise, and went in pursuit of the offenders; presently coming in sight of them they opened fire, but fortunately none were killed.

One who went by the name of "The Tory Van Vleet" lived back of Newtown, in the present town of Rochester. He was taken prisoner at Minisink, and forwarded without much ceremony by the various captains from one military post to another until he was brought up before Captain Kortright, of Rochester. That stern old patriot did not deem it best to let Van Vleet pass his hands without some ceremony suited to the times and the occasion. He ordered out a portion of his company with a fife and drum. Then stripping his prisoner, he caused a liberal allowance of tar and feathers to be applied to his person, and a long yoke with a bell was fastened to his neck by way of distinguished compliment. A negro then went ahead with a rope attached to the yoke, by which he was led along to the next station, which was at Mill Hook. The Rogue's March was struck up, and a few soldiers with charged bayonets followed to spur him up occasionally. Sometimes the negro would give the rope a jerk, when the bell would give a melodious tinkle, blending beautifully with the martial music.

There was another Tory by the name of Joe Westbrook, whose father lived in Minisink. On his way home from the war, Joe stopped at Andrew Bevier's, at Napanock, and made some enquiries, as though he were a stranger in those

The Tories After the Revolution.

parts. It has been well observed that hypocrisy is ever addicted to overacting its part, and Joe's conduct at that time was no exception to the truth of the proverbial remark. In short his attempted deception was the occasion of adverse comment, and aroused the sentiment still more against him. A few warm-hearted patriots in and about Napanock embarked in a wagon and drove down the Mamakating valley in time to reach Minisink early in the evening. They looked in at the window, and saw the old man and his son Joe sitting and talking at the fire. Joe was boasting of his exploits against the Whigs in the late war—at least so thought the Napanock patriots. They surrounded the house, while Jacobus Chambers, a brave and hardy veteran, was chosen to enter.

The moment the tap at the door was heard, Joe ran into an adjoining room. In response to a question from Chambers the old man solemnly declared "he

A TORY TARRED AND FEATHERED, YOKED AND PELLED.

had not seen his son Joe since the war." Chambers replied, "Give me a candle and I will show you your son." "But I have no candle," persisted the old man. Chambers retorted. "I don't want your candle;" and producing a tallow dip from his pocket he proceeded to light it, and then moved towards the door where Joe had secreted himself.

"*Loop, jongen, loop!*" (run, boy, run) sang out the old Tory, at the top of his voice. The boy started for the window, but two or three stalwart men were guarding it, and the poor fellow cried out, "Yes, dad, but it's full here too." Joe was taken in the wagon back to Napanock, where a council of war was convened to deliberate on his case. Some were for hanging him outright as no more than a just recompense for his past misdeeds, while a few counseled a less rigorous punishment. It is said, while the deliberations were progressing, that Joe trembled and shook as did Belshazzar at the hand-writing on the wall of his palace, and could not conceal his pleasure when he saw the tar-bucket and feathers brought in, and judged by the preparations that it had been determined not to hang him. He was accordingly tarred and feathered, yoked and belled, in lieu of the paint which he had formerly used. From the yoke a rope was passed to a man on horseback, by which he was led out of town. On being released, he hired a negro in Rochester to clean him for fifty cents, and then returned to his home in Minisink.

TOM QUICK, THE INDIAN SLAYER.

THOMAS QUICK emigrated from Ulster county about the year 1733, and was the descendant of respectable and affluent ancestors, who came over from Holland previous to 1689. He located some valuable lands at Milford, Pennsylvania, where he built a log cabin, and settled down with none but Indians for neighbors. He depended largely on hunting and fishing for his subsistence, and in this respect his habits differed little from those of the wild Indians about him.

It was not long before other settlers were attracted into that locality. Among the few white maidens that had ventured so far into the wilderness was a comely lass whom Thomas Quick prevailed on to share his fortunes in life's thorny pathway. Though the bride's *trousseau* may not have come from Paris, though guests in silks and rich brocades may not have graced the occasion, we question whether loving hearts did not beat as fondly as though surrounded by the demands and restraints of fashionable life; and whether the plain and homely fare of corn-bread and venison was not as thoroughly relished as the most elaborate wedding-feast of modern days. Here, in due time, several children were born to them, among the number Thomas Quick, the subject of this chapter. The Quicks had wisely chosen the location of their home. The family prospered, became the owners of mills, and the possessors of much valuable real estate.

Notwithstanding that the wealth and social position of the Quicks would assure Tom a welcome to the best society of those border settlements, his tastes led him in another direction—a wild life in the forest and the companionship of the savages by whom he was surrounded proving much more to his liking.

At this time the various tribes of natives held undisputed sway along the banks of the Delaware and its tributaries, except the settlement at Peenpack, on the Neversink; and they frequented the house of Quick, who had early won their confidence, and who, from the first, had treated them with generous hospitality. They took quite a fancy to young "Tom," and "made him presents of plumes of feathers and other articles." He frequently participated with the young Indians in their sports, became their companion in their hunting expeditions, and learned to speak the Delaware tongue with as much fluency as the Indians themselves. So much did he incline to a hunter's life that he could rarely be induced to follow any other vocation. His associations developed in him all those characteristics of the natives which inclined them to a life of wild abandonment, and he grew to be totally unlike his brothers and sisters; while he ranged the woods, they attended a Dutch school that had been established to meet the demands of the neighborhood. During this period, however, he was familiarizing himself with the country at the headwaters of the Delaware and its tributaries; most of these streams he had traced to their sources, and thus acquired a knowledge that proved of essential service to him in after years.

As has been before stated, the Indians were on very intimate terms with the Quicks, "many of them almost living in the family." But these friendly relations were not of an enduring character. While the Quicks studiously avoided giving any offense to their savage neighbors, and invariably treated them with open-hearted hospitality, there were other influences at work which induced the Indians to forget the kind offices of their benefactors; and while the latter felt their past favors merited some consideration, the natives were plotting for the total extinction of the white settlement.

The Indians had become alarmed at the increasing demands and encroachments of the whites. The Delaware country was the favorite haunt of the red man; the bones of their fathers were interred in its most pleasant places, and within the sound of its waters the clans had gathered, from time immemorial, to celebrate their annual festivities. Now the prospect was that the pale-faced, land-loving race would soon occupy the whole country unless some decisive step was taken; that their hunting-grounds would be spoiled, and the graves of their forefathers desecrated by the white man's plow.

Though the Quicks had been uniformly kind to them, the fact could not be denied that this family was the first to locate on the Indian lands at Milford, and that it was through their influence that other settlers were induced to come. Some of the latter were not over-scrupulous in their dealings with the Indians, and the Quicks were in a measure held responsible for their acts. It has been hinted that the cupidity of the savages was another predisposing cause of their subsequent atrocities, being excited by the great possessions of the Quicks, which would fall into their hands in case of open hostilities. Frequent and open threats were made to expel the whites out of the territory.

This was at the time of the breaking out of the French and Indian war; and under such circumstances it was an easy matter for the emissaries of France to rouse the Indians against the adherents of Great Britain, and endeavor to drive them back to their old bounds. Each party feared and distrusted the other. A few whites having been killed or captured at exposed points, it was resolved to increase the defenses of the settlement by erecting block-houses, and procuring additional arms and ammunition. The settlers sought to avoid provoking open hostilities, and hoped the fears of a general uprising of the Indians were groundless.

Owing to the changed attitude of the Indians, Tom Quick had withdrawn from association with them, and had become quite domesticated in the family of his father; and while thus situated an event occurred which crystalized Tom's life, and changed his whole being into one of implacable hatred of the Indian race.

The savages had plotted the destruction of Milford, and were then secreted in the neighborhood waiting the approach of night, under cover of which to put their plan into execution. Unsuspicious of such a critical state of affairs, Tom, together with his father and brother, went into the woods across the river for the purpose of cutting hoop-poles. The river was frozen, so they passed over on the ice, and were soon busily engaged in selecting and securing the poles. As they proceeded around a ridge near the river, they were discovered by an out-post of the ambushed Indians. The latter determined to attack the Quicks, even at the risk of alarming the settlement, and thus defeating the main object of the expedition.

When Tom and his companions had approached sufficiently near, they were fired upon, and the father fell mortally wounded. The Quicks were unarmed: their only course was to fly. Neither of the sons were hurt, and, taking hold of their father, they endeavored to drag him after them as they ran. Being too closely pressed by the pursuing savages, the dying man prevailed on them to leave him to his fate, while they ran for their lives.

The only avenue of escape involved the hazardous experiment of crossing the Delaware river on the ice, within full view of the Indians, and at close rifle range. The dash was made; but before they had reached half way, the savages appeared upon the bank behind them. There was no protection against the murderous rifles of the yelling demons, any of whom could hit a deer nine times in ten while it was bounding through the forest; but by running in zigzag course, and by keeping as far apart as possible, the fire of the Indians was less effective. Presently a ball hit Tom, and he fell; at which the savages set up a loud shout. But the next moment he was up again, and running as rapidly as ever. The ball, as was afterward ascertained, only hit the heel of his boot, but with such force as to knock his foot from under him. Again the balls whistled past the fugitives; but, coming to the river bank, they were soon out of danger. The brothers were both fleet runners, and trained in backwoods life. Another circumstance contributing to their escape was, that on leaving their father, they had sought the cover of an overhanging rock, and by striking an oblique direction were well across the river before the savages could get a shot at them.

Finding they were not pursued, Tom and his brother crept back to the river bank to see what was going on. They heard the scalping-whoop, and witnessed the rejoicings of the Indians over the remains of their father. It was at this juncture that Tom, rendered frantic by their fiendish conduct, made a solemn vow that he would never cease from a war of extermination as long as an Indian remained on the banks of the Delaware. This oath of vengeance Tom fulfilled to the letter. It is known that he slew at least twenty of the hated race, while some writers have placed the number of his victims at a hundred.

With Tom the killing of Indians became a kind of religious duty, in which he undertook to redress the great wrong of his father's murder. He pursued his bloody work with all the fervor of a fanatic. In after years he would relate his exploits, and give the harrowing details with no more show of feeling than if they related to the most trivial affairs; and without any apparent misgiving that his work involved a grave moral question.

According to his own statement, Tom destroyed an indefinite number of the hated race while hunting. On hearing the report of a gun in the woods, he would creep cautiously to the point whence the sound proceeded, and was generally rewarded by finding an Indian skinning a bear or a deer. It was then an easy matter to send a bullet on its fatal errand; and when in after years a hunter came upon the bones of an Indian and a deer bleaching together in the woods, he would ejaculate "Another victim of Tom Quick's vengeance."

The sight of an Indian seemed to suggest but one thought to Tom, and that was how the savage could be dispatched with the greatest facility. He was many times involved in serious personal danger in the execution of his vow, and seems to have had little regard for his own safety whenever an opportunity was offered him of killing an Indian.

At last old age came upon Tom Quick, the Indian slayer, and his increasing infirmities compelled him to relinquish his former habits. At this time he lived with James Rosecrans, about three miles below Carpenter's point. Here he was kindly treated, and furnished with every comfort he could desire. He was regarded by those who knew his history with a kind of deferential awe; and was spoken of with as much enthusiasm by his admirers as was ever accorded to any hero of modern times.

He is described as being six feet in height; gaunt and angular; with high cheek bones; bright and restless gray eyes; and his hair, before it was silvered with age, was of a dark brown. He was quiet in his demeanor; his features were grave and dignified, seldom relaxing into a smile. So long as he was able, he visited each summer the scenes of his adventures. At such times he stopped temporarily at the house of a friend at Mongaup island, or in a hut near Hagan pond.

Tom carried his favorite rifle on his shoulder until the stock was worn through. Outlawed and alone he waged war against a race that had incurred his hatred, until the Indians were driven from the territory, leaving him in possession of their hunting-grounds. Tom died at the house of Rosecrans about the year 1795, regretting to the last that he had not shot more Indians.

If tradition is to be believed, it is true of Tom Quick, as was said of Samson of old, that "he slew more of his enemies at his death than he destroyed during his whole life." By a strange fatality, Tom was brought down by that dreadful malady—small-pox. The Indians, having learned the place of his sepulchre, dug up the body of their deceased enemy, and distributed the portions among the clans throughout the vicinity. Great pow-wows were held, every man, woman and child of the several clans were assembled, and the sections of Tom Quick's body were burned with great ceremony. No more effective plan could have been devised to spread the disease, and its ravages were not checked until the tribe had been nearly exterminated.

If the death of any man was ever avenged, the death of Tom Quick's father certainly was.

TOM QUICK AND THE INDIAN MUSKWINK.

NOT long after the close of the French and Indian war, an Indian by the name of Muskwink returned to Peenpack, in the lower valley of the Neversink. He was an idle, drunken vagabond, and spent much of his time at Decker's tavern. One day Tom happened at the tavern while Muskwink was there. As was usually the case, the savage was intoxicated; but he claimed Tom's acquaintance, and asked him to drink. The latter replied with some vehemence, which brought on a war of words. The savage, with no apparent design other than to irritate Tom, began to boast of his exploits in the late war, and of his participation in the killing of Tom Quick's father. He declared that he tore the scalp from his head with his own hand; and then proceeded to give a detailed account of the whole affair, dwelling at length upon the old man's dying moments, interspersing the narration with unfeeling and irreverent remarks. As if that was not enough to arouse the demon in Tom's heart, the Indian mimicked his father's dying struggles, and even exhibited the sleeve-buttons worn by him at the time he was killed.

Tom was unarmed. Suspended on some hooks over the fire-place, in accordance with the custom of border settlements, was a rifle. Tom walked deliberately across the room, removed the rifle from the hooks, saw that it was loaded and primed, and then cocked it. Before those present divined his purpose, or the savage could retreat or resist, Tom pointed the muzzle directly at his breast, and ordered him to leave the house. The Indian sullenly complied, and resigned himself to the guidance of Tom, who drove him into the main road leading from Kingston to Minisink. After proceeding about a mile in the direction of Carpenter's point, Tom exclaimed, " You Indian dog, you'll kill no more white men;" and pulling the trigger, shot the Indian in the back. Muskwink jumped two or three feet from the ground and fell dead. Tom then took possession of the sleeve-buttons that had belonged to his father, dragged the body near to the upturned roots of a tree, and kicking some loose dirt and leaves over it, left it there. He then returned to the tavern, replaced the gun on the hooks, and left the neighborhood. Several years afterward the Indian's bones were exhumed by Philip Decker while plowing this land, who gave them a Christian burial. It does not appear that any attempt was made to arrest Tom for the murder of Muskwink; if any such were instituted he eluded them. The frontiersmen generally applauded his action, believing the aggravating circumstances under which he acted were a full and sufficient justification.

Not long after this tragedy occurred, Tom was hunting in the vicinity of Butler's rift. As he was watching at the foot of the rift, either for wild beasts or Indians, he was rewarded by the sight of some savages, coming up the river in a canoe. The party consisted of an Indian and squaw, and three children— the youngest an infant at the breast. They were quietly passing up the stream, unaware of the presence of Tom, who lay concealed in the tall reed-grass growing upon the shore. As they approached, Tom recognized the Indian as one of those who had visited his father's house before the war, and had been engaged in several outrages on the frontier.

When they had arrived within gun-shot, Tom rose from his recumbent posture, and ordered them to come ashore. The Indian had heard of the killing of Muskwink; and when he recognized Tom, he "turned very pale," but he dare not disobey, and approached the place where Tom stood. The latter then made some inquiries, asking them whence they came and where they were going, to all of which they made respectful answer. Tom next coolly informed the savage that he had reached his journey's end; that his tribe had murdered his father and several of his relatives during the war, and that he had sworn vengeance against his whole race. The Indian replied that it was "peace time;" that the hatchet was buried, and that therefore they were now brothers. Tom replied there could be no peace between the redskins and him; that he had sworn to kill every one that came within his power. He then shot the Indian, who jumped from the canoe into the river, where, after a few convulsive throes, he died. Then wading out to the canoe he brained the squaw with a tomahawk:—the mother, true to her instinct, essayed to fly to her youngest child after the murderous instrument had cloven through her skull. Next the two oldest children shared the fate of their mother. Tom said he had some difficulty in dispatching them, as they dodged about so, and "squawked like young crows." When he came to the babe, and it looked up into his face and smiled, his heart failed him for a moment; but remembering if he let it live it would grow and become an Indian, he did not spare even the babe. In his old age when asked why he killed the children, his invariable reply was, "Nits make lice."

Tom's next duty was to secrete the bodies of his victims. If the affair became known, he would incur the enmity of his own people, as they would stand in fear of some retaliatory measure from the Indians with whom they were then at peace. He brought a number of stones; then with some ropes of basswood bark he tied a stone to each of the bodies, and conveyed them one after the other to the deep water of the rift, where he sank them to the bottom. When all the bodies were thus disposed of, Tom destroyed the canoe, and no evidence of the crime remained. As soon as it was safe to do so, he related the foregoing facts to his nephew Jacob Quick, of Callicoon, from whom the historian Quinlan received them. It is said that Tom would relate the circumstances of the affair in an exultant manner, as though he thought himself entitled to credit. The incident illustrates the extremes of cruelty and barbarity

TOM QUICK KILLING A FAMILY OF FIVE INDIANS.

to which a person may be led by a constant brooding over wrongs, real or imaginary, and by the still more reprehensible habit of harboring thoughts of revenge.

TOM QUICK AND THE BUCK WITH SEVEN SKINS.

DURING the months of summer, Tom Quick followed his favorite avocations, which alternated between the business of hunting and that of killing Indians. Sometimes in company with a boon companion, but more frequently alone and unattended, he ranged the forests about the head-waters of the Delaware, now pursuing the bounding deer, and again following with stealthy and cat-like tread the trail of the Indian hunter, whom he sent without warning to the Indian's paradise His winters were usually spent at the house of some congenial spirit in the vicinity of his hunting-grounds. He always paid well for his entertainment, for he kept the family, with whom he was quartered, fully supplied with venison and bear meat. While hunting late one autumn on a distant fork of the Delaware, he awoke one morning to find the forest buried in deep snow, and the rigors of winter at hand in all their severity. It was with difficulty that he made his way to the house where he purposed to spend the winter. So sudden and severe had the season set in that Tom had not secured a supply of winter venison. He knew a place out some distance from his friend's residence where he could find abundance of game, and only waited a favorable change in the weather to go and secure it.

About this time an Indian came into the neighborhood, and Tom was not long in making his acquaintance. Together they talked of the chase, and related their hunting exploits around the fireplace of the settler, protracting their story-telling long into the night. Tom at length set out upon his hunting expedition, accompanied by the Indian. They had agreed to hunt in company, Tom proposing to take the venison for his share, and the Indian the skins. They arrived at the destined locality at the close of a day's march, when they bivouacked for the night in the snow. The next day they had unusual good luck for they killed seven deer. The Indian had as many skins as he could carry, consequently he did not want to hunt any more at that time; so he got them together, placed them upon his back, and started through the snow for his cabin. It was destined he should never reach it, however, for as he started off, a ball from Tom Quick's rifle penetrated the seven skins, and entering the back of the Indian killed him instantly. When Tom reached the settlement with all the skins and the venison, his friends, who knew the arrangement that had been made in regard to the division of the spoils, asked him how he came by all the pelts. Tom replied that after he and the Indian had got through hunting, "he had shot a fat buck in the woods with seven skins on his back."

TOM CAPTURES SIX INDIANS.

The Indians suspected that Tom was concerned in the mysterious disappearance of so many of their hunters, and frequent attempts were made to kill him. Notwithstanding they had numerous opportunities, they missed their mark so often that they were inclined to believe he had a charmed life, and could not be hit by an Indian bullet. One day Tom was splitting rails for a man named Westbrook, on land now included in the village of Westbrookville, in the Mamakating valley. As he was driving in a wedge, he was suddenly surprised and surrounded by six dusky warriors. Tom caught up his gun, which was always within his reach, and prepared for a fight even at such odds. The Indians did not want to kill him, preferring to take him alive if they could do so. A parley ensued, in which Tom told the savages that he would go with them provided they would first help him split his log. They were so pleased at getting him without a fight that they threw down their guns and came forward to where Tom was at work. According to his directions they ranged themselves, three on a side, and thrusting their hands into the split, pulled while Tom drove the wedge. Instead of driving the wedge in, Tom directed a peculiar blow which caused the wedge to fly out, and the six Indians were held by their fingers in the cleft as with a vise. He then brained them at his leisure.*

At the close of one cold winter day an Indian came to the house where Tom Quick was stopping, complained of fatigue, and requested permission to stay all night. He professed to be very friendly, but Tom suspected he was an enemy in disguise. During the evening he casually mentioned that he had seen a number of deer during the afternoon, and asked Tom if he would not like to go with him next day and get them. Tom readily assented to the proposition, and they agreed to start at an early hour next morning. During the night Tom managed to get hold of the Indian's rifle. He drew out the charge, substituted ashes in place of the powder, replaced the ball, and restored the gun to the position in which he found it. The next morning Tom detected the Indian covertly examining the chamber of his rifle and the priming, with which he seemed satisfied. This and other circumstances confirmed Tom in the belief that the savage contemplated mischief.

There was a deep snow on the ground, and the hunters found difficulty in making their way through it. The Indian, apparently in good faith, proposed that one should go ahead and break the path. To this Tom readily assented; and furthermore offered to be the first to go in advance, at which the Indian seemed greatly pleased. In this way they had proceeded a mile or more, and had arrived at a lonely spot, when Tom heard the Indian's gun snap, and the powder whiz in the pan. He turned round and asked the Indian what he had seen. "A fine buck," was the reply. The Indian reprimed his gun and they went on. Pretty soon Tom heard another snap and another fizz "Well, brother Indian," he inquired, " what did you see this time?" "I saw an eagle sweep over the forest," replied the other as he again primed his gun. "Brother Indian," said Tom, "the snow is deep, and I am tired. You go ahead." "The Yankee speaks well," said the savage, and he sullenly took his station in advance. Tom leveled his rifle. "Lying Indian dog," exclaimed he, "what do you see now?" "I see the spirit land," said the savage gloomily; and bowing his head and drawing his blanket over his face, calmly awaited his inevitable fate.

TOM QUICK'S INDIAN EXPLOITS.

TOM was one day wandering through the woods without his rifle, which was very unusual for him, when he encountered a young Indian who was armed. Tom spoke to him in a friendly manner, and they were soon on good terms. "Brother Indian," said Tom, "would you like to see

---

* A lady residing at Westbrookville pointed out to the writer the precise spot where this is said to have taken place. The historian Quinlan, from whose writings the above facts are taken, was informed that an early settler had seen Indian bones at the spot, and believed the story to be true.

Tom Quick?" The young savage intimated that he felt a strong desire to do so, and Tom agreed to show him the Indian slayer. After a long walk which terminated at the brink of a high ledge, Tom told his companion to wait a few moments and he would show him the person he desired to see. Tom went to the edge of the precipice and peered over to the highway below. Here he watched intently for a few minutes, and then suggested to the Indian to take his place. The Indian cocked his rifle and hastily advanced to Tom's side. "Where is he?" eagerly demanded the red man. "There," said Tom, pointing so that the Indian would project his head and shoulders over the brink in his desire to shoot the enemy of his race. "Further, a little further," whispered Tom. The Indian hung as far over the precipice as he could without losing his equilibrium. Tom quickly slipped around, and grasping the shoulders of the savage from behind, shouted —"Shoot *me!* shoot *me*, would you!" and with those words he hurled the Indian over the precipice, where he was dashed to pieces among the rocks.

Two Indians once surprised Tom in his sleep. They bound him securely, and after plundering the cabin in which they found him, set out for their own country by way of the Delaware. One savage, with Tom's chattels upon his shoulders, walked in advance; Tom came next, with his arms securely tied behind him; and the remaining savage, with his rifle and that of his companion, brought up the rear. One of these rifles was kept cocked in readiness to shoot Tom if he attempted to escape. Their route led them over a high ledge of rocks, where they were obliged to take a very dangerous path far up on the cliff. At times the path was very narrow, and at one point lay directly on the brow of the precipice. When they reached the narrowest and most dangerous part of the path, Tom feigned to be very dizzy, and refused to proceed further, although the blows of the Indian fell thick and fast upon his shoulders. He leaned against the bank on the upper side, and shuddered when he cast his eyes toward the river. The savage next attempted to push him along, when by an adroit movement Tom got between him and the precipice, and the next instant with a loud "ugh-whoop," the savage was making an air-line descent towards the river. He fell fifty feet or more and lodged in the fork of a sycamore, where he hung helpless, and roaring lustily for his brother savage to come and help him out. The rifles fell into the river. Tom relied on his heels for safety, and ran pinioned as he was with astonishing celerity for home, which he reached without further incident.

Tom was in the habit of concealing in the woods the guns he had taken from the murdered Indians; and this circumstance on one occasion was the means of saving his life. Two Indians had captured him, and were taking him off by the Grassy Brook route. His arms were pinioned with deer-skin thongs. It commenced to rain, and Tom was gratified to find that the moisture caused the thongs to stretch, and ultimately they became so loose that he could, when he chose, free his hands. He was very careful to conceal this fact from the savages. Near the path they were pursuing was a very large chestnut tree;

and in the side of this tree furthest from the path was a large hollow space. In this trunk Tom had shortly before concealed several guns, a flask of powder, and some bullets. When they reached this tree Tom expressed a great desire to go to it, and gave such a good reason therefor that he was allowed to go. The Indians both stood by with guns ready aimed, to guard against any attempt on his part at escape. Once behind the tree which concealed his movements, he loaded two of the guns with inconceivable rapidity, and fired upon one of the savages, who fell dead. His companion attempted to get behind the nearest tree, but he never reached it.

Tom was too quick for him and he shared the fate of his comrade.

Tom Quick was often the guest of John Showers, in the town of Lumberland. On one occasion Quick and three or four other white hunters had sought the shelter of Showers's bark roof, when a savage entered and asked to stay all night. He was told he might lodge there. After spending the evening pleasantly, chatting around the ample fireplace, the party wrapped themselves in their blankets and lay down upon the floor. All were soon asleep except Tom Quick, who remained awake for a sinister purpose. When the deep breathing of his companions announced that they were unconscious, Tom got up and cautiously secured his gun. In a few minutes the hunters were aroused by an explosion, and found the savage dead in their midst. After the fatal shot was given, Tom immediately left for the woods. As the Indians were then the almost exclusive occupants of that part of the country, and would avenge their brother if they knew the whites were responsible for his death, his murder was concealed for many years.

INDIAN STRATAGEM TO SLAY TOM QUICK.

THE owner of the cabin at which Tom was staying kept a hog. An Indian had formed a plan to make this hog an instrument to effect Tom's destruction. One night, when no one but Tom was in the cabin, this Indian got into the pen, and by holding the hog between his knees caused it to squeal as lustily as though in the claws of a wild animal. This he supposed would lead Tom to conclude a bear had made a raid on the hog-pen, and that he would come to the rescue. But the wily hunter was not thrown off his guard by this ruse. He cautiously peered through a crevice of the cabin; the pig continued to keep up a great outcry, while Tom could see nothing that would indicate the assailant was not an animal. Presently he was rewarded with the sight of an Indian's head above the top log of the pen. The hog proved to be of the perverse sort, which the Indian had hard work to manage and at the same time keep a lookout for Tom's appearance. The hunter, on discovering the nature of the aggressor, prepared to greet the Indian's head should it appear again. The opportune moment arrived; the ball was sent on its errand; the porker was speedily released, and with a wild yell of pain, the savage broke for the woods. But he had received a fatal wound, and Tom soon overtook him, and put a speedy end to his life.

Once, when Tom was in a field at work, he was accosted by an unarmed Indian, who said he had discovered something "just over there" that he very much wished him to go and see. Tom left his work, but did not fail to notice the look of satisfaction on the Indian's countenance, as he started to accompany him. This plainly indicated the design of the Indian and put Tom on his guard. The scheming native had hid his gun in the woods, and hoped to entice Tom into the vicinity unarmed, when he could be dispatched. Tom had gone but a short distance when he discovered a hemlock knot, which he thought would be a very good weapon in a rough-and-tumble fight. He stooped to pick it up; but the savage perceiving his intention, sprang upon him; and although he got hold of it he could not use it. A severe and protracted struggle ensued for the possession of the weapon, with varying advantage; and blows were given and received with the grim determination of men who fight to the death. Tom finally came off victor; but he was often heard to declare that this was the most severe fight in which he was ever engaged. When the affray was over, and the Indian lay dead on the field, Tom was so exhausted that it was with difficulty he made his way to the house at which he was temporarily stopping.

Another native Indian attempted Tom's life while he was at work in the saw-mill. Tom, always on the alert, had been made aware of the presence and intention of his enemy, and so arranged his hat and coat as to deceive him. The Indian sent a ball between the shoulders of the coat supposing Tom was inside of it, at which the latter stepped out from his place of hiding and shot the helpless and trembling savage through the heart.

Tom was once ranging the woods on the lookout for Indians, and came upon one unexpectedly. Both parties sought shelter behind trees within gunshot, where they remained a long time, each endeavoring to get a shot at the other without exposing himself. Various stratagems were resorted to with the hope of drawing the other's fire, but each found they had a wary foe to deal with. Tom at length thrust his cap cautiously from behind the tree, when the report of the Indian's rifle was heard, and Tom fell to the ground as though grievously wounded. The Indian dashed forward to rescue the hunter's scalp, when Tom sprang up and aimed at his breast. As the Indian saw the muzzle of the gun within a few feet of him, he exclaimed in dismay, "Ugh—me cheated!" and fell dead at Tom's feet with a ball in his heart.

THE SAVAGES PLAN TOM QUICK'S CAPTURE.

AT last, exasperated beyond measure at the death of so many of their braves, three Indians banded together and pledged themselves they would not return until Tom's death or capture was effected. They lay in ambush all one season at one of Tom's favorite hunting-grounds; but their intended victim not making his appearance, the approach of cold weather compelled them to seek winter-quarters. With the coming of the next season of flowers they resumed their station and watching. A white man was one day observed coming up the river in a canoe. The Indians presently made out it was not the one for whom they were watching, but a Tory for whom they entertained a friendship. This Tory was, however, an intense hater of Tom, and had more than once threatened to kill him. From him the warriors learned that Tom was at Handsome Eddy, to which point they resolved to go, and be governed by circumstances.

There they learned that Tom was living with one of his friends, and that he was in the habit of going into the woods every night after a cow, and that a bell was on the cow. The next day the three Indians went to the place where the cow was pastured, and secreted themselves. Towards evening they took the bell from the cow and drove the animal back into the woods. They then took their station near Tom's residence where they could observe what was going on without being themselves seen, and commenced ringing the bell.

Just before sundown Tom started for the cow, rifle in hand as usual. As soon as he heard the bell it occurred to him that its ring was unusual. This admonished him to caution; and instead of proceeding directly toward the sound, he took a wide circuit, during which he encountered the cow. He now carefully crept forward and came up in the rear of the Indians, whose attention was absorbed in the direction of the house, where they momentarily expected Tom to show himself. As Tom approached from behind he saw that one of the Indians had the bell, while the other two held their arms in readiness for the conflict. He determined to attack all three. He passed cautiously from tree to tree, so as to bring them within range, with a view to kill two at the first shot. Before he got into position he unfortunately stepped on a dry twig, which snapped under his foot. Instantly the bell stopped ringing, and the Indians turned toward him with their rifles cocked; but he had dodged behind a large hemlock which screened him from view. They saw nothing but the cow which was quietly grazing and walking towards them. Supposing her to have been the cause of their alarm, they again commenced ringing and watching. Tom then left the shelter of the friendly hemlock and reached his objective point. He took deliberate aim, and the two armed savages were killed or disabled, and the bell-ringer wounded, but not sufficiently to prevent his escape. But in his hurry he forgot to take his rifle.

The Indians were more exasperated than ever when they learned the fate of the two braves. They organized a band of fifteen or twenty others, and determined to spare no efforts to capture or slay Tom. Having found his retreat, and a storm of rain accompanied by a dense fog favoring their purpose, the Indians were enabled to surround the cabin of which he was the solitary occupant, before he was aware of their presence.

When they had finally secured him, the joy of the redskins was unbounded. As night was approaching and rain falling in torrents, the party determined to spend the night in Tom's cabin. Tom's skins and other goods were prepared for transportation, but his favorite rifle, standing in a dark corner of the garret, escaped their notice. Among the things which pleased them best was a keg of brandy, a liquid that Tom seldom used, but of which he generally had a supply in his possession. They drank of it freely, and its effect soon became visible; the crowd grew uproarious, and menacing looks and gestures began to be directed by three or four of the party towards their unfortunate prisoner.

It had been the leading object among the Indians to take him alive, so that the whole tribe might participate in torturing him. It was to be feared that some of the more ill-natured savages, under the inspiration of the fire-water, would anticipate the action of the tribe and kill him on the spot. To put Tom out of reach of danger, and at the same time relieve all from the restraint of standing guard over him, it was proposed to bind him with additional thongs to a rafter in the garret—a proposition that was heartily approved by all.

From his position Tom could hear what was transpiring in the room below. He overheard an animated discussion, as to whether it was best to take his scalp at once, or reserve him for the torture. Tom remained in an agony of suspense, revolving in his mind, the while, the probability of making his escape. But so desperate was his situation that hope died within him. He even meditated suicide that he might deprive his captors of the pleasure they anticipated in his torture, but he was too securely tied to admit of even this alternative. About midnight the savages relapsed into a state of quiet. So far as Tom could judge, they were either asleep or too drunk to do him any harm. Ere long he heard the sound of steps, and some one seemed to be ascending the ladder. A moment afterward the head of a savage appeared above the floor. In one hand he held a brand of fire, and in the other a formidable knife. He approached with unsteady feet, and stood before his intended victim, with features distorted from the effects of his potations, and with eyes gleaming and snakish. With knife uplifted, and his body swaying to and fro, he regarded Tom an instant and prepared to strike. The moment was a trying one to Tom, thus helplessly bound; but instinctively he fell flat upon his face, and the knife passed harmlessly over him. The drunken savage, having missed his mark, and unable to preserve his balance, fell headlong, striking his head so heavily against the log wall of the garret, that he lay in a stupid and senseless heap upon the floor.

Having waited long enough to ascertain the noise did not awaken those below, Tom essayed to get possession of the Indian's knife; but the thong which was tied to his neck was too short to enable him to reach it. In the effort to resume his erect position his foot came in contact with the object he sought. Having secured it, and taking the handle between his teeth he soon freed his ankles, and cut the thong that bound him to the rafter. He next thrust the knife in a crevice so that the blade projected firmly from the log; then, by turning on his back, his hands being tied behind him, he managed to cut the remaining fastenings. Once free, he got possession of his rifle, and having removed some of the bark which composed the roof, leaped to the ground and reached Minisink entirely destitute.

EARLY SETTLERS OF THE SHAWANGUNK REGION.

ON the shore of Pleasant lake, in the town of Thompson, Nehemiah Smith bought a tract of land at the beginning of the present century, built a log house, and constructed barracks in which to store hay and grain. After putting in some winter cereals, Smith returned to Southeast, Putnam county, where his family resided. The following February, he started for his new home in the wilds of Sullivan, accompanied by four of his neighbors and their families. His own household consisted of his wife, two children, and a nephew, a lad of thirteen years.

Crossing the river at Newburgh, they there hired teams to take them to the end of their journey. The Newburgh and Cochecton turnpike was then good as far as Montgomery; beyond that point the roads had no existence except in name. After leaving Montgomery, they traveled the first day as far as the Barrens, where the accommodations were meagre for so large a party—one room and an attic. The next night they reached Thompson's Mills, where was a backwoods tavern. Here the facilities for entertaining travelers were much better. Beyond this point the road was only a line of blazed trees.

The snow was deep, and the path unbroken; had the ground been bare they could not have driven their team over the route on account of its roughness. Up and down ravines, across streams, and under the sombre foliage of hemlocks so dark at times that the sky could not be seen, the party plodded; and they were obliged to look sharp about them to keep the marked trees in view.

Slowly the jaded horses labored through the snow, sometimes sinking almost to their backs, now plunging over the side of a cradle hole, or stumbling over the trunk of a fallen tree. When the sleigh threatened to upset, then there was a panic among the women and children; but it was quickly remedied when the strong arms of the men came to the rescue. They were obliged to leave one sleigh load in the woods, where the goods remained until the men returned and carried them on their backs to their destination. At this time there was no house in Monticello, nor even a line of marked trees to that point.

The dwellings of these settlers were very primitive structures, built of logs with bark roofs. The floors—as soon as they could afford that luxury—were made by splitting logs in half, and laying the flat side uppermost. The fireplaces were commodious affairs, without jambs, into which a back-log ten feet in length could be rolled. For windows they at first used paper, previously rubbed with hog's lard—a kind of glazing that shed a most beautiful light when the sun shone on it. The chimneys were made of stones plastered with mud; the same primitive cement was used in stopping up the chinks between the logs. When the room was lighted up of an evening by the glowing fire extending nearly across one side of the house, there was an air of comfort within the interior of that log-cabin that is not to be found in the most sumptuous apartment. And when to the music of the winds in the tall pines that grew by the door, there are added the lonely howl of the wolf and the scream of the panther, while within all was safe and snug, with the children sweetly sleeping in their cots—the picture is complete.

There was no cellar under the floor. Potatoes and other vegetables were stored in holes or dirt cellars close by the house. A mound of earth was heaped over these depositories, and it seems these mounds were a favorite resort for wolves. Fifty years afterwards the wife of Nehemiah Smith used to tell of having seen them there at night, when the moon made them visible. These animals were a source of great terror to the women and children, and their howlings were generally continued long into the night.

Sheep were a necessity, as their wool was the chief reliance of the settlers for winter clothing; but it was impossible to keep them unless they were put into a safe enclosure every night. A single wolf would destroy a whole flock in a few minutes, its instinct leading it to rush from one victim to another, giving each a snap in the throat, which was always fatal.

The bedsteads were made in the most primitive way, with but a single post —let all who believe that four posts are essential take notice—holes bored into the logs of the apartment serving the purpose of the missing legs. A bit of clapboard, riven from the red oak, supported on wooden pins driven into the wall, contained the pewter dishes and spoons. The spinning wheel was an essential adjunct to the family outfit, while a few chairs, some pots and kettles, and an eight-by-ten looking-glass completed the furniture.

A majority of the inhabitants of this period were of upright characters, bold, energetic, and generous-hearted. Although subject to privations, their lot in life, as a whole, was not an unhappy one. Said one of them; "When I look back upon the first few years of our residence in the wilderness, I am led to exclaim, Oh, happy days of primitive simplicity! What little aristocratic feeling one brought with him was soon quelled, for we soon found ourselves equally dependent on one another; and we enjoyed our winter evenings around our blazing hearths in our log huts cracking nuts much better than has fallen to our lots since the distinctions and animosities consequent upon the accumulation of wealth have crept in among us." The following is said to have been an actual occurrence:

In one of the back-woods settlements a visit was arranged by some of the ladies, by way of paying their respects to a neighboring family who lived a little out of the way. The lady of the house was very much pleased to see them, and soon commenced preparing the usual treat on such state occasions—a cup of tea and accompaniments. As the good woman had but one fire-proof vessel in the house—an old broken bake-kettle—some time would be consumed in the preparation of the repast. In the first place, some pork was tried up in the kettle to get lard; secondly, some doughnuts were made and fried in it; thirdly, some short cakes were baked in it; fourthly, it was used as a bucket to draw water; fifthly, the water was boiled in it; and sixthly the tea was put into it, and an excellent beverage made. Thus with the old cracked bake-kettle a delicious meal was prepared, and a very agreeable " social tea " was the result

Bears were formerly quite plenty in Sullivan county—probably wintering on the lowlands which border on the lakes, and wandering into the hills in summer. One of Nehemiah Smith's neighbors was a man by the name of Bailey. Bruin was frequently seen passing through Bailey's premises. He seemed to have a special fondness for hog's flesh, and sometimes raided Bailey's pig-pen to satisfy his appetite. One night when Mr. Bailey was from home, Mrs. Bailey was putting the little ones to bed when she heard a terrible squealing out among the pigs. She understood what that meant—a bear had got into the pen. She well knew the danger incurred by going out, but she could not endure the thought of losing a fat pig. So bidding the children be quiet until she returned, she took some blazing fire-brands and rushed out to the sty, where a huge bear confronted her. The heroic woman shouted with all her might, and pelted the bear with her blazing brands, so that bruin was beaten off without getting his pig. Having the satisfaction of seeing the hungry intruder run off into the woods, she returned to the house and resumed her household duties.

Another neighbor of the Smith's, by the name of Warring, went out one night to shoot deer. While chopping a few days before in the vicinity of Dutch pond, he had noticed that deer-tracks were very plenty, and that two runways passed within rifle shot of a large rock. He promised himself some fine sport the first moonlight night. Such a night soon came; and, telling his family he might remain away all night, but that they could expect some venison steak for breakfast, he shouldered his rifle and started for the woods. In due time he took up his position on the rock. There was snow on the ground, and the bright moon overhead so lighted up the earth that he could see a passing object distinctly.

He watched the two runways very patiently, but saw no game, and heard no sound except the hooting of an owl in an adjacent grove of hemlocks. His vigil was becoming dull and tedious; the night was waning; he was about making preparations to go home, when pat, pat, came the sound of rapid steps, and he noticed a dark object coming up the path. Without waiting to discover what the animal was, he fired. The creature gave a howl of mingled pain and rage, rushed at the hunter furiously, and attempted to jump upon the rock where he stood. It would have reached him, and the snarling jaws would have closed upon him, only that he made a vigorous thrust with his rifle and pushed the animal back. Again and again it leaped at the man on the rock, and was as often beaten back. At last the animal, whatever it was, ran one way and the hunter the other. Warring reached home at an unexpected hour, but brought no venison. He visited the place the next morning with his boys, and ascertained by the blood and tracks around the rock that he had shot and

MRS. BAILEY AND THE BEAR.

wounded a very large wolf. Though wolves were very numerous at the time, it was rare that they were so pugnacious as this one showed himself to be.

Another settler in the vicinity of Pleasant lake was very much annoyed with wolves. They seemed to gather at a certain pond about a mile away, and every night would make the woods ring with their howling. One day this settler slaughtered a cow, and hung up the meat in the attic of his log cabin. That night the wolves gathered in numbers under his very eaves, and the father being absent, the mother with the children went up into the attic, drawing the ladder after them, being greatly terrified as they heard the hungry beasts leaping against the door, and snarling and snapping under the windows.

The first inhabitants of Sullivan had another source of annoyance—the bark roofs of their cabins could not always be depended upon. On one occasion, during the temporary absence of Nehemiah Smith from his home, there occurred a great storm of wind and rain. When the storm was at its height, the roof of their house was blown away, and the family were left at the mercy of the elements. Mrs. Smith put the children where they would be partially sheltered and was diligently sweeping out the water when the neighbors came to her relief.

One winter's night the family were gathered around the ample fire-place, in which glowed a section of a tree that would have put to shame the traditional yule-logs of our British ancestors. The night was tempestuous; snow had been falling all day, and lay piled up in the woods to the depth of several feet, but within all was snug and comfortable. The labors of the day were over; the children were at their games; the older members of the family were relating Revolutionary stories and incidents of frontier experience; in short, the storm outside was unheeded, except when an unusual blast swept along, rattling the windows and doors, and screeching dismally down the chimney. The hour was approaching that the family were to retire to rest, when sounds of disintegration were heard. The roof was giving way above them. Mr. Smith slowly and cautiously ascended the ladder by which they reached the loft—stairs were a luxury unknown at that time in Sullivan county—when there came a crash! One half of the roof had slid over the outer side of the house, leaving that part of the dwelling roofless; and the other half of the roof, together with two feet of snow that had accumulated on it, had fallen in upon the puncheons of the upper floor. Had the catastrophe occurred an hour later, the rafters and snow would have fallen upon the children, whose beds were in the attic. This was an unfortunate dilemma for a stormy night, with a family of little children, and the roads impassable. Yet the family lived through it; and in after years used frequently to relate the incident to crowds of eager listeners.

Jehiel Stewart was another pioneer settler of Sullivan county. He came originally from Middletown, Connecticut; he first settled in Ulster county, and after remaining about a year, he again emigrated, this time journeying over the Shawangunk mountain. He travelled down the Beaverkill, crossing and recrossing that stream twenty-five times before he reached the Big Flats, where he concluded to settle. He cut his way through the woods with an axe. His family and household goods he transported on ox-sleds, driving his stock before him as he progressed. He camped out each night, improvising some tents to protect them from the night air and from the rain.

One evening after he had located his encampment and made preparations for the night, he found that his cows were missing. Mounting a rock near by, he saw some animals at a distance quietly feeding in a small opening, which he supposed to be the missing cows. He called to his children to go after them; but as the children approached the opening, the animals winded them and ran off, making a peculiar rattling noise with their hoofs as they ran. They proved to be a drove of elk.

It was during this journey that his little daughter got lost in the woods.

Night came, and she did not return. The father and mother hunted for her all night, and their fears were great when they heard the wolves howling in the woods, and also the noises made by other wild animals. Morning came, and still no traces of the child; they made up their minds she had been torn in pieces and devoured by the wild beasts they had heard during the night. They renewed their search next morning with sorrowing hearts and fearful forebodings, lest they should come upon her mangled remains in the forest; what was their great joy presently to see her coming toward them alive and well. In answer to their eager inquiries as to how and where she had spent the night she said "Alongside a log, sleeping." With childlike faith she had gone to sleep in the wilderness, undisturbed by the noises around her.

Jonathan Hoyt, who, in 1804, moved into the town of Thompson, was another representative pioneer settler. He came from Norwalk, Connecticut, and his family consisted of a wife and three children. In April of that year he started for his new home in the wilds of Sullivan, his caravansary consisting of a span of horses, a yoke of oxen, and an immense butterfly cart.

In the broad and flaring box of the cart were bestowed the household goods of Mr. Hoyt, including sundry small canvas bags filled with coin and placed inside the family chest. On top of all, when on their journey, were perched the wife and children, who climbed to their elevated position by means of a ladder. They first journeyed to a port on Long Island sound, where the family, the teams, the butterfly cart and all, were put on board a sloop, and in due time were landed at Newburgh.

Here the more serious obstacles of the journey were encountered. The oxen and horses were attached to the cart, and the movement was made westward on the Newburgh and Cochecton road. The turnpike, so far as completed, had been but recently made; besides, the frost was only partially out of the ground, so that their progress was slow. Sometimes the wheels would sink so deep into the slough-holes that it became necessary to partially unload the cart before the team could proceed. At other times one wheel of the cart would remain firm on the partially thawed soil, while the other would sink to the axle, causing the elevated wings of the vehicle to lurch with an energy that threatened to hurl the women and children into the mud. So forcible was this side movement that the chest was broken in pieces, and the silver money it contained scattered over the bottom of the cart-box. Fortunately the box had been so well constructed, and of such good materials, that the money was found all safe when they reached the Neversink.

Towards the close of the sixth day from Newburgh the journey was made down the west side of the Shawangunk mountain. There at the foot was a broad, turbid, and impassable river. The Basha's kill was swollen with the spring freshet, the turnpike was submerged, leaving nothing visible but the bridge. There was not at that time a solitary building on the western slope of the mountain that would afford them shelter—not even a barn. They could neither advance nor retreat, so they spent the night where they were, in the mud, homesick and heartsick, and doubtless contrasting the wilds of Sullivan with the pleasant home they had left in the land of plenty and comfort.

The next day the floods subsided so that Mr. Hoyt mounted on one of his horses, crossed the kill, and went in search of assistance. At the west side of the Mamakating valley an enterprising individual had opened a log tavern. Here Mr. Hoyt obtained an extra team, with which he returned to his family. With the united efforts of the three strong teams the cart was safely brought over the stream. That night the family found more comfortable quarters in the log tavern.

When they reached the vicinity of their new home on the east bank of the Neversink, Mr. Hoyt learned that the cabin he had built was untenable: the snow of the previous winter had broken down its bark roof, and it was little better than a ruin. The settlers informed him there was a small log structure on the opposite bank of the Neversink that had been used as a school-house, but was at that time vacant. Into this he moved his family until he could build another house. The tracks of all sorts of wild animals could be seen around the cabin when the Hoyts arrived there.

There was a saw-mill at Katrina falls, and Mr. Hoyt commenced hauling white-pine lumber from this establishment. Settlers were scarce in the vicinity, but money was much more so; and Mr. Hoyt having brought with him a goodly supply of silver coin, men were found who were willing to leave their own farm work to get it. In two weeks' time Mr. Hoyt's new house was so far completed that he moved his family into it.

For several years the wolves annoyed them very much, and he found it very difficult to rear cattle or keep sheep. On one occasion the wolves killed eighteen sheep near the entrance to his door yard, where he found them lying about on the snow next morning. It was quite common for him to find the carcasses of yearlings in his fields, and occasionally his cattle would come home bleeding from wounds inflicted by the blood-letting and stealthy brutes.

A few years of labor brought comparative competence to the early settlers, whose privations for a time were very great. Here and there, throughout the valleys, was a small clearing, literally choked with stumps and stubborn roots; and in the midst of the clearing stood a little, low, bark-roofed, mud-plastered log-cabin, with a stick-and-mud chimney, with a hole sawed in the logs that served as a window. Near this was a log pen, open to the blasts and snows of winter, in which the pioneer stored whatever of hay or grain he could gather for the subsistence of his shivering cattle. These "children of the wilderness" had no difficulty in procuring meat, as the surrounding woods abounded in deer and bears, which could be had fresh from the shambles in a few hours' time. Wherever the beech-nut flourished the sweetest pork could be fattened, in which toothsome edible bears often came in for their share with the settlers. Wheat could be raised in sufficient quantities alongside the charred stumps, but to get it converted into flour was the great difficulty. It often required a journey of days to reach a flour mill, and then each customer was

ST. JOHN'S EPISCOPAL CHURCH AND RECTORY, MONTICELLO, N. Y.

required to await his turn for his grist, which sometimes consumed a day or two more.

Samp and coarse meal were made at home in various ways. Some had a heavy wooden pestle fastened to a spring pole, with which a half bushel of corn could be pounded at once. This was thought to be a great institution. Later on, small mill-stones, made from the "grit" of Shawangunk mountain, and operated by hard labor, were introduced into the settlements, by which laborious and tedious operation a semblance of flour could be obtained

Even the water-mills of the most approved pattern of those times were cumbersome and unsatisfactory affairs. One of these was put up in Sullivan county by a man named Thompson, and was facetiously dubbed Thompson's samp-mortar by the early settlers. The whole building would shake and quake to such an extent when the stones were revolving that even venturesome boys would flee from it.

A BORDER ALARM.

THERE is nothing that will excite the sympathies of a border settlement more than the alarm of a child missing or lost in the woods. The uncertainty as to its fate, compassion for its agonized parents, and a realizing sense of the feelings of the little one, exposed to Indian capture, or to be torn in pieces and devoured by wild beasts, or to the slower process of perishing by cold and hunger,—all call forth the deepest human sympathy.

In 1810 the entire population of Bethel * town turned out, and for eight days searched the woods for little Johnny Glass, and did not relinquish their efforts until all hope of finding him alive was abandoned.

The lad was living with his parents near White lake. His mother sent him to carry dinner to his father, who, with some men, was chopping wood about a mile away. He reached them safely and started for home, but for some reason got bewildered and lost his way. When the lad did not return in the afternoon, his mother felt no anxiety, as she surmised Johnny had got permission from his father to remain in the woods with the men until they returned at nightfall. But when the father arrived in the evening and reported that the lad had immediately started on his return trip, the dreadful truth flashed upon the minds of the household

Every parent can imagine the scene that ensued—the distress of the mother, the wild energy of the father. Hastily summoning his nearest neighbors, the father spent the night in a fruitless search in the woods, while the mother remained at home rendered frantic by the intensity of her grief.

By the next morning the tidings had spread far and wide, and a thorough

---

* Quinlan.

and systematic search was instituted—all the settlement joining in the work of beating the swamps and thickets. The search was continued from day to day, until all courage and hope were lost. No trace of the boy could be found, and the supposition was that he had perished from terror, cold and hunger, or that he had met with a more speedy and less dreaded death by being devoured by wild beasts, which were then numerous and ferocious.

As was afterward ascertained, when little Johnny left the path he traveled almost directly from home. When night overtook him, bewildered, weary and hungry, he lay down by the side of a fallen tree and cried himself to sleep. where he slept until morning. On awakening he again started to find his way out of the woods, wandering at random. In this way he continued to travel ten days, with nothing to eat except wild berries, and seeing no living thing except the beasts and wild birds of the forest.

One night as he lay in a fevered sleep on his couch of leaves alongside a log, he was aroused by the bleating of a deer in distress; then he heard the angry growl and snarl of a catamount, and knew the ferocious animal was drinking the blood of his harmless victim. He lay very quiet, as he did not know how soon he might meet with a similar fate.

On the eleventh day of his wanderings he was a pitiable object. His clothes were tattered; his body emaciated and cheeks sunken; his limbs had scarcely strength to carry his body about, while his feet were so sore and swollen that he could scarcely bear his weight on them. He was about to lie down exhausted, first calling the name of mother, as he had done scores of times before, with no answer save the echoes of the forest, when his ears were greeted with the tinkling of a cow-bell. The sound gave him renewed life. It nerved him for one more effort. With difficulty he slowly made his way in the direction of the sound, leaving marks of blood on the leaves at every step. He soon came to a clearing in which were several cattle feeding At sight of him the animals started for home. It was near night and he knew if his strength lasted he could find succor. Finally he was obliged to crawl on his hands and knees, and thus he proceeded until he came in sight of a house. This proved to be the dwelling of a Mr. Lain, who lived on the Callicoon.

When Mrs. Lain started to milk the cows she discovered the lost boy on the ground near her door. She took him in her arms and carried him into her dwelling. The good woman had a kindly heart and a sound head, and she treated the wanderer as she would her own son, and with as good judgment as though bred a physician. She bathed him, dressed his sores, put him into a warm bed, judiciously fed and cared for him until he had revived sufficiently to tell his name and residence. News of his safety was then sent to his parents, who for ten days had mourned him as dead. He lived to be an old man, but he never fully recovered from the effects of the adventure, and ever after needed the controlling influence of a mind more sound than his own.

In the town of Forestburg, years ago, there lived a little girl named Mary Frieslebau. She was a lovely child, full of life and animation. One day she went to the house of a neighbor on an errand with some other children. It was in winter; a deep snow lay on the ground, and the wood-choppers and lumbermen had cut the woods up into roads in all directions. In playing hide-and-seek on their way home, Mary became separated from the other children, and they lost sight of her altogether. Calling her by name, and receiving no answer, the children returned without her, and supposing she would immediately follow, did not mention the circumstances when they reached home. An hour or more afterward, when her parents sought for her, the children pointed out the spot where she was last seen; and although a score or more engaged in the search, they failed to find her.

It so happened that a quack doctor by the name of Heister was living in Orange county, who was looked upon with suspicion by the people of this neighborhood where he sometimes came on professional visits. Inasmuch as he was seen to pass along the road with his wife about the time of Mary's disappearance, they surmised he was concerned in abducting her. Some children having reported they had seen Mary in Heister's sleigh, served to confirm their suspicions; and accordingly a warrant was made out, and the doctor and his wife were arrested and brought to Forestburgh for examination. Two days were spent in investigating the affair by a Justice of Peace, and the evidence was so much against the prisoners that all believed them guilty; they were therefore held for trial and were required to give bail

A rain had meantime fallen, which carried off a portion of the snow with which the ground was covered, with the result of exposing a portion of the dress of little Mary, where she lay in the snow with her face downward. She had fallen down exhausted after being separated from her companions, and was concealed from view by the snow which at the time was rapidly falling. She had probably perished before her parents had set out to look for her.

This chapter would not be complete did it not include the adventures of Mrs. Silas Reeves, the wife of an early settler of Fallsburgh. Her husband manufactured mill-stones and was absent from home most of the time. Mrs. Reeves was one of your true women, who met the hardships and privations of frontier life with a courage undaunted. At one time she traveled several miles to the house of a neighbor and brought back living coals to replenish her fire.

One evening, her cows having failed to come home, she bade her children remain in the house while she went after them, and told them not to be afraid of the dark, as she would be gone but a little while. Taking up the chubby babe and kissing it, she gave it and its little sister into the charge of their elder brother, a bright lad of six; then shutting and securing the door behind her, started on her errand. As it began to grow dark the smaller ones showed symptoms of fear; but the little fellow was equal to his charge. As the hours went by, and the mother did not return, he gave them their frugal supper and put them both to bed; not, however, without a protest from the babe, who wanted to sit up till his mamma came home. Then propping himself up in his chair, the whole household was soon wrapt in slumber.

Early next morning, a neighbor in passing found the children alone, and heard their story. The two younger were clamoring lustily for their mamma, while the boy was offering such consolation as he was able. The children were at once sent to the house of a relative to be cared for, while the neighborhood was aroused and search made for Mrs. Reeves. For three days the inhabitants

MRS. REEVES AND THE WOLVES.

far and near were ranging the woods looking for her, and when they at last found her, she was exhausted and almost speechless, having lain down to die. One night she climbed to the top of a high rock to get out of the reach of the wolves that were on her track. Here she was serenaded all night, during which they made many unsuccessful attempts to reach her; nor did they leave her until the dawn of day, when they vanished into the forest.

SAM'S POINT, OR THE BIG NOSE OF AIOSKAWASTING.

THE traveler in the region of the Shawangunk has not failed to notice that remarkable feature of the mountain known as Sam's Point. Even when seen at such a distance that the mountain looks like a blue cloud suspended above the earth, this promontory stands out in full relief against the sky. The name has its origin in one of those quaint legends with which the vicinity abounds. The story as handed down by tradition, and still related by the residents of the neighborhood, is as follows:

Samuel Gonsalus was a famous hunter and scout. He was born in the present town of Mamakating; was reared in the midst of the stirring scenes of frontier life and border warfare, in which he afterward took such a conspicuous part; and was at last laid to rest in an unassuming grave in the vicinity where occurred the events which have caused his name to be handed down, with some lustre, in the local annals.

He lived on the west side of the mountain, a locality greatly exposed to Indian outrage, and his whole life was spent in the midst of constant danger. His knowledge of the woods, and his intimate acquaintance with the haunts and habits of his savage neighbors, rendered his services during the French and Indian War of inestimable value. He possessed many sterling qualities, not the least among which was an abiding devotion to the cause of his country. No risk of his life was too imminent, no sacrifice of his personal interest too great, to deter him from the discharge of duty.

When the treacherous Indian neighbors planned a sudden descent on an unsuspecting settlement, "Sam Consawley," as he was familiarly called, would hear rumors of the intended massacre in the air by some means known only to himself, and his first act would be to carry the people warning of their danger. At other times he would join in the expeditions against bands of hostiles: it was on such occasions that he rendered the most signal service. Though not retaining any official recognition of authority, it was known that his voice and counsel largely controlled the movements of the armed bodies with which he was associated, those in command yielding to his known skill and sagacity.

His fame as a hunter and Indian fighter was not confined to the circle of his friends and associates. The savages both feared and hated him. Many a painted warrior had he sent to the happy hunting-grounds; many a time had they lain in wait for him, stimulated both by revenge and by the proffer of a handsome bounty on his scalp; but he was always too wary for even the wily Indian.

In September of 1758 a scalping party of Indians made a descent into the country east of the Shawangunk. The warriors were from the Delaware, and had crossed by the old Indian trail * leading through the mountain pass known as "The Traps;" their depredations in the valley having alarmed the people, they were returning by this trail, closely pursued by a large body from the settlements. At the summit of the mountain the party surprised Sam, who was hunting by himself.

As soon as the savages saw him they gave the war-whoop, and started in pursuit. Now was an opportunity, thought they, to satisfy their thirst for revenge. Sam was a man of great physical strength, and a fleet runner. Very few of the savages could outstrip him in an even race. But the Indians were between him and the open country, and the only way left was toward the precipice. He knew all the paths better than did his pursuers, and he had

---

* During the spring of 1887, the writer followed this old war trail for a considerable distance, it being still plainly visible.

already devised a plan of escape, while his enemies were calculating either on effecting his capture, or on his throwing himself from the precipice to avoid a more horrid death at their hands.

He ran directly to the point, and pausing to give a shout of defiance at his pursuers, leaped from a cliff over forty feet in height. As he expected, his fall was broken by a clump of hemlocks, into the thick foliage of which he had directed his jump. He escaped with only a few slight bruises. The Indians came to the cliff, but could see nothing of their enemy; and supposing him to have been mutilated and killed among the rocks, and being themselves too closely pursued to admit of delay in searching for a way down to the foot of the ledge, they resumed their flight, satisfied that they were rid of him. But Sam was not dead, as some of them afterward found to their sorrow. To commemorate this exploit, and also to bestow a recognition of his numerous services, this precipice was named Sam's Point.

Sam had a nephew by the name of Daniel Gonsalus, who was captured by the Indians when he was about five or six years old. The savages were lurking in the vicinity of Mamakating farms; and being too feeble in numbers or too cowardly to make an open attack, they sought to effect their purpose by making secret reprisals. One day the boy, having ventured too far from home, was captured and carried away. He was soon missed, and search made for him, but all to no avail; and after some days his parents gave him up as lost. Whether he had been carried off by some strolling band of Indians, or had become bewildered in the woods, and so perished, was to his agonized parents merely a matter of conjecture.

The Indians, on leaving the valley, stopped and rested at a lake in the mountains, where they remained several days. The boy became the adopted son of a warrior and his squaw; he formed an acquaintance with several of the young Indians, and engaged with them in their sports. Among other things they brought together some small stones and made a miniature wall. After this the band wandered from place to place, and Daniel lost all knowledge of the direction in which his parents lived.

For a time he was watched closely; but eventually was regarded as fully adopted into the tribe, and was suffered to go where he pleased. After some time had elapsed, the band again encamped by a lake, when Daniel discovered the little wall of stones he helped build when he was first captured. His love for his white friends had not diminished, nor had his desire to return to them abated. He would have made his escape from his captors long before, only that he did not know which way to go. Here was a discovery that made plain the way to home and friends.

Waiting a favorable opportunity he set out on his journey, reaching the residence of his father safely after an absence of three years, where he was received by the family as one raised from the grave.

Elizabeth Gonsalus, another relative of Samuel, was captured by savages when she was seven years of age. She was carrying a pail from her father's house to a field near by. Her way led through bars; the rails were all down but the upper one; and as she stopped to pass under this, she was caught by a painted Indian. He so terrified her by threats that she could not give an alarm, and conveyed her to his party encamped near by. In company with other captives she was taken several days' march in a southwest course over the mountains and along the banks of the rivers until they reached a town in interior Pennsylvania. Here she remained a prisoner twenty years.

Her disappearance from home had been so sudden and mysterious, that her friends were in deep distress as to her probable fate. Had she wandered into the woods and perished? Such instances were comparatively frequent. Had she been killed and devoured by wild beasts? Such a fate was by no means uncommon in a country abounding with wild animals. Or, worse than all, had she been carried off to become the unwilling slave of a brutal savage? These questions had been asked for twenty long years. Her father inclined to the theory that she had been captured by the savages, and continued, year after year, to make inquiries of those who had been among the Indians, in the almost despairing hope that he would yet find tidings of his lost daughter.

At last he heard of a white woman who was with a clan near Harrisburgh, the circumstances of whose capture led him to suspect she might be the one long sought. He lost no time in searching for the clan, with whom he had the good fortune to find the white woman. Twenty years of a life of servitude, with brutal treatment, had so changed her appearance that he could trace no resemblance in her to the little girl he had lost so long before. He listened to her story, some particulars of which led the father to claim her and carry her back to his home. She had entirely forgotten the names of her family. When taken to the house in which she was born, she went directly to the bars where she was taken prisoner by the Indian. The shock and fright of her capture twenty years before had fixed the locality so firmly in her memory, that she pointed out the place where the Indian seized her, and gave some of the details attending her capture. There was no longer any doubt—the lost one was restored to the fold.

"GROSS" HARDENBURGH.

A NARRATIVE OF EARLY LAND TROUBLES.

THE man whose crimes and subsequent history form the subject of this chapter was a resident of the Neversink valley. The deeds of violence attributed to this man are yet traditionary in that locality, and still serve as themes to while away many a winter evening as they are told by the fathers to the younger members of the family, seated by the firesides of the log-cabins and cottages of the neighborhood.

Near the beginning of the present century the people of this valley were agitated over the question of title to lands. The settlers had very generally paid for the farms they occupied, the title to which they had acquired under the Beekman patent, and had made considerable improvements in the way of clearing up wild lands, and putting up comfortable log-cabins and barns, which greatly enhanced the value of the property. They had settled down with the purpose of obtaining a competence that would assure them a serene and comfortable old age; and now they were threatened with the loss of the fruits of years of trial and sacrifice by a defective title. These pioneers would not look with favor on any one who sought to dispossess them of their farms, even were he a man of sterling qualities, and in possession of a valid title; but it does not appear that Gerard, or "Gross" Hardenburgh, who figured as a rival claimant to the land, enjoyed either of these qualifications. Gross Hardenburgh—we take the liberty of using the name by which he is usually spoken of—was the son of Johannis Hardenburgh, and was born in Rosendale, Ulster county. He was of a haughty and willful temper, and greatly addicted to drink. In early life he married Nancy Ryerson, an estimable lady, by whom he had several children.

During the War of the Revolution he espoused the cause of the Colonies with a devoted patriotism, and frequently imperiled his life in the struggle. His time, his means, and his influence were thrown without reserve into the scale. Quinlan, whom we quote largely, says he organized two companies of infantry, both of which were engaged in defending the frontier against the incursions of the savages, one of them being commanded by him in person.

At the attack on Wawarsing, in 1781, it will be recollected that Captain Hardenburgh hastened forward to the relief of the settlement; and having thrown his detachment into a small stone house, he with a force of only nine men bravely withstood the advance of nearly four hundred Indians and Tories. So stubborn was the defense of the little garrison that thirteen of the enemy were left dead on the field. This Captain was none other than Gross Hardenburgh, by whose courage and leadership Wawarsing was saved from utter annihilation.

As he advanced in years his habits of dissipation grew upon him to such an extent, that his existence was little better than one continuous debauch, which tended to confirm and inflame his evil propensities, while it obscured what was commendable in his disposition. He became morose, impetuous, tyrannical and uncongenial in the extreme. It is said of him that in his old age, when traveling about the country, he would order the innkeeper with whom he lodged to cover his table with candles and the choicest liquors, and taking his seat solitary and alone, drink himself into beastly insensibility.

Owing to his vicious and morose ways, his father disowned him, and devised his share of the paternal estate to the heirs of his wife, Nancy Ryerson. This act of the elder Hardenburgh seemed to extinguish the last spark of manhood that lingered in the heart of his eccentric son.

The death of Nancy Ryerson antedated that of her husband, and several of her children died unmarried; consequently the purpose of the father was defeated, the dissipated son inheriting the property of his deceased children. Gross Hardenburgh is said to have made the impious and heartless boast. that while his father disinherited him, the Almighty had made all right by removing some of his own children. Such were the antecedents of the man who was about to enter upon the work of evicting the settlers of Sullivan. Little hope of mercy could any expect who were in his power.

His controversy with his father, his wife, his children, and the settlers of the Neversink valley, had the effect of arousing a spirit of antagonism against him which time has scarcely softened, nor the teachings of charity perceptibly modified; few, even at this late day, choosing to say a word in his defense. He hated his family, and defied the world. When he at last met his fate there was not one left to mourn his loss; while many could not conceal their joy that his presence would no longer afflict them.

Before proceeding to extreme measures, Hardenburgh made a general offer of one hundred acres of wild upland to each settler of the disputed territory for his improvements; but the occupants of the valley met his overtures with defiance. They had purchased the bottom lands of the Neversink in good faith, and were not disposed to yield up their improvements for wild mountain lands. They believed that Hardenburgh's claim was fraudulent; or should it prove otherwise, that the state would provide a remedy for the difficulty.

Meanwhile, finding that his offers were refused, Hardenburgh instituted suits of ejectment against several of the settlers. Without waiting, however, for the courts to decide the question, he took the law into his own hands, and commenced the work of seizing upon property and forcibly dispossessing the inhabitants. In the fall of 1806 he took six hundred bushels of grain in bulk, and all the growing crops, from James Brush and his three sons. The grain was placed in a grist-mill owned by himself, which stood on the site of the Hardenburgh saw-mill.* Gross also owned a house and barn in the vicinity, and his son also owned some buildings there. Among the latter was a barn in which was stored three hundred bushels of grain, which had been forcibly taken from the settlers.

It was not long before the mill, houses, and barns, were all destroyed by fire. Under such circumstances it was strongly suspected that the dissatisfaction of the settlers had an intimate connection with the burning of the property, and that a terrible vengeance awaited upon the patentee. Some of the Hardenburgh family were then residing near by, but became so alarmed that they soon left the neighborhood.

During that same year it is asserted that Hardenburgh forcibly set the family of James Brush out of doors, and kicked Mrs. Brush as she went, though

---

*Quinlan's "History of Sullivan."

only three days before she had given birth to a child which she then held in her arms. During the absence from home of a neighbor, Jacob Maraquet, his family were ejected, Mrs. Maraquet being dragged from her home by the hair of her head. She died a few days afterward from the effects of her treatment.

During the two years following, outrage followed outrage. Hardenburgh was excited to frenzy, and the blood of the settlers was fully aroused. The usurper of their lands was looked upon as a common enemy, whose death would prove a public blessing.

In November, 1808, Gross Hardenburgh passed through the Neversink valley. He was at that time seventy-five years of age. Notwithstanding he had led a life of dissolute habits, he was still active and energetic, and controlled his spirited and somewhat perverse horse with skill and boldness. He was, withal, possessed of a magnificent physique, on which neither time nor dissipation had made perceptible inroads; and he boasted of a weight of two hundred and fifty pounds. He feared neither man nor beast and appeared to entertain no respect for his Creator.

Calling on his way along the valley at the house of one of the Grants, he made the emphatic declaration that "he would raise more hell in the next seven years than had ever been on earth before."

When passing along what is locally known as the "Dugway," he noticed that the chimney of a house owned by him, and occupied by a man named John Coney, was not completed. Calling Coney from the house he upbraided him in a towering passion, and concluded with the remark that "unless the chimney was topped out when he came back he would throw him out of doors." Coney immediately employed the services of a neighbor, and the chimney was finished next day.

Hardenburgh spent that night at the house of his son, and soon after sunrise on the following morning he started to go up the river. About an hour afterward he was found in the road, helpless and speechless. His horse was caught about a mile above. Hardenburgh was taken to a neighboring house, where he lingered until about three o'clock the next morning, when he died. He did not know that he had been shot, and those about him did not think best to acquaint him with the fact. Before he died he was heard to remark, that his friends had often told him his horse would throw and probably kill him, "and now," said he, "he has done it."

While preparing his body for burial, a bullet-hole was found in his coat, and a wound in his shoulder. His friends were unwilling to admit he had been murdered, and were on the point of burying him without an inquest. An old soldier standing by, who had seen many wounds received in battle, declared that nothing but lead could have made the hole in the dead man's shoulder. A coroner was sent for, and the nearest physicians (one of them Hardenburgh's son Benjamin) were requested to be present

A crowd of people surrounded Van Benscoten's house where the inquest took place, and was attended with scenes and incidents almost too shocking for credence. Some of them brought jugs of whiskey to make merry over the death of their enemy, and drunkenness became the order of the day. One, who had just come from butchering hogs, as he beheld the dead man prepared for dissection, exclaimed: That is fatter pork than I have killed to-day." The speaker bore unfriendly relations to one of the physicians; and, while the dissection was going on, he continued: "That is more than I ever expected to see—my two greatest enemies—one cutting the other up!" When the body was opened, and the heart exposed, he cried: "My God! that's what I've longed to see for many a day!"

Another composed and sang an obscene and irreverent song, in which he described the death of Hardenburgh, the feeding of birds on his body, and other indelicate details. This greatly pleased the assembled multitude, and was repeated so often, that some can yet recite parts of the composition

Quinlan, from whom we glean most of the preceding, says that a woman of the neighborhood, whose descendants are among the most respectable citizens of Fallsburgh, declared that "Gross had gone to - -, to fee more lawyers." One of the witnesses, on being asked if he knew who shot Hardenburgh, answered that he did not; but expressed regret that he did not himself do the deed, as "Doctor Benjamin had offered two hundred acres of land to have his father put out of the way."

These remarks evoked shouts of merriment from the crowd. Vain were all efforts to preserve order; decorum and decency were set aside; the rejoicing of the settlers, inflamed by the all-potent rum, took the form of the revels of Pandemonium.

From evidence elicited at the inquest and from subsequent developments, it is supposed the assassins were three in number, and that they were posted behind a tree about eight rods from the road, where they had cut away some laurels that had obstructed their view. The ball had entered the victim's shoulder, and passed through, breaking the back-bone; and the shock to his nervous system was such as to instantly deprive him of sensation. This accounts for the circumstance of his not hearing the report of the gun.

Several were suspected of being implicated in the murder, some of them being arrested either as principals or accessories; it is probable that a number of individuals in the "infected" district could tell more than they were willing to disclose. When the fatal shot was heard in the valley, one of the men who was at work on the chimney at the "Dug-way," slapped his hands and remarked, "That's a dead shot! An old fat buck has got it now!"

A tradition is current in the neighborhood that a suspected person moved west, who, on his death-bed, confessed that he assisted at the murder, but stubbornly refused to disclose the name of any of his accomplices. If the death of Gross Hardenburgh was the result of a conspiracy involving a number of persons, the secret has been well kept; and guilty souls, blackened with the horrible crime, have gone down to the grave with the burden of their unconfessed transgression. After the assassination, such of the settlers as had not removed from the valley, found no difficulty in making satisfactory terms with the heirs of Hardenburgh. Thus was ended what the old settlers termed the "Hardenburgh war," a term by which it is usually spoken of to this day by the residents of the valley.

LITTLE JESSIE MITTEER AND THE BEAR-TRAP.

"BE sure and start for home early; you know I don't like to have Jessie out after dark, when there are so many wild animals about. You remember it was only a night or so ago that we heard the wolves howl dreadfully over by the creek; and I heard to-day they killed some sheep of Job Jansen's."

Such was the parting injunction of Mrs. Samuel Mitteer, as her husband and little daughter Jessie set out one afternoon on an errand to the house of a neighbor some three miles distant. The husband bade her not to disturb herself on that account, assuring her that he would be home before nightfall; and the little girl, first kissing her mamma good-bye, took her father's hand and departed in high spirits.

They reached their destination, but were obliged to wait a short time for the neighbor to return. The business being arranged, the men engaged in a friendly chat, and the moments flew by unheeded. The sun had already disappeared behind the wall of forest to the west when Samuel bethought himself of his promise to his wife. Still, he did not dream of any more serious result than a little anxiety on the part of the good woman; and taking his daughter by the hand, set out on their homeward journey as fast as her little feet could carry her.

Her merry voice rang through the woods, now growing dim and solemn with the gathering darkness; and they had already passed the Hemlock wamp, and were more than half way home, when their ears were greeted with a sound that made the father involuntarily clutch the arm of his little companion with an energy that could not fail to alarm her. Again the sound came through the darkening forest aisles and echoed from hill to hill, and at last died away to a whisper.

"What is it, Papa?" exclaimed the child, whose quick glance noted the strange demeanor of her father; "is it anything that will hurt us? I do wish I was with Mamma!" Without deigning a reply, Samuel caught the child in his arms, and ran in the direction of home with all his might.

Reader, did you ever hear the howl of a wolf in the woods of a still night— when some old forester opens his jaws and sends forth a volume of sound so deep, so prolonged, so changeful, that, as it rolls through the forest and comes back in quavering echoes from the mountains, you are ready to declare that his single voice is an agglomerate of a dozen all blended into one? Then as you wait for the sound to die away, perhaps, across the valley, another will open

Little Jessie Mitteer and the Bear-Trap.

his mouth and answer with a howl as deep, and wild, and variable as the first; then a third and a fourth will join in the chorus until the woods will be full of howling and noise? If you have heard this weird music of the forest, far from home, without means of protection, and with helpless beings in your charge, then you may realize the feelings of Samuel Mitteer as he fled along the path with the speed of a deer.

Mr. Mitteer hoped he might reach home before the first wolf had time to call the others to its assistance, as he understood their habits sufficiently to know these animals seldom attack singly. He was within a mile of his house, and less than half that distance from the clearing. So great was the effort he was making in his flight, encumbered by the weight of the child, that he began to show signs of exhaustion; he feared lest his strength should fail entirely before he reached a place of safety.

To add to his terror he knew by the well-known sounds that the pack had collected, and that the hungry brutes were upon his track. The disclosure added new energy to his frame. He was a powerfully built man, and rock and tree flew by as he sped on in his flight. Yet his were the efforts of sheer despair, as he heard the din of snarling beasts, and knew they were rapidly gaining in the race.

He thought of home; he wondered if his friends heard the howling of the pack, and knew that he was making a race for life. He imagined what would be their feelings when they should find his fleshless bones in the woods next day; and even calmly conjectured as to what would be the sensation of being torn limb from limb by the fierce brutes.

Nearer, ever nearer, came the howling and snarling of the pack. He realized that his moments were numbered if he depended on the speed of his flight alone. By abandoning his child he knew he could climb a tree beyond the reach of his pursuers; but he could not do so with her on his shoulders. Rather than leave her to her fate he would die with her—the little one whose arms were then encircling his neck, and whose breath came thick and fast against his cheek. Ah, that death shriek, when at last her form would be crushed in the jaws of the bloodthirsty brutes—would it strike him dead?

"I see them coming, Papa," said little Jessie, who from her position could look back over her father's shoulder, "and, oh, Papa, there are so many of them; you won't let them hurt me, will you?" A scarcely audible groan was the only response.

While every means of escape was being canvassed in the mind of the agonized parent with a rapidity that is possible only in times of great danger, he bethought himself of a bear-trap he had seen in the vicinity but a short time before. Could he reach the trap? It was worth the trial. All that human energy could do he would accomplish. Striking obliquely from the path he bounded away. The door to the trap was raised when he last saw it; if still in that position he believed he could place the child inside and spring the trap; but if the door was down, he knew he would not have time to raise the ponderous weight, and all would yet be lost. It was a forlorn hope at the best.

What is that object looming up directly in his path? It is the bear-trap. But the door! the door! The shadows of the forest render the vision indistinct. He cannot tell whether the door is shut or raised. It appears to be shut. A few more steps will decide. Already he hears the panting of the brutes at his heels, and expects each moment to feel their sharp claws in his flesh. There is a mist before his eyes. He feels that his strength is failing. One moment, and—"Thank God," he cries, "the door is raised." With a wild energy begotten of despair he tears the terrified child from his breast, thrusts her through the opening, touches the spindle and down comes the ponderous door with a thud. Then seizing an overhanging limb he swung himself up out of reach just as the jaws of the foremost wolf came together as he snapped after his prey.

JESSIE MITTEER AND THE BEAR-TRAP.

Now that the necessity for immediate exertion no longer existed, the reaction was so great that Mr. Mitteer feared he would fall from the tree from sheer exhaustion; to prevent such an occurrence, he tied himself securely with his cravat and handkerchief. All night long the wolves perambulated about that bear-trap and tree, and made the night hideous with their howling. It was a night ever to be remembered by both father and child. They were sufficiently near to one another to converse, so they could cheer each other during the long and tedious hours.

The trap in which little Jessie lay was built so strongly that the largest bear could not get out after it had once sprung the door. The father had told her to keep as near the centre of the pen as she could, and she would be safe. Though out of reach of harm, her position was far from enviable, with the ferocious brutes all around and over her prison, thrusting their noses and their sharp claws into the crevices between the logs in their frantic efforts to reach her. Morning came at last, but Mr. Mitteer dare not leave his perch for fear their late assailants might yet be lurking in the vicinity.

The people in the village of Liberty where he resided had heard the unusual howling of the wolves during the night, and much anxiety had been felt, as it was feared they were on his track; the wife and mother had been inconsolable. She had spent the whole night in alternately going to the door of her log cabin to listen to the wolves in the forest through which her husband and child were to return, and then throwing herself upon the bed and giving way to violent paroxysms of grief. Before sunrise a party was sent in search of the wanderers. Proceeding along the Hurley road the relieving party hallooed the names of the missing ones, and presently were rewarded with an answer. Then, following up the direction of the sound, they came upon Mr. Mitteer still in the tree, and little Jessie safe and sound in her bear-trap. The wolves had gone, but had left behind abundant evidences of their visit. The father and child were speedily restored to their friends, who had given up all hope of ever seeing them alive. Though Samuel Mitteer lived many years after this occurrence, he ever after exhibited an almost childish terror at the howling of a wolf.

A RIVAL OF ISRAEL PUTNAM.

EVERY schoolboy has heard the story of Israel Putnam and the wolf. Comparatively few have heard of the similar experience of a lad in a panther den at Callicoon. Without detracting from the glory of Putnam, we think the story of little William Lane, of Callicoon, worthy of honorable mention.

In the spring of 1843 the track of a very large panther was discovered, and a party of hunters turned out and followed it to its den in a ledge of rocks. Closing up the entrance to the cave carefully, they went home, proposing to return next day with reinforcements.

The following day they were on the ground and found everything as they had left it. They first dislodged the rocks for about twenty feet, or half way to the extremity of the den, so as to admit the passage of a man to that point; beyond this they found the hole too small and the surrounding material immovable. A small lamp was tied to the end of a pole and thrust inward far enough to enable the "fiery eye-balls" of the monster to be seen. A candle was next placed so that the light would shine on the barrel of a rifle, and thus enable the daring man who attempted to shoot the panther to take sure aim. The first shot was fired by William Adams, who wounded the game, causing it to scream so terribly that every one fled from the spot, fearing the enraged creature would emerge and rend them in pieces. Except a few contusions, caused by a hasty scramble over fallen tree-trunks and scraggy rocks, no damage was incurred. One by one the hunters returned and obtained a furtive view of the scene of terror. All seemed quiet, and after a hasty consultation, the entrance was again securely walled up and the place abandoned for the night.

On the third day all the men and boys that the surrounding country afforded were assembled to witness the sport. They were armed with an endless variety of weapons,—rifles, shot-guns, bayonets, hatchets, axes, crowbars, and butcher knives. It was agreed to resume the plan of operations adopted the day previous. The boulders were once more rolled away from the entrance, and the lights properly placed. A brother of William Adams, the hero of the previous day, went into the passage as far as he was able and fired. The same scene followed as on the second day, the screams of the panther causing a panic in the whole crowd, and the forty men and boys ran as if life depended on the celerity of their flight.

The company rallied sooner than on the former occasion, however, and John Hankins fired the third shot, prostrating the panther in his lair. But how to get him out was the difficulty. None but a lad could enter; and now was a rare opportunity to test the bravery of the boys. One lad volunteered but at the last moment his courage failed him. Next a spirited little fellow named William Lane threw off his coat, hat and vest, and arming himself with a hunting axe and dirk, went into the den, accompanied by Mr. Hankins as far as the latter could get. While his friends remained outside in breathless suspense, young Lane cautiously crept through the narrow passage, pausing occasionally to listen. The panther still exhibited signs of life, as the boy could see by the faint light of his lamp. As soon as young Lane was within reach he buried the blade of his axe in its brain, and then applied the dirk to its throat—a very hazardous experiment. The young hero then ended his adventure by hauling out the body of the panther, which proved to be the largest of its kind.

PANTHER HUNTING AT LONG POND.

NO sports are more thoroughly enjoyed by robust men than those of hunting and trapping. The freedom from restraint; the mountain air and vigorous exercise; living in constant communion with Nature, with just enough of danger to add relish to a calling full of excitement and adventure —these are among the causes that lend to such an existence a char mthat no other life can give.

Cyrus Dodge had a thrilling adventure at Long Pond, one of the many beautiful sheets of water found in the county of Sullivan. This pond was conspicuous, in times gone by for its large trout, and for the numbers of deer found in its vicinity. One day in mid-summer, Dodge went to this lake to look for deer. He sat under some huge trees that grew near the shore, waiting for the deer to come to the water. While thus engaged, his attention was directed to a suspicious noise overhead. Looking up he saw a large catamount on a limb just above him. The animal was watching him intently, as though mentally discussing the relative merits of a man or deer for dinner. Believing there could be no merit in procrastination Dodge brought his rifle to his shoulder and fired. The next instant he heard a dull thud on the ground at his feet, and saw that the turf and dead leaves were being crimsoned by the blood of a panther in its dying throes.

The report of his rifle started other lithe forms into activity among the tree-tops, and, as Dodge declared afterwards, he believed the woods were full of panthers, and realized that he was in great peril.

Knowing the aversion of the cat-tribe to water, he waded out into the lake waist deep. As he loaded his gun he counted no less than five panthers among the trees that lined the shore. They were probably a mother and her young; and the latter, though nearly grown, had continued to follow the old one. The hunter kept up a fusilade from his position in the water until three more panthers were brought down. The other two ran off and were seen no more. He then waded ashore, skinned the four panthers and made the best of his way homeward, sensibly concluding that it was a dangerous locality for deer hunting.

One day in mid-winter a hunter by the name of Sheeley discovered the track of a large animal not far from a cabin occupied by a widow. He followed the track until it led to a den in the rocks. He examined the entrance carefully, but did not care to explore the interior alone. The next day, in company with a companion, he revisited the place. The passage into the lair of the animal was very narrow, so that a person could enter only by creeping on his hands and feet. Procuring a sapling, they tied a birch bark to one extremity, and thrust the lighted end into the hole. By the light they discovered a very large panther quietly reposing in the cave. A rifle-ball speedily deprived the animal of life, and the hunters started home with their game. On their way they came upon the half-devoured carcass of a large buck, which the panther had killed, and had been feeding upon.

William Woodward, while roaming through the woods in the town of Rockland, discovered a panther's den. Though entirely alone he crept into it. The lady of the house was not at home, but was absent foraging, leaving her children to take care of themselves. Woodward took up the little panther kittens, thrust them inside his torn shirt, and carried them home. Had the old mother panther discovered him in the act of purloining her little ones, this story would have had a different ending.

Peter Stewart and a young friend were once hunting in this town, but with no success. Game seemed to be scarce. They examined the mountain runways, and the crossings in the soft spongy soil of the valleys, without finding the print of a hoof. While passing near a ledge they discovered a hole in the rocks, near which were a number of bones of deer and other animals. This they concluded was the lair of some wild beast, which was in the habit of bringing food home to its young. Examining carefully the priming of their guns, they secreted themselves within easy gun-shot of the hole, and awaited the development of events.

In a few moments they saw a bear come out of the hole with a young panther in his mouth. As Stewart's friend was about to shoot, the other signaled him to withhold his fire. The bear quickly crunched the life out of the kitten, went back into the hole, and presently issued forth with another one struggling in his teeth. Bruin had come upon a panther family in the absence of the old ones, and had thought this was his opportunity. As he crushed this second kitten between his jaws, it gave a loud squeal. The cry was heard by its mother who happened to be returning home. Soon there was heard the sound of swift feet, and the crashing through brush and dry branches of some rapidly moving body. Then a large panther merged into view, with eyes blazing and hair bristling—boding dire vengeance on the despoiler of its home.

The bear saw the panther coming, and his animal instinct took in the situation. He saw he was about to reap the fruits of his indiscretion. He made an awkward effort to shamble away, but was too closely pursued by the infuriated beast; to escape he took refuge in a tree. But the tree afforded no asylum from the sharp claws and teeth of the panther. The bear rolled himself into a ball and dropped to the ground, and again essayed to shuffle off. His antagonist was once more upon him; and forced to extremities Bruin turned to fight and a fierce and bloody conflict ensued. The hunters were meanwhile looking on with breathless interest while the actors in this drama of the forest were contributing to their entertainment. However, the end was soon reached. The bear proved no match for his adversary, and the feline monster, fastening its teeth in the shoulder of his victim, with its hind feet ripped out his intestines. The hunters now both fired upon the panther and killed it. Then skinning both animals, they hung the bear meat out of the reach of wolves, and went for assistance to take the carcass home.

BEAR HUNT ON THE MONGAUP RIVER.

THE pioneers of the region of the Shawangunk, who were, by turns, lumbermen, farmers, hunters and soldiers, as inclination led or occasion required, were a robust race of men, fearless and active, who thoroughly enjoyed forest life. Encounters with the fierce denizens of the forest were frequent, always exciting, and occasionally hazardous in the extreme. This territory abounded in wild game, and was a famous hunting-ground for both white and red men, even after the country adjacent had settled down to civilization. After the War of the Revolution it is said that "John Land, the Tory," trapped enough beaver in the town of Cochecton to pay for four hundred acres of land. David Overton used to tell of standing in his father's door in the town of Rockland, and shooting deer enough to supply the family. Once he counted thirty of these animals at one time in a pond near the house. Five or six of the larger ones seemed to be standing in a circle and pawing the water with their forefeet.

In the winter of 1819, three young men by the name of Burnham, Horton and Brown, residing in Forestburgh, engaged in a bear hunt. Burnham, while returning from his work in the woods, discovered fresh bear tracks in the snow, and engaged the others to go with him and capture the animal. Armed with rifle and axe, before daylight the next morning they were on the trail, which they followed for several hours until the track came to a flat on the Mongaup river. Here the snow was very much trampled, and they judged the bear's winter-quarters must be in the vicinity. The three commenced to search, when Burnham found a hole near the centre of the flat under some large rocks, with bear tracks leading to and from it. He called out to his companions that he had found the den, and presently all three were peering into it, but could see nothing

They then cut a pole and thrust it into the opening, when they found the end of the pole came in contact with some soft substance. Burnham then split the end and twisted it vigorously against the substance, and was rewarded with some short, black hairs, which were held in the split. They had found the bear, and the animal was within reach of the pole. One of the men suggested they would better go home, but Burnham utterly refused to leave until he had killed the bear.

His next move was to make the stick very sharp, with which he punched the bear with all his might. Immediately there was an angry growl within, with a scrambling of feet and scratching of claws; the bear seized the sharpened end and pushed the pole outwardly, carrying Burnham with it. Burnham dropped the pole, stepped back, caught up his rifle, and aimed it just as the bear reached the entrance. As he showed his head at the hole, Burnham fired, and the bear fell back into his retreat.

At first they could not determine whether or not the bear was dead; a few vigorous punches with the pole satisfied them on that point. They then tried to get out their game with crooked sticks, but their efforts were fruitless. Then Burnham went head-first into the den, and taking hold of the bear's shaggy coat, his companions, by pulling on his legs, drew out both him and the bear

While waiting to get breath, they heard a noise under the rocks, and presently the head of another bear was thrust forth, which speedily met the fate of its companion.

It was now dusk and they were occupied with the question as to how to get the bear home. The feet of the small bear were tied together and slung across the shoulder of one of the party. The large bear was suspended from a pole and carried by the other two. In this way they reached the road, a mile distant, just at dark, where they met a team with an empty sled, on which they were permitted to deposit their game. On reaching home, tired and hungry as they were, they would not eat until a steak was cut from one of the bears and prepared for their supper.

Zephaniah and Nathan Drake, also of the town of Forestburgh, once had an adventure with a bear. They were out hunting and the dogs had driven Bruin up a tree. The hunters came up and saw the bear seated on a limb thirty feet or more from the ground, calmly eyeing the dogs. Zephaniah quickly brought his rifle to bear upon the animal, when Nathan meekly advised him to be careful and make a sure shot. "Why," said Zeph., a little vexed at the suggestion, "I can shoot the critter's eye right out of his head." The ball, however, missed its mark, but it shattered the upper jaw so that the bear's

ZEPHANIAH DRAKE AND THE BEAR.

nose and about half of its upper teeth turned up over its forehead. The bear fell to the ground, and the dogs fell upon the bear. The bear caught one of the dogs between his paws and attempted to crush it; when the other dog bit the black brute so viciously, that he dropped the first dog and turned his attention to the other. Thus the battle went on back and forth, the animals being so mixed up that the brothers dare not shoot, for fear of killing their dogs.

Zephaniah finally sailed in with his hunting knife, when the bear left the dogs and attacked his human assailant. The man retreated as the animal advanced upon him. His heel caught in a laurel bush, down he went upon his back, with the bear on top, and the dogs on top of all. For a brief period there was a lively tussle among the bushes. Every actor in that drama was in earnest, as much so as though thousands were witnessing the progress of the fight. From impulse Zephaniah threw up his hand to keep off his assailant as much as possible, and thrust his finger into Bruin's mouth. The bear's jaws, torn and mangled, as they were, closed on one of the fingers and crushed it.

Finally, as Zephaniah was about giving up for lost, the bear, by some means not now known, was killed; but the hero of this bear fight ever afterward exhibited a crooked finger.

CASUALTY ON BLUE MOUNTAIN.

ONE method adopted by the early settlers in clearing up timber lands was by "jamming." This consisted in partially cutting through the trunks of a number of trees, and by felling some of the outside ones against the others, all would be brought down, and a considerable saving of labor effected. In a few months the interlaced limbs would be sufficiently dry, when fire would be applied, and usually nothing but the charred stumps and prostrate trunks would remain.

Other farmers would first cut the brushwood and small trees, while the larger ones were girdled and left standing. The latter, particularly the hemlocks and other evergreens, the foliage of which would remain green too long after girdling, were sometimes trimmed from the top downward. This method was adopted to save the labor of gathering the trunks into heaps for burning, a very laborious undertaking where the timber is large. When the limbs and brushwood had become thoroughly dried, and no rain had fallen for several days, the refuse was set on fire. If the result was "a good black burn," the ground was ready for planting. When the standing trunks began to decay, fire was again applied, and in a few years all was thus consumed. Sometimes, however, the burning was not good, when the fallow would be abandoned, and allowed to be overrun with briers and other rubbish. These "fallow fires, gleaming in the spring time," are still a feature of Sullivan county.

Years ago, in the town of Liberty, there occurred an incident that is still fresh in the minds of the people residing in the locality. One of these abandoned fallows was on Blue mountain, near the residence of Nathan Stanton. This fallow had come to be a famous spot for blackberries, and the children were in the habit of visiting the place to fill their baskets and pails with the fruit. It was near the middle of August, and the day mild and pleasant, that the four children of Nathan Stanton went thither to gather berries. While there one of the trees toppled and fell, and, in its fall, struck against another, until a number of the immense trunks were brought to the ground. When the children heard the first sound of warning, they ran for a place of safety, only to be caught under the wide-spreading branches of the trunks that were falling all around them. Two of the three boys were killed outright, and the sister was injured badly. The children had gone forth happy and joyous, and before the hour set for their return, two had met a violent death, and a third was dangerously if not fatally injured, by a casualty so remarkable and unprecedented as to appear like a dispensation of Providence. The dead bodies were extricated, and taken to the house of mourning, where soon the neighbors gathered to witness the sad occasion of bereavement, and to bestow such aid and consolation as it was in their power to give. It was an affecting burial scene at the little rural grave-yard on Blue mountain, when the settlers assembled about the open graves of the Stanton children and participated in the last sad rites of their sepulture.

What added to the impressiveness of the occasion, was the superstitious awe with which the early settlers regarded the mysterious phenomenon which led to the children's death. Those trees had withstood the blasts of the previous winter and spring, and on a bright day in midsummer, when scarce a breath of air was stirring, they were laid prostrate. What unseen hand caused them to fall? What unknown agency in nature made those forest giants to quiver and reel and then come rushing headlong to the ground, when to mortals there seemed to be no cause? Is it the result of some chemical change in the atmosphere, or are we to await a solution of the problem until the supernatural is unveiled to our understanding?

Though no one has yet explained away the mystery, it is a well-attested fact that trees do thus fall. When the sun is shining brightly, and all nature seems to repose in the beams of the morning; when not a zephyr fans the cheek and no unwonted sound disturbs the ear, lo! a monarch of the forest suddenly begins to tremble, and totter, and then falls crashing to the earth. Now, far away, a dull heavy roar will arise; and again nearer at hand, comes the rushing sound of the bushy top of some lofty pine, as one patriarch after another yields to its fate. It seems as if the direct agency of God produced these effects; and the hunter, untutored though he may be, as he beholds these evidences of the power and incomprehensibleness of the Infinite, breathes a silent prayer of adoration.

NELSON CROCKER AND THE PANTHERS.

NELSON CROCKER was a noted hunter, of whose adventures in the woods many interesting stories are told. It is said that when he accompanied a hunting expedition his companions felt certain of bagging their game. The following narrative, which is given by Quinlan, is highly illustrative of early life in the wilds of Sullivan.

Northwest of Big pond in the town of Bethel, there is a tract of low, wet land known as Painter's swamp. In former times this ground was as good for deer hunting as any in the country; and where deer were found, panthers generally abounded. This was, consequently, a favorite hunting-ground for Crocker; but on one occasion he found more panthers than he wished to see.

While rambling one day with his dog on the outskirts of the swamp, he counted the tracks of no less than seven of these ferocious animals. As they are generally found singly, or at most in pairs. Crocker could not conjecture why so many were together. He followed the tracks until he was hungry, and then sat down to eat his luncheon. Dividing this into two parcels, he proffered one to his dog; but the latter instead of sharing the tempting meal, showed his teeth, and seemed bristling for a fight with an unseen enemy. Just as the hunter swallowed his last mouthful, a large panther sprang by him, almost grazing his shoulder as it passed. Crocker caught up his rifle, fired at the beast at random, and saw it disappear unharmed. An instant afterward his dog was fighting another of the monsters at a little distance; but the dog was soon glad to get out of reach of the claws of his antagonist and run to his master for protection.

As Crocker was reloading, he saw a third panther coming toward him. He shouted at the top of his voice, and it ran up a tree. This one he shot and killed. As soon as he could reload he caught sight of another, which he also shot and brought down from its perch in a tree. Here the fright of the dog, which seemed to feel safe nowhere but between his master's feet, and the screaming of the panthers in every direction, caused Crocker to lose heart. To get out of that swamp without delay he believed to be his first and supreme duty. He ran with all his might for safe ground, and did not stop until he believed himself out of the reach of danger.

The next day Crocker returned to the scene of this adventure for the purpose of skinning his game. While thus engaged he discovered a large male panther in the crotch of a tree. He fired at the beast and it fell; but it immediately ran up a sapling until the top was reached, when the sapling bent with the weight of the beast until its branches reached the ground. As the panther came down, the dog, forgetting the rough usage of the previous day, stood ready for battle. A rough and-tumble fight ensued, in which the dog was speedily whipped, when he fled yelping toward his master, closely pursued by the panther. Crocker's rifle was unloaded; and as he had no relish for a hand to-claw encounter he concluded to run too. A race ensued in which the dog was ahead, the hunter next, with the panther in the rear, driving all before it. Crocker expected every moment to feel the weight of his pursuer's claws on his shoulders, and consequently made excellent time. Finding his rifle an encumbrance, he dropped it as he ran. This proved his salvation; for the beast stopped a moment to smell at it, and decide whether it should be torn in pieces. This enabled Crocker to get out of the swamp before the panther could overtake him, and the beast did not seem inclined to follow him to the upland.

After waiting some hours, Crocker, armed with nothing but his hatchet and hunting knife, started once more for the swamp from which he had twice been driven ingloriously. Recovering his gun, he reloaded it carefully, and endeavored to induce his dog to follow the panther's track; but he declined, having had enough of panther hunting. As they were leaving the swamp the dog commenced to howl. The panther answered with a loud squall, and started towards the hunter, repeating the challenge as it came, evidently bent on a fight. The dog crouched close to the feet of the hunter, while the latter coolly awaited the approach of the ferocious monster. When it was within one bound of him, and about to spring, Crocker sent a ball crashing into its brain. Without further adventure he skinned the game he had shot during his two days' hunt, and returned home.

THE DISAPPOINTED GROOM.

WALTER MANNING was a native of Ulster county. At the age of twenty he fell heir to a property of several thousand dollars. Disregarding the advice of his friends to let his inheritance remain in real estate, he converted most of it into cash, and started for the west to make a more colossal fortune. In due time he arrived in California. His talkativeness soon apprised the people of the town that he was a young man of property, which he proposed to invest when a desirable occasion offered. It was not long before a speculator, who had landed property on his hands that was quite slow of dividends, by dint of much flattery and persuasion, convinced young Manning that his was just the property he required, and that it was certain to bring rich returns in the near future. The result was that Walter paid a large portion of his patrimony for the estate, and set up his pretensions as a landed proprietor. The next essential for house-keeping was a house-keeper, and Walter cast about him for a wife. A young man of reputed wealth, with a large estate and money in bank, good looking and accomplished, ought to be in no lack of young ladies willing to share his fortunes. And so it proved in the case of young Walter. Mothers with marriageable daughters vied with each other in their attentions to the young landholder; he was invited to teas, plied with calls, and in short was lionized by the female world generally.

But Walter Manning, with all his wealth, his devotion to the sex, and the largeness of his philanthropic soul, could not marry them all. He must needs single out one of the number of his admirers, and content himself with the love and adoration of her alone, so unreasonable and circumscribing are the marital regulations of modern society. Among the most beautiful and accomplished of those damsels, he thought Virginia Green the most to his liking. She was a blonde, possessed a petite figure, bore the reputation of a superb dancer, and withal was an excellent conversationalist. As soon as Walter's preference became known, he was no longer invited to afternoon tea-parties. The mothers of marriageable daughters were fain to pass him unrecognized. But if he had lost caste in the eyes of the feminine public, he was more than compensated by the smiles and caresses of Virginia Green. Not a day passed but he was found in her society; and what his passion overabounded in intensity, ber affection counterbalanced in devotion. In short they became engaged. And now that the matter was settled, why delay the day of nuptials? When love was so fervent, the mansion in want of a mistress, and a bachelor heart so much distressed for lack of a ministering angel, procrastination was a loss to all concerned. Walter pressed his suit for an early wedding, and the young lady, after a show of reluctance which amounted to nothing, appeared to bend to his desires.

"But," said the young lady, "you know that fortune is fickle, more inconstant even than affection. Why not bestow upon your future wife a marriage portion? It will be yours to enjoy as though held in your own name, and should fortune fail you, you will have something saved from the wreck, to fall back upon. Besides, it will be a slight token of the sincerity of your professions of love to me." "That I will readily do," said Walter. "I'll give you the deed to this estate, to be given you at the altar on the day of your nuptials, to be celebrated at the parish church next Thanksgiving Day, two months hence;" to which she assented in tones of never-dying affection.

Now followed the busy note of preparation. Numerous journeys to the metropolis, a half score of milliners, dressmakers, hair-dressers, and assistants were found necessary to bring out a trousseau suitable for the future mistress of Redwood Hall. The coming wedding absorbed the talk of the town; and Walter thought himself fortunate in that he could now revenge himself for the slights of his former admirers, by leading the most beautiful of them all to the altar. Every body received cards of invitation, and no less than three clergymen were invited to be present, that there might be no hitch in the ceremony.

Thanksgiving Day arrived at length, and a most auspicious day it proved. The air was bland, the sun shone brightly, and nature seemed to don a holiday attire in keeping with the occasion. The church was gaily trimmed; carpets were spread from the doors to the carriage-way, and the pews were literally crammed with people clad in fashionable attire. The organ pealed forth its most joyous wedding march, and presently a flutter in the audience showed that the contracting parties had arrived. As the bride swept up the aisle, a bewilderment of feathers, lace and white satin, a murmur of admiration ran through the entire assembly. And, too, the manly bearing of Walter was such as to cause a perceptible flutter in the hearts of more than one damsel present.

As they took their places in front of the altar, and just as the highest flourish of the Wedding March was reached, Walter took a package from his pocket and gave it to the woman at his side. It was the deed of Redwood Hall, made over to Virginia Green, made to her before she was his bride, as a husband may not transfer real estate to his wife.

The last notes of the organ died away in semiquavers among the arches of the ceiling when the minister stepped forward and in solemn tones said, "Let the parties join hands," and in a moment continued. "If any one have reasonable objection to the marriage of Walter Manning and Virginia Green, let him now make it known, or forever hold his peace."

A pause ensued in which the silence became oppressive. Presently a voice was heard. It was that of a young man in the rear of the audience. "I object to the bans." All eyes were turned in the direction of the speaker. "State the grounds of your objection," said the officiating clergyman with forced composure. "On the ground that the lady at the altar is already my wife," was the calm reply. And then all present knew a wrong had been done that robbed Walter Manning, in one moment, of a bride and an estate. In one hour's time, the disappointed groom had arranged his pecuniary affairs, and was on his way with the remains of his fortune to his home in the east.

The statements in the foregoing narrative are based on facts. The names only, for obvious reasons, are fictitious.

NEW PALTZ.

ON the 26th of May, 1677, an agreement with the Esopus Indians was made, pursuant to a license from the Hon. Governor Edmund Andros, dated 28th of April, 1677, concerning the purchase of land "on the other side of the Rondout kill," known in history as the "Paltz Patent."

Matsayay, Wachtonck, Senerakan, Mayakahoos and Wawawanis acknowledged to have sold Lewis Du Bois and his associates the land within the following boundaries: Beginning at the high hill called Moggoneck [Mohonk], thence southeast toward the Great river to the point called Juffrow's hook in the Long beach, by the Indians called Magaat Ramis [point on Hudson river on line between the towns of Loyd and Marlborough]; thence north along the river to the island lying in the Crum Elbow at the beginning of the Long Reach, by the Indians called Raphoos [Pell's island;] thence west to the high hill at a place called Waraches and Tawaeretaque [Tower a Tawk, a point of white rocks in the Shawangunk mountain]; thence along the high hill southwest to Maggoneck, including between these boundaries, etc." This tract the Indians agreed to sell for the goods specified in the following list:

40 kettles, 40 axes, 40 addices, 40 shirts, 100 fathoms of white wampum, 100 bars of lead, 1 keg of powder. 60 pairs of socks, 100 knives, 4 ankers of wine, 40 guns, 60 duffel coats, 60 blankets, 1 schepel of pipes, etc.

Having thus extinguished the Indian title to this tract by the present of articles valued by the red man, the settlers of New Paltz enjoyed a comparative immunity from savage outbreak during the early wars. In order to arrive, however, at a more complete understanding of the history of this settlement, reference will be made, in brief, to an event in the chronicles of the old world.

The French Protestant Huguenots were celebrated for their love of liberty and zeal for their chosen religion. Persecutions against them were temporarily abandoned during the reign of Henry IV, King of Navarre, from 1589 to 1610,

FIVE SUCCESSIVE CHURCH EDIFICES OF THE DUTCH REFORMED CHURCH AT NEW PALTZ.

SIX STONE DWELLINGS IN NEW PALTZ, N. Y., BUILT SOON AFTER 1700.

especially after he proclaimed the celebrated Edict of Nantes in 1598. Louis XIII repeatedly violated its stipulations; and a formal revocation of the Edict was made in 1685, which cost the lives of 10,000 of the Huguenot people, who perished at the stake, gibbet, or wheel. Thousands fled to other lands for refuge, especially to the Lower Palatinate, or Pfaltz, along the river Rhine. Some of the persecuted Hollanders likewise fled to the Lower Palatinate, and when they subsequently returned to Holland the Huguenots accompanied them, and both finally emigrated to America. These two peoples were attracted to each other by reason of their adoption of the same religion, and this fellowship was rendered still more firm in consequence of the free intermarriage among them. This accounts for the presence of Dutch physiognomies with French names, observable, even at the present day, among the congregations in localities where are found the posterity of the once persecuted Huguenots.

There seems to be no definite information as to the course the Huguenots took in coming to America. They were hospitably received by the Dutch at Wiltwyck, or Wildwyck, the modern Holland for wild retreat, or wild parish, from its primitive and rough appearance. Soon after the granting of the New Paltz patent the Huguenots set out for their new home in the wilderness. Their weary way lay through the trackless forests; and their families and household goods were conveyed in wagons so constructed as to answer the double purpose of transportation and shelter. Arriving at a broad meadow on the banks of a limpid stream they named the place "Tri-Cors," Three Cars, in allusion to the three primitive vehicles in which the possessions of the exiles were transported. The river itself they named Walkill, probably from *Wael*, one of the branches into which the Rhine divides itself before emptying into the North Sea, and *Kill*, the Dutch for river; while to the settlement was given the appellation of New Paltz, in remembrance of their ever dear Pfaltz—their ancient home on the Rhine. Here, in the midst of the beautiful alluvial valley, the crystal waters of the river at their feet, the blue dome of heaven above them, and the towering hills a gallery of attendant witnesses, the Huguenot refugees opened the Bible brought from their old homes, read a lesson from the holy book, and with faces turned toward France, joined in a hearty and joyous thanksgiving to the God that had led them safely thus far, and had permitted them once more to breathe the air of religious freedom.

The first conventional act having been that of public worship, it was resolved that their first building should be a church. This was built of logs, and was also used as a school-house. Temporary residences were at first put up on the west bank; but the Indians advised their removal to the higher ground on the opposite side, as the place first chosen was subject to overflow during the spring freshets.

From a minute in French, still in possession of the church, we find that on January 22, 1683, M. Pierre Daillé, Minister of the Word of God, arrived and preached twice at New Paltz. He proposed that the people choose, by a vote of the fathers of families, an elder and a deacon, to aid the minister in the management of the church. They chose Lewis Du Bois, elder, and Hugh Frere, deacon. Thus was organized the Walloon Protestant Church of New Paltz, and for fifty years service was held in the French language. But the Holland tongue had become the vernacular in Ulster and adjacent counties, and gradually became adopted by the Huguenot settlers of New Paltz. The first Dutch entry in the church bears date of the 6th of July, 1718. During the period intervening between 1709 and 1730, there was no stated supply at New Paltz; the earnest Christians were obliged to go to Kingston to attend preaching—whither they often went on pious pilgrimage.

Rev. Stephen Goetschius accepted a call from the congregation, at New Paltz and New Hurley. His ministry healed the breach that threatened to disrupt the church at New Paltz. He is described as small in stature, and bent in form. He boarded at the house of Lewis Du Bois, and married his daughter. He was a sound preacher, and occupied a high place in the estimation of his people. His vacant Sabbaths were spent at Wawarsing. At that time the Indians were visiting the defenseless inhabitants with fire and slaughter. Goetschius writes of preaching in a pulpit cut and disfigured by the tomahawks of the savages; the church itself showing evidences of having been set on fire by the same agency, but which providentially went out. He further writes: "At the close of the war I perceived there were places where new congregations might be gathered. I did undertake to collect the people together, and under the blessing of God organized nine churches." At that time Goetschius was the only minister in the Dutch church in Ulster.

The log church was soon found to be unequal to the demands of the growing colony. A new church was built of stone, "of small dimensions," the records say, "and finished with brick brought from Holland. Its form was square, each of the three sides having a large window, and the fourth a door inclosed by a portico. In the centre of the steep and pointed roof was a little steeple, from which a horn was sounded for religious services." This was dedicated December 29, 1720. October 25th, 1771, it was resolved to erect a third house of worship. The site of this edifice corresponds nearly with the location of the present church, and is described as having been a "substantial, well-proportioned stone building, with a hipped roof, surmounted with a cupola, and a bell." The building was dedicated in 1773. The old square church was broken down, and the material used in the construction of a school-house, which was afterward converted into a residence. It is worthy of note that both churches were built while the people were without a pastor.

It was during the ministry of Rev. Douw Van Olinda, a gentleman of marked executive ability, that the New Paltz academy was erected and put into active operation; and he was largely instrumental in carrying forward the project to a successful termination. During his pastorate the third church was taken down and a new brick church erected on its site, which constitutes the eastern extension of the present house of worship.

There were twelve original proprietors of the New Paltz patent. These twelve patentees exercised the governmental control of the colony, one of their number presiding, constituting what was known as the "Dusine," a primitive form of civil administration, out of which sprang the Town Meeting of New England. Most of them constructed substantial stone dwellings along one street, now known as Huguenot street. Six of these stone edifices are yet standing, and are shown in the accompanying illustrations. The Holland bricks, the quaint little Dutch windows with glass set in lead, and the ancient port-holes in the walls of the houses, are yet shown to curious visitors, and yearly attract scores of antiquarians to the locality.

NEEDDERDUYTSE TAAL TE SCHAWANKONK.

LOW DUTCH CHURCH OF SHAWANGUNK.

THE Reformed Church of Shawangunk was organized in 1750, and the present church edifice—the oldest in the consistory—was built the same year. The society first worshipped in the "Owl house," a temporary structure near the kill. Johannis Mauritius Goetschius came over from Switzerland and organized the infant church in the wilderness. Barent Frooman, a native of Schenectady, was called to the pastorate at Shawangunk, New Paltz and Walkill [Montgomery], February 4th, 1751. He was sent that same year to the University of Utrecht, where he remained two years. He started home in company with Jacobus and Ferdinandus Frelinghuysen, and Johannis Schunneman. The first two died on shipboard of small-pox. Frooman preached at New Paltz August 26, 1753, at Shawangunk September 2, and at Walkill [Montgomery] September 9. No record is given of any installation. His salary was fixed at £90, one-third to be raised by either church. He lived at Shawangunk, now Bruynswick, a house and one hundred acres of land having been set apart there for his use. He married Alida, daughter of David Vanderhyken, of Albany. He was called to Schenectady in 1754, and died at that place in 1784, in the sixtieth year of his age.

Rev. Johannis Mauritius Goetschius was born in the Canton of Thorgan, Switzerland, in 1724. He studied and practiced medicine before he entered the ministry, but was drawn to the study of theology and began to preach without due authority in 1754. He was a warm advocate of the Coetus principles, and three years later was called to the pastorate at Scoharie at a salary of £60, parsonage house, one farm, and 40 schepels of wheat.

Goetschius was called to Shawangunk and New Paltz in 1760. He lived in the Shawangunk parsonage, then one story high, and was paid a salary of £80, one-half borne by each church. He died at the parsonage March 17, 1771, of dropsy. He was long sick, and was a great sufferer. He preached the last time at New Paltz September 9, 1770. During the ten years of his ministry he baptized 320 persons at Shawangunk, and married 75 couples; at New Paltz he baptized 212 persons, and performed 41 marriage ceremonies. He was buried under the pulpit of the Shawangunk church, in accordance with the ancient custom of the society, where his ashes still repose. His widow, Catherine Hager, continued to live at Shawangunk, and married her husband's successor, Rev. Rynier Van Nest.

Van Nest, the third minister, was early converted, but studied late in life for the ministry. He was for several years clerk in a country store at Bound Brook. He was licensed by the Synod of Kingston October 7, 1773, receiving his call to preach at Shawangunk and New Paltz April 16, 1774. His stipulated salary was £60 and parsonage; New Paltz was to pay £20, and the service was to be divided accordingly. The records say he baptized 384 persons at Shawangunk, and 45 at New Paltz. His labors seem to have extended to Montgomery, where he performed 307 baptisms. His pastoral connections were dissolved by the Classis in April, 1785. His personal appearance is described as follows: height, five feet, ten inches; fleshy as he advanced in age; wore a wig, and was very neat and particular in dress; possessed regular features, with a somewhat prominent nose; he spoke with a loud voice, and was considered a good preacher when speaking in Dutch, but never succeeded well in English. He was held in high estimation. The fourth minister was Rev. Moses Freligh, who was licensed to preach in 1787 by the Synod of New York city, called to preach at Shawangunk and Montgomery February 20, 1788, and was ordained in the Shawangunk church the same year by Rev. Blauvelt Rysdyk, Steven Goetschius and De Witt. First baptism at that place was a child of George Upright and Maria Rhinehart; first baptism at Montgomery, a child of William Christ and Elizabeth Decker. Freligh married Sarah Varick, of New York, in 1788, and died at Montgomery February 10, 1807, at the age of 54 years.

Rev. Henry Polhemus next succeeded to the ministry. He was born at Harlingen, N. J.; was licensed by the Classis of New York in April, 1798; called to Shawangunk January 23, 1813; installation service June 13th of that year, Rev. Moses Freligh preaching the sermon. Polhemus died in November, 1815. He had been to New Jersey, and on his way home was attacked with bilious fever. His remains were deposited under the pulpit, along with those of Goetschius.

The next in succession was Rev. G. B. Wilson, who was licensed by the Classis of New Brunswick, and was called to Shawangunk and Paughcaughnaughsink [New Prospect] in January, 1816. He was dismissed in 1829 on account of feeble health. The following is a list of ministers up to the present time, with the date of settlement; Henry Mandeville, 1831; John H. Bevier, 1833; John B. Alliger, 1845; Charles Scott, 1851; Cyril Spaulding, 1868; P. K. Hageman, 1882.

The stone edifice of this church has been subjected to changes suggested by modern taste. The ancient pulpit, beneath which the remains of the two faithful pastors, Goetschius and Polhemus, were deposited, was located on the north side of the building, and the entrance was opposite the pulpit. An extension, surmounted by a spire, and partially enclosing the present entrance to the building and a stairway to the gallery, has more recently been added to the west end, and the pulpit moved to the east side of the structure.

THE TRAPS.

THERE is a singular and romantic formation on the top of the Shawangunk mountain known as The Traps. Quite a village has sprung up within its sheltering bosom, and boasts of a hotel, store and chapel. Benj. Burger and his wife Helena were among the first settlers. They put up a log cabin and commenced housekeeping in a primitive way. At first the wild animals were so fierce that fires had to be kept at night as a protection to their cattle. A colt was killed by the blood-letting brutes, and the mare was badly bitten and torn. Burger sometimes worked for the farmers in the valley, and when he returned home at nightfall he was obliged to carry a torch to keep off the wolves. He used to tell of seeing their teeth as they gathered about him in the darkness and followed him up the mountain, growling and snarling, yet keeping at a safe distance through fear of his blazing pine knots.

On the east side, near to the highway leading over the mountain, there still stands a straggling building known as The Traps Tavern. Many years ago, a number of young men from the vicinity of High Falls were at this tavern, and were having a grand frolic. Their visit was protracted far into the night; and as the company seemed in no humor to depart, one of their number named Hill determined to go home. So, mounting his horse, he set out alone over the mountain road. While passing leisurely down on the opposite side, his horse began to prick up his ears, and exhibit other symptoms of alarm; and presently young Hill detected the stealthy tread of some animal that was moving in the underbrush by the roadside. He at last awoke to the fact that wolves were on his track; and, giving the reins to his horse, the frightened animal went galloping down the rugged mountain road at a breakneck speed. The iron shoes of his horse sent the sparks flying at every step; and the clatter of hoofs, the shouts of the rider, and the sharp quick cries of the wolves in close pursuit, startled the night air and awoke the sleeping echoes among the mountains. A false step, or a failure to retain his seat, and all would have been over for young Hill. In this way the cavalcade went dashing down the defiles, and finally brought up before another hotel at the foot of the mountain. Here the pack turned off into the forest, and the panting horse and terrified rider sought the friendly shelter of the hostelry until morning.

Some thirty years since the neighborhood of The Traps was the scene of a startling tragedy. Ben. Gosline, a man of middle age and married, became intimate with a young mulatto girl by the name of Maria Cross. One Sabbath afternoon he invited her to take a walk, and their rambles led them along the brink of one of the dizzy precipices with which the locality abounds. Arrived at a point of the rocks where the crag juts out three hundred feet in perpendicular height over the base, Ben remarked to his companion that he knew where was an eagles' nest, and asked if she would not like to see it. Stepping aside he went to the brink, and, holding by a small sapling, leaned forward over the frightful chasm until he could see the face of the precipice. Presently he called out that he could see the nest, and that there were some young eagles in it. Unsuspicious of treachery, Maria took his place, and leaned over the edge as far as she dared, but failed to see the nest. "Stand a little nearer," said Ben, "I will not let you fall." So, taking his hand, she took a step forward until her head and shoulders hung over the beetling crag; at this moment Ben loosened his hold, gave her a gentle push, and, with a piercing shriek, the girl went over the precipice.

Providentially a hemlock tree grew out of the face of the rock, near to the bottom, into the thick branches of which the girl chanced to fall. The momentum of her descent was thus broken, so that she was not killed by the shock when she struck at the foot of the precipice. She managed to drag herself the distance of a few yards, where she lay in her agony until morning.

During the night she observed a light moving among the rocks where she fell, as though a lantern were being borne in the hand of some person there. Maria came to the conclusion it was her seducer and would-be murderer, searching for her mangled body. In the belief that Ben would yet kill her if he found her alive, she lay very quiet; and her visitor, after clambering a long time among the rocks, went away. In all probability it was Ben Gosline, who had come to remove all traces of his double crime. He doubtless concluded that she had escaped alive, or that some one had discovered and removed the body; in either case his only safety lay in immediate flight. Ben was never seen in the vicinity afterward.

The next morning, by dint of great exertion, Maria crawled over the broken ground towards the nearest house, when her cries of distress were fortunately heard. When found she was nearly exhausted, and her bowels trailed upon the ground as she urged her way along. Strange to say, she recovered from the effects of her fall; and it is believed is yet living in comfortable circumstances. Her child, born not long after the above adventure, lived to grow to maturity. The incidents of the attempted murder, and her miraculous escape from instant death, form themes yet fresh in the minds of the residents of the locality.

One day, late in autumn, the wife of Calvin Burger thought she heard the whir of a rattlesnake under the floor of their log cabin. She told her husband of the circumstance on his return, but he affected to believe she must have been mistaken. The snake continued to sound his rattle every day during the winter, whenever the heat from the stove warmed his snakeship into something like life; still the husband maintained at least an outward show of incredulity, knowing that any other course on his part would necessitate the taking up of the floor to search for the snake, or removing from the cabin. At length there came a mild day in spring. It chanced that Burger was obliged to be away from home on that day, but he directed his wife to watch for the snake, as he would most likely come out into the sunshine. Mrs. Burger kept a close watch, and was rewarded by seeing a large rattlesnake crawl out through a chink in the foundation wall of her cabin. She found means to dispatch it, and proudly exhibited the remains of her late unwelcome guest to her husband on his return. The snake proved to be one of the largest of its species.

In the vicinity of The Traps are vast crevasses in the rocky ledges, some of them of unknown depth. These fissures vary in width from a few inches to as many feet, and constitute a feature of the natural scenery of the region. Table Rock is a cliff that apparently has been partially detached from the parent mountain by some convulsion of the past, but still maintaining its position, and rearing its head high among the surrounding elevations. At an early day an active and intrepid hunter by the name of Decker chased three deer to the edge of the precipice, two of which leaped from the rocks and were dashed in pieces at the bottom. The third, a huge buck, took up a position on Table Rock, and facing about, boldly defied his pursuer. Decker had thrown down his rifle in the haste of his pursuit, and had nothing but his hunting knife. Undaunted, he closed in with the buck, and a desperate conflict began Grasping the deer by the horns, Decker essayed to cut the animal's throat. The latter attempted to throw off his assailant, repeatedly lifting the hunter from his feet, at times suspending him over the brink of the precipice, so that he hung dangling by the buck's horns. Again the hunter was obliged to exert his strength to prevent the deer from falling over. Long and uncertain the battle waged; at length the courage and agility of the hunter prevailed, and the life-blood of the buck reddened the face of the rock.

At the foot of the mountain, near The Traps, many years ago, lived a man by the name of Evans. In his employ was a negro boy named Jed, some nine or ten years of age. One afternoon Jed was sent up in the back lots to bring home the cows. Not returning after the usual absence, Evans went to look for the lad, and was horrified to find him bound to a bar post in a standing position by a huge black snake, and stone dead. The snake had probably attached himself to the post, and, as the boy attempted to pass through, it had taken a turn around the lad and squeezed him to death.

SHANKS BEN.

JOHN MACK was an old resident of Wawarsing. John Mentz, his son-in-law, lived on the east side of the mountain. The only communication between the two families was by an Indian trail leading over the mountain, known as the Wawarsing path. Some time during the Revolution Mack started on a visit to his daughter, Mrs. John Mentz, accompanied by his younger daughter, Elsie. On their way they called at the house of a neighbor. While there, Elsie, who was dressed in white, catching a view of herself in the glass, declared that she "looked like a corpse." As she was of a vivacious temperament, the remark impressed itself on the minds of her friends, some regarding it as a premonition of some evil that was to befall her. Without further incident they accomplished their journey, and made the contemplated visit.

On their return, John Mentz accompanied them as far as the top of the mountain, with two horses for the old man and his daughter to ride. Mentz proposed taking along his rifle, but was dissuaded from so doing by Mack, who thought it was not necessary. On arriving at the summit where they were to separate, the father and daughter dismounted, the former seating himself upon a log and lighting his pipe. Presently strange movements of the horses indicated they saw something unusual: and looking down the path over which they had just come, Mentz saw two Indians advancing, while a third, whom he recognized as the notorious Shanks Ben, was taking a circuitous route through the woods, so as to get in advance of them.

Mentz understood the significance of this movement, and realized the danger of their situation. He bitterly regretted he had not followed his own counsel, and brought along his rifle. He might easily have killed the two Indians in the path at a single shot. He had formerly been on intimate terms with Shanks Ben. They had hunted in company, and together had engaged in the labors of the farm; but a quarrel about a dog, and the bitter feeling engendered by the war, had contributed to destroy their friendship, and they were now sworn enemies. The old man, knowing it would be vain for him to attempt escape, sat still, resigned to his inevitable fate. Mentz started with Elsie in a direction designed to elude pursuit; coming to a precipice, he was obliged to leave the girl, in spite of her earnest entreaties that he would not abandon her, and save himself by jumping off the ledge some twenty feet in height. In his leap he injured his ankle badly, but succeeded in making good his escape. Mentz said he might have saved the girl had it not been for a little dog that followed them and kept constantly barking.

When Mentz came in sight of Colonel Jansen's, he saw a number of men collected there. A relief party was immediately made up and dispatched to the mountain, where they found the bodies of the old man and blooming maiden, side by side, covered with purple gore, and mutilated by the tomahawk and scalping knife their immortal spirits gone forever! The scene was solemn beyond description; and it was with difficulty that, in after years, Mentz could be induced to speak of it; and he never related the story without shedding a flood of tears.

At the time of the murder of John Mack and his daughter Elsie, Shanks Ben and his associates were returning from Col. Johannes Jansen's. Lured by the prize offered by the British for the scalp or person of the doughty Colonel, the wily savages had attempted to ambush Jansen as he was leaving the house in the morning. The Indians were discovered by some of the family, and the alarm given. The Colonel ran with all his might for the house, hotly pursued by Shanks Ben, and closed the door just as the latter hurled a tomahawk at his head. This door is still preserved as a relic of the past, bearing the prints of the Indian's weapon. Failing to enter the main building, the assailants plundered the kitchen; and hearing Mrs. Jansen call out as if the neighbors were coming, they hastily left the place.

A young white girl, named Hannah Grunenwalden, daughter of a neighbor, was that morning coming to spin for Mrs. Jansen, and was approaching the house as the Indians were engaged in their plunder. Mrs. Jansen called to her to go back, but Hannah misunderstood the warning, and fell an easy captive. The Indians also took with them two negro boys, that were never heard of afterwards. Fearing her screams would guide pursuers, Shanks Ben and his companions soon killed and scalped the girl.

red spot on the top of a large rock on a farm belonging to Brundage Peck is still shown as the place where Hannah met her fate—a stain which the storms of a century have not effaced. When the remains of Hannah, together with those of John Mack and his daughter Elsie, were deposited in their last resting-place, the whole community, on either side of the mountain, mingled their tears in the common sorrow.

There is a tradition in Shawangunk that some time after the close of the war, John Mentz went off into the woods with his rifle, and for more than a year he was not heard of by his family or friends; that he would never give a satisfactory account of his absence; that he shook his head mysteriously when Shanks Ben was mentioned, and that the latter individual was never again seen.

Shanks Ben, at this time, was about forty years of age. He was tall and athletic; hair jet black, and clubbed behind; forehead wrinkled, and brown eyes deeply sunk in their sockets, and his cheeks hollow and furrowed. The natural frightfulness of his visage was heightened by an accident; and when arrayed for war, he was one of the most hideous specimens of humanity the eye could rest upon.

One day Shanks Ben and two other savages came upon a log cabin in the town of Shawangunk. The man was not at home; but his wife saw them approaching, and escaped to the woods, leaving an infant sleeping in its cradle.

One of the Indians raised his tomahawk, and was about to slay the child, when it looked up into his face and smiled; even his savage heart was touched and he restored the tomahawk to his belt. With a fierce oath Shanks Ben thrust his bayonet through the innocent babe, and ran about the place holding up the child impaled on the cruel instrument, in the hope that its screams would entice the mother from her concealment. Failing in this, Ben dashed out the little one's brains against the door-post; and the marauders departed, first appropriating what they could conveniently carry away.

During the Revolution, Cornelius Decker was one day at work in a field near the present village of Bruynswick, when he felt a strange oppression, as though some great personal danger were impending. He could not shake off the feeling and presently returned to the house, where he was laughed at for his caprice. After the war was over, Shanks Ben came through the neighborhood. In an interview with Decker and others, Ben pointed to a log in the field above mentioned, and remarked that he one day lay behind that log with the intention of shooting Decker when he came to his work; but that the latter, having always deported himself as a friend, he could not find it in his heart to take his life. On comparing the day and hour of Ben's concealment behind the log, it was found the time coincided precisely with that of Decker's feeling of presentiment.

In 1784, Shanks Ben and two other Indians visited their old camping grounds on the Delaware to fish and hunt. They were first seen at Cochecton, where they were advised to go no further, as there were some dangerous characters below—Tom Quick among the number. They did not heed the advice, however, but went as far down as Shohola, where a hunter named Haines discovered them. Haines urged them to visit his cabin, setting apart a day for the purpose. In the meantime Haines communicated with Tom Quick and a man named Chambers, and a plan was arranged by which Shanks Ben and his companions were to be killed while they were his guests.

Accordingly Haines proposed to Ben and his companions to fish at the Eddy, taking up their position on a rock near which Quick and Chambers, by previous agreement, had secreted themselves. Presently two rifle shots were heard. One of the balls wounded Ben's companion, who ran to Haines and claimed his protection; but Haines seized a pine knot, exclaiming--" Tink, tink ! how you ust to kill white folks ! ' Pent, 'pent ! I'll send your soul to hell'n a moment !" and dispatched him by beating out his brains. Even Tom Quick was shocked at the perfidy of Haines and shouted as he came up, " D — a man that will promise an Indian protection, and then knock him on the head !" Shanks Ben, who was unharmed, jumped into the river, and made good his escape.

FACTS AND FANCIES.

THE Rondout *Freeman* is responsible for first giving publicity to the following story. Some slight changes are here made to conform more closely to the facts. Up back of Lackawaxen lived Farmer Cole. While at work in his field one day, with his man Olmstead, word came that a bear had raided his pig-pen, and was carrying off a pig; and presently the Babel of sounds in the direction of the house announced that something unusual was transpiring. Cole and his man made a dash for the scene of the disturbance. The former caught up a hay-knife which happened to be lying near, while Olmstead had secured a stout hickory club from the wood-pile. On reaching the house the bear was seen crossing the orchard back of the sty, walking

UP BACK OF LACKAWAXEN.

upright on his hind feet, and carrying a pig in his fore paws. The pig was squealing lustily, and struggling to get away. Close upon the heels of the bear came the sow and the rest of the litter, which seemed to know all was not right and made a great uproar. Next followed Mrs. Cole and her three daughters, armed with brooms and such other weapons as they in their haste could secure. Farmer Cole, his two sons and the hired man joined in the pursuit, and a formidable force was presented. At the back of the orchard was a fence. The bear climbed over with his pig, but the fence prevented the sow and her litter from following; the rest, however, followed on, and carried the war into the adjoining field. Farmer Cole gave the hay-knife into the hands of his son James, caught a rail from the fence, and running ahead of the bear, he and the hired man by taking hold of either end tripped Bruin up. The bear did not lose his hold of the pig, but gathered himself up and made off towards the woods. The rail was held as before, and a second time was he tripped up. This enraged the bear, and he dropped the pig, which was now dead, and made a dash for Farmer Cole. A third time was the animal thrown to the ground, and the men, by holding with all their united strength against the rail, held the bear down until James came up with the hay-knife and cut his throat.

In Southern Ulster there is a burial-ground that in times gone by was set apart for the interment of slaves. The headstones were selected from the fields; and though partially hidden from the casual observer by grass and shrubbery, the mounds and rude monuments can yet be located. Some of the older in-

THE SPECTRE.

habitants say that apparitions are sometimes seen loitering among the graves; and that on very dark and stormy nights a figure is seen to rise and soar away into space. In former years, it is said, the ghostly visitant used to frequent a house in the vicinity, and disturb the quiet of its occupants. Sometimes steps could be heard ascending the stairs. Then there would follow the creaking of a door on its hinges, though no door could be seen to move, and a figure in white would advance to the centre of the room, and pause as if intently looking for some object, and then vanish out of sight. The more knowing ones shake their heads when the subject is mentioned, and aver that if the dead could speak, some great wrong would be exposed; that by reason of this great wrong the spirits are not allowed to rest in their graves, but are forced to do penance as punishment for the acts committed during life. It is related that the good dame who once lived there used to punish her diminutive but somewhat refractory husband by doubling him up into a bucket, and letting him down into a deep well, until his spirit was reduced to something like submission. Be that as it may, there are those living in the vicinity, who, when they have occasion to pass the graveyard in the night-time, keep an eye over their shoulder until they get well beyond the ghost-haunted spot.

Yannaker Rosecrans, a domestic in the family of Col. Jansen, was a character in her way. She had a wen growing on her neck half as large as a man's head. She frequently stood sentry at the house of her employer. One night she detected a number of Indians lurking in the currant bushes near the house. She fired two or three shots in the direction of the sound, and declared some of them were hit, as she presently heard the noise of tomahawks, and supposed the Indians were cutting poles to carry the wounded away. Old people claim she could hold up a barrel of cider and drink out of the "gunnel." She boasted that no two men could take her alive. It is said that Shanks Ben once lay in ambush for the purpose of taking her prisoner as she came to fodder the cattle; but at the sight of her, armed as she was with a huge pitchfork, he declared his heart went "pitty-patty," until she was out of reach. At another time, while the Colonel had taken refuge in the chimney, she kept the Indians away from the fire-place by throwing hot suppawn at them with a spoon.

It was one of the most melancholy features of the battle of Minisink, that the friends of many of the patriots engaged in that sanguinary conflict were left in painful solicitude as to their fate. Whether killed in the heat of the strife, massacred in cold blood by the marauding savages, left to perish in the wilderness, or carried away captive,—to many of the kinsfolk about Goshen these were questions of conjecture, which only the judgment day will reveal. Major Wood was among the number who failed to return home with the remnant of the little army, and of whom the survivors were able to give little or no account. It could not be determined whether he was among the slain, or of the number taken prisoner. As years went by, and one by one a few returned from their captivity, the wife eagerly sought for tidings of her husband. Her inquiries were all in vain, and she finally felt constrained to give him up as lost. After the lapse of several years the widow had a favorable offer of marriage. Though she had no positive proof of the death of her husband, there was little probability of his being yet alive; so acting under the advice of friends, she accepted the offer. The second marriage proved a happy one, and two children blessed the union. Twelve years after the battle of Minisink, Major Wood returned to his home. He had been kept a close prisoner during all that time, and had not once heard of his family. He embraced the first opportunity to escape from captivity; and returned to find that he had long been mourned as dead; that his wife had married again, and had another family growing up around her. Much as it pained him to break the ties that bound the new family together, she was still his wife, for the law would not recognize the second marriage, now that the legal husband was known to be alive. But the way out of the difficulty was reached in an unexpected manner. The second husband went from home, ostensibly on business, and a few days afterward his hat and some of his clothing were found on the banks of the Delaware. Whether he really committed himself to the mercy of the water with suicidal intent, or only sought to convey the impression that he was dead, while he left for parts unknown, has never been told. Those who knew him best incline to the view that, from motives of compassion for the feelings of his family, he chose the latter alternative. Major Wood lived many years after his return, and his descendants are held in high estimation at the present time.

One of the greatest curiosities, in point of the mysteriousness of its origin in the county of Ulster, is that bit of ancient masonry in the town of Plattekill known as the "Indian Dam." It is located on what is known as the Levi Bodine farm, now occupied by J. S. Terwilliger, jr. The dam in question consists of two stone walls joined at an obtuse angle, and is about one hundred and fifty yards in length, eight or ten feet in height at the highest part, and four feet in width at the top. It is built across a stream at the outlet of a heavily timbered swamp, and would submerge about one hundred acres. As there is scarcely any perceptible fall, the dam could hardly have been built to furnish water power, hence the question as to the purpose of its construction has never been satisfactorily answered. What is stranger still, when the first settlers came into the vicinity, more than a century ago, the dam was there in the same condition in which it is now found; nor could they ascertain when, by whom, or for what purpose it was built. Though called the Indian Dam, it is not probable the Indians had anything to do with its construction, as they were not given to wall-building. Its origin may have been coeval with that of the ancient roads in the vicinity of the Shawangunk mountain, called the "Mine Roads," indications of which may yet be seen at various points at the foot of the declivities on either side, of which neither history nor tradition can give a satisfactory account.

www.ingramcontent.com/pod-product-compliance
Lightning Source LLC
Chambersburg PA
CBHW020828190426
43197CB00037B/730